APPORTIONMENT AND REPRESENTATIVE INSTITUTIONS

THE MICHIGAN EXPERIENCE

APPORTIONMENT AND REPRESENTATIVE INSTITUTIONS

THE MICHIGAN EXPERIENCE

By

KARL A. LAMB
WILLIAM J. PIERCE
JOHN P. WHITE

THE INSTITUTE FOR SOCIAL SCIENCE RESEARCH
CONTINENTAL BUILDING
WASHINGTON 5, D.C.
1963

Printed in the United States of America
by
Hennage Lithograph Company, Washington, D.C.

THE AUTHORS

Karl A. Lamb:
Assistant Professor of Political Science, University of Michigan; on leave, 1963-64, to serve at the University of California, Santa Cruz. Professor Lamb is the author of "Michigan Legislative Apportionment: Key to Constitutional Changes" in Malcolm E. Jewell (editor), *The Politics of Reapportionment,* and other articles in the fields of American and Michigan politics.

William J. Pierce:
Professor of Law and Director of Legislative Research Center, University of Michigan Law School. Professor Pierce's works include *Atoms and the Law* (with E. B. Stason and S. D. Estep).

John P. White:
Professor of Political Science, Arizona State University. A member of the Department of Political Science, University of Michigan, from 1954 to 1963, Professor White is the author of several works on Michigan politics, including *Parties, Group Interests, and Campaign Finance: Michigan '56* (with John R. Owens).

James K. Pollock:
Murfin Professor of Political Science, University of Michigan. Professor Pollock is the author or co-author of several books, including *Party Campaign Funds* and *Germany in Power and Eclipse.* He was President of the American Political Science Association (1950) and President of the International Political Science Association (1955-58). Professor Pollock was a delegate to the Michigan Constitutional Convention, 1961-62, and served as chairman of the Convention's Committee on Declaration of Rights, Suffrage, and Elections.

APR 18 1964

FOREWORD

The case of *Baker* v. *Carr,* handed down by the United States Supreme Court in 1962, has given unprecedented stimulation to the study of the apportionment of representatives in legislative bodies. For more than a decade before this decision, the subject had been pushed to the forefront of public discussion largely because of the great growth in the population of urban areas all over the country. The 1960 census of population showed nearly two-thirds of the entire population of the United States residing within the 212 recognized metropolitan areas—112.9 million persons of the nation-wide total of 179.3 million. These areas accounted for 84 percent of the increase in the nation's population during the last decade. It was, therefore, quite natural that these areas should press for change in the power structure of the various states. Aided by party and group interests, the movement for greater urban representation, especially in state legislatures, gained momentum in the decade of the fifties and finally erupted in a series of court cases leading to the epoch-making decision in *Baker v. Carr.*

The country, the courts, and the people were ill prepared for a discussion of apportionment. Despite several limited studies of apportionment in a few states, political scientists in particular had not conducted much research in depth into the effect of differing apportionment formulas. The great complexity of the subject was little realized. Politicians and legislators had played around with the subject for decades, and the place of apportionment in the total election picture and its relationship to representative government had been discussed by theorists, but not subjected to thoroughgoing empirical research.

As is so frequently the case with politics, pat formulas and political polemics took the front of the stage. When egalitarian forces could make no headway with electorates, they turned to the courts, and here action, explosive and immediate, occurred. But the courts which had heretofore considered apportionment a "political" question, now tumbled over each other in a head-long endeavor to rectify old injustices and establish equitable representation. But such an important political question required more research than the courts had been able to give to it.

In the midst of these significant developments, one state was in the process of developing a new state constitution. Michigan, which had wrestled with apportionment problems in the 1952 referendum election, now, after much civic effort, had summoned a constitutional convention to consider among other things, the whole basis of its representative system. The delegates chosen directly by the people in existing legislative districts were thus given the opportunity and responsibility of reconsidering all aspects of the apportionment picture in the light of population and party changes in the decade since the referendum of 1952. The convention was nearing the end of its deliberations when the case of *Baker* v. *Carr* was decided. Thus, a popular assembly in a key urban state has within recent months reviewed all aspects of the apportionment problem and made its proposal to the people for approval. This recent experience of Michigan in apportionment matters has great relevance to and provides much valuable background for any study of reapportionment problems throughout the country.

With this thought in mind my colleagues and I welcomed the encouragement and support of The Institute for Social Science Research in undertaking a comprehensive research project into all aspects of apportionment in the State of Michigan, historical, legal, statistical, and political. The results of this research are found in the monographs within these covers. Michigan's whole reapportionment history is reviewed and evaluated. The complicated facets of apportionment formulas are revealed. Also the apportionment problems of local government bodies are investigated and what would happen if the strict population formula were applied to other governmental units, is discussed. The court adjudications are reviewed, and finally, the actions and deliberations of the recent constitutional convention are carefully scrutinized and analyzed to see what value they have in identifying basic problems in apportionment and in developing solutions for them.

Recognizing that "apportionment is part of a system of elections in a representative government" as Professor Alfred de Grazia so well puts it, the authors have subjected to analysis every aspect of apportionment formulas, procedures, methods, and practices. What is reflected in an apportionment? Must apportionments be drawn in terms of any one theory of representation such as strict population, community or neighborhood groupings, economic or regional similarities, political or historical traditions? What criteria did the Michigan Constitutional Convention use in preparing its formula? How can this formula be expected to work now and in the foreseeable future? Does it have any relevance or usefulness to other states? Does it meet the test of "equal protection" under the fourteenth amendment?

These significant questions—and many more—are treated in the studies prepared by Professors Lamb, Pierce, and White of the University of Michigan. They are presented with the thought in mind that they can provide a necessary insight into the whole apportionment problem. It is possible that as a pilot project they may be duplicated and emulated in other important states to the end that legislatures and courts may have some basic research on which to base their actions.

There is at present so much confusion and such broad generalizations are made that heroic action must be taken if we are to avoid a genuine political catastrophe. Will we be permitted to follow our historic road of experimentation in our respective states so that a strong federal system will continue to be the backbone of our constitutional order? Are the courts going to set rigid formulas and order strict compliance with their decisions, or will they merely set the norms which must be followed in ways which can be adjusted to each state's condition? What apportionment schemes are invalid as a denial of equal protection of the law? If the scheme is approved by the people of a state, does it have validity? If rational departures from strict population are permitted, assuming there are no "invidious distinctions," what is rational?

In any event, the United States Supreme Court in reviewing the cases now before it has an opportunity to speak definitively on the role of the equal protection clause in relation to apportionment. This they cannot prudently do, however, until more pertinent data is available to them. Certainly the present research casts doubt on some of the standards suggested and even applied judicially in evaluating existing apportionments.

In this connection the recent report of the Advisory Commission on Intergovernmental Relations is very apropos. Without dissent this new, unique body which has members representing all levels of government, urged that,

> . . . state and federal courts confine their apportionment roles to adjudicating and enforcing the constitutionality of apportionment actions and should refrain from the prescription by judicial decree of specific apportionment formulas or the geographic composition of legislative districts.

It went further by recognizing that some effective means for enforcing reapportionment provisions are necessary, and that "the people of the state should be provided the opportunity to react at the polls at any time to the continuance or change of apportionment formulas."

After all, an apportionment plan must be evaluated in terms of its effects. No apportionment plan is neutral. It benefits certain people or interests or areas and disadvantages others. To ascertain precisely what it does can only be secured after extensive and basic research such as is included in our study.

Perhaps this Michigan study and the apportionment plan in the new constitution will provide a system of guaranteed apportionments for both houses under a set of standards which are unequivocal and clear, and which eliminate the possibility of "invidious discrimination." In any case the careful and penetrating research which is presented here endeavors to lay bare the complicated problems which are involved in accomplishing a reapportionment, and to point out the shallowness of some arguments and the pitfalls to be avoided.

It is hoped that a new face will be put on the problem of apportionment and representative government by these studies, and serious mistakes will be avoided. There is no doubt that the courts are now dealing with a problem fraught with grave consequences for this old republic. Playing with power is always dangerous and to bring about a veritable political revolution in the distribution of political power in states and local governments, is a responsibility of the gravest character. We trust that whatever is done will be done carefully, after acquiring all the facts, and with the benefit of exhaustive deliberation.

JAMES K. POLLOCK
Murfin Professor of Political Science
University of Michigan

Contents

List of Tables

List of Figures

LEGAL SETTING: PRE-BAKER v. CARR

By William J. Pierce

ONLY INFREQUENTLY DO DECISIONS of the United States Supreme Court affect the body politic. Even more rarely do they have ramifications involving the foundations of state government. Such, however, may be the effect of the decision rendered on March 26, 1962 in *Baker* v. *Carr*,[1] the Tennessee apportionment case. In that case it was alleged that an apportionment based on a Tennessee statute deprived qualified voters of equal protection of the laws. The Supreme Court held that this case was justiciable. In so doing, it has opened the doors of the courts

[1] 369 U.S. 186 (1962).

for judicial review of the validity of the representation schemes employed in most states.

The decision has sown the seeds of change, and, as we shall see, in some cases the harvest has already been reaped. How many of the seeds will germinate and be harvested still remains in doubt. Only through the process of judicial decision on a case-by-case basis—the traditional method of constitutional law development—will we be able to draw any definitive conclusions regarding the totality of the impact of *Baker* v. *Carr* on our constitutional system.

The major question which the majority opinion in *Baker* v. *Carr* did not answer and to which, hopefully, the Supreme Court will address itself in future cases is: What, if any, apportionment schemes violate fourteenth amendment guarantees to equal protection of the law? One might well ask why the decision has been hailed as one of the most momentous of the century if this seemingly fundamental question was not answered by the majority of the Supreme Court. The significance of the *Baker* v. *Carr* decision can perhaps best be explained in terms of the legal situation prevailing at the time it was rendered. The legal setting involves a number of complex relationships. These include the specific provisions of the state constitutions relating to apportionment, the role of the courts in litigation involving coordinate branches of government, the ability of the courts to handle issues which are often basically political in nature, the ability of courts to fashion appropriate legal relief, and the substantive requirements imposed by the equal protection clause of the fourteenth amendment to the United States Constitution.

STATE CONSTITUTIONAL PROVISIONS
GOVERNING APPORTIONMENT

IN STATE COURT LITIGATION challenging the validity of apportionment statutes, the provisions of the state constitution govern, unless, of course, the state constitutional provisions violate the federal constitution. Moreover, as we shall see, compliance with the state constitutional apportionment provisions may be an important factor in determining whether or not federal constitutional requirements have been breached. At the same time it may prove significant in determining the nature of the judicial relief to be afforded if constitutional invalidity is found. A summary of the state constitutional provisions will also help in evaluating the practical effect of the decision in *Baker* v. *Carr*. It may also provide some guidance for predicting the course the United States Supreme Court may follow in apportionment cases.

Bases of Apportionment

As of December 1961, only eight state constitutions provided for the apportionment of the entire legislatures exclusively on the basis of population.[1] In Indiana both houses of the legislatures are to be apportioned on the basis of male inhabitants over 21 years of age. In Massachusetts and Tennessee both houses are to be apportioned on the basis of legal voters and qualified voters, respectively. In eight states, the senate is to be apportioned on the basis of population,[2] and in four states the lower chamber is to be apportioned on the basis of population.[3]

Apportionment of Senate

In 14 states, the constitutions either specifically establish senatorial districts or, in effect, have frozen senatorial districts created in some prior apportionment, or they allot one senator to each county.[4] In three states the senate is to be apportioned on the basis of population, but each county is to have at least one member.[5] In each of these three states, the total membership of the senate is fixed with the result that substantial discrepancies in the population of individual districts may result. In contrast, the senate in eight states is to be apportioned on the basis of population or qualified voters, but a limitation is placed on the number of senators from any single county or both a mini-

---

[1] Colorado, Minnesota, Nebraska, Oregon, South Dakota, Virginia, Washington, and Wisconsin. See Appendix, p. 39.

[2] Alabama, Kansas, Kentucky, Louisiana, Missouri, North Carolina, Oklahoma, and Utah. See Appendix, p. 39.

[3] Alaska, California, Illinois, and Michigan.

[4] *Specific districts:* Arizona, Delaware, Hawaii, Illinois, and Mississippi; *Frozen districts:* Arkansas and Michigan; *One senator per county:* Idaho, Maryland (six districts in Baltimore), Montana, Nevada, New Jersey, New Mexico, and South Carolina.

[5] Connecticut, Vermont, and Wyoming.

mum and maximum number of senators is prescribed.[6] In Alaska, geographical area is the predominant factor in apportioning the senate, but population factors are also considered. In Georgia, senatorial districts are to be composed of counties with no more than one member per district. West Virginia divides the state into 12 districts with two members per district, but if the district is composed of two or more counties, no more than one senator can come from any single county. In Ohio, population is the major factor for determining apportionment of the senate, but discrepancies in population ratios among senatorial districts are resolved by fluctuations in total membership of the senate over a decennial period.[7] Finally, in New Hampshire, membership in the senate is apportioned on the basis of direct taxes paid.

Apportionment of Lower House

In addition to Nebraska, which has the nation's only unicameral legislature, and the ten states which apportion both houses on the same basis (population, male inhabitants, or qualified voters), four states provide for apportionment of the lower chamber on a population basis.[8] New Hampshire's lower chamber is based on population, but each town or ward is entitled to a representative at least once every ten years. Maine apportions its lower house on a population basis, but no town may

---

[6] California (no county or city and county may have more than one senator and no more than three counties may be in a district); Florida, Iowa, and Texas (no county more than one senator); Maine (no county less than one, nor more than five senators); New York (no county more than one-third of senators nor more than one-half of senators to two adjoining counties; the provision is not operative); Pennsylvania (no county or city to have more than one-sixth of senators); Rhode Island (minimum of one and maximum of six per city or town).

[7] Ohio Constitution, article XI, sections 6-10 (1851). A proviso to section 6a specifies that "no additional senator . . . shall be elected if his election would result in his senatorial district having as members of the next following general assembly a number of senators in excess of its number of full ratios plus one." The population ratios are established by dividing the population of the state by 35. Original senate districts were established by groupings of counties.

[8] Alaska, California, Illinois, and Michigan.

have more than seven members unless it is a consolidated town. Texas utilizes a population basis, but no county may have more than seven representatives unless its population exceeds 700,000. In Maryland, representation in the lower chamber was frozen in 1948, but previously apportionment was to be based on population with a minimum of two and a maximum of six members from each county and district of Baltimore. Arizona apportions its house on the basis of the number of votes cast for governor in the preceding general election, but has a savings clause making the 1930 election a minimum basis. Nineteen states require apportionment of the lower chamber on a population basis, but also require that each county have at least one member.[9] The requirement that each county have one member when coupled with a common provision fixing the maximum number of members has the effect, of course, of creating large population discrepancies between districts. Kentucky uses a population basis, but no more than two counties may be joined in a district. The Idaho Constitution specifies that each county is entitled to at least one representative, but the remaining seats are to be apportioned as provided by law; the constitution does not prescribe the basis to be utilized by the legislature. Florida and Georgia allow additional representation for more populous counties but the number is fixed.[10] Iowa allows additional representation to the nine most populous counties only on the basis of population ratios. Oklahoma utilizes population ratios with counties having one-half a ratio being entitled to a representative and no county may elect more than seven members. Rhode Island utilizes population but assures each city or town at least one representative, and no town or city may have more than one-fourth of the total house membership. Connecticut allows

---

[9] Alabama, Arkansas, Hawaii, Kansas, Louisiana, (each ward of New Orleans and each parish), Missouri, Montana, Nevada, New Jersey, New Mexico, New York (other than Hamilton County), North Carolina, North Dakota, Ohio, Pennsylvania, South Carolina, Utah, West Virginia, and Wyoming.

[10] Florida: 3 to 5 largest counties, 2 to next 18, 1 to remaining: Georgia: 3 to 8 largest counties, 2 to next 30, and 1 to remaining.

two members for each town having over 5,000 population, but other towns are to have the same representation they had in 1874. Vermont allows a representative to each inhabited town. Mississippi allows each county one representative, but then divides the state into three groupings of counties with each grouping never to have less than 44 representatives. Only the Delaware Constitution has prescribed the boundaries of its districts with each district being allowed one representative.

Significance of Constitutional Provisions Governing Apportionment

From this rather abbreviated description of the state constitutional provisions governing legislative apportionment, it readily can be seen that the state constitutions present a bewildering array of variation in the principles of apportionment. One should not overlook the fact that the constitutions often contain other provisions affecting apportionment. One such is a limitation on joining parts of two or more counties to form a legislative district. Others require that districts be composed of contiguous counties and that no county be divided to form a district. All of these tend to place practical limitations on apportionment according to population if equal population districts is the major principle to be followed in apportioning one or both houses of the legislature. Therefore, the constitutional structure of each individual state must be examined; for it is only by joining the several pieces of the puzzle that definitive conclusions can be drawn regarding the actual basis of apportionment prescribed.

By looking at the totality of state constitutional provisions, however, we are able to draw some general conclusions concerning the bases of apportionment of state legislatures.

In the first place, 39 of the 49 states having bicameral legislatures provide different bases for apportioning the two houses. Thus in the vast majority of states, the legislative houses are apportioned, it may be argued, in a manner which will tend to make the "checks and balances" features of bicameralism effective. In most of these cases the population factor is predominant in the apportionment of one house and representation of political subdivisions in the other. The analogy to the Congress is obvious in terms of the "checks and balances" feature. The analogy in terms of representation of political subdivisions, however, is not as valid because the political subdivisions are not and never were sovereign in the same sense that the states are sovereign within the federal system.

Second, 49 states in some way recognize population as a factor in apportioning one or both houses of the legislature. In a representative democracy, the conclusion would seem inescapable that people are to be represented in some way. Even in Delaware where the boundaries of the districts are fixed, they were originally developed in light of population distribution. However, despite the apparent universality of the population standard, the fact remains that compliance with other constitutional limitations and requirements in 39 states results in legislative districts having wide population discrepancies.

Third, 34 states employ the standard of affording representation to political subdivisions, although in many instances population is also considered. The apparent objective is to afford people grouped together for local governmental purposes and services some minimal representation to provide them an effective voice in the legislature. The desirability and necessity of representing local governmental units would appear more pronounced where those units have little autonomy in the conduct of local affairs so that state legislative action is required on numerous occasions. Even in states allowing considerable local autonomy the demands to enact general legislation dealing with local governmental affairs are great in each regular session of the legislature. Furthermore, much of the so-called general legislation is actually specific in nature for, in practical effect, it applies only to a single local governmental unit.[11]

---

[11] See John M. Winters, *State Constitutional Limitations on Solutions of Metropolitan Area Problems* (Ann Arbor: Legislative Research Center, University of Michigan, 1961).

Fourth, the state constitutions (with the possible exceptions of such states as Alaska, Delaware, and Illinois where the boundaries of legislative districts in at least one house are fixed) do not seem to recognize area in terms of the number of square miles per district, as a significant factor in apportionment. However, a provision assuring each county a member might be rationalized in part on the ground that it assures that legislative districts will not be too large geographically. With modern transportation and communication devices facilitating election campaigning, such limitations appear to be less relevant as a basis of apportionment.

Fifth, demographic factors, other than population, have not been significant in formulating state constitutional apportionment provisions. Apparent exceptions exist in four states which have based apportionment on factors roughly corresponding to population, such as male inhabitants over 21, legal voters, qualified voters, or votes cast for governor. Conceivably, legislative apportionment based on legal voters, for example, could result in less representation for suburban areas having large numbers of children than would be afforded if the total population was utilized in apportioning legislative seats. Also a basis of votes cast for governor could lead to results representing significant disparities in terms of total population. These bases, however, could be rationalized in terms of effective citizen participation or ability to participate in the affairs of government.

Sixth, economic factors, as such, are not specifically recognized as apportionment bases except possibly in the apportionment of the New Hampshire Senate which is based on direct taxes paid. Since the direct taxes are property taxes, the New Hampshire scheme may be said to represent wealth. However, because the base reflects property tax valuations, only a portion of wealth is recognized and studies of the system indicate that the basis closely parallels population. As a practical matter different economic interests are represented in state legislatures, but this

9

stems from factors other than ecomonic ones reflected in the constitutional provisions.

Finally, one must not overlook the fact that state constitutional apportionment provisions resulted from the political process characterized by compromise among various political groups and interests. Often relevant was the prospective ability of a political party to control the affairs of state government. The constitutional framers undoubtedly also considered the representation of economic, social, and sectional interests. Because of the compromise among political forces, a single, precise, logical scheme of apportionment seldom emerged from the deliberations of constitutional conventions. Moreover, the circumstances underlying the compromise inevitably changed. For example, a fairly old constitutional system recognizing representation of each county may not at the time of its creation have resulted in any egregious departure from the principle of equal citizen representation. The ravages of time and the rapid urbanization of certain areas of a state, however, have brought about substantial discrepancies of population between districts. Therefore, the underlying premises of the original formula have disappeared, and the problem remains of providing rationalizations which the framers would not necessarily have advanced for the constitutional provisions. The resulting "political thicket" is not easily rationalized in many instances.

Requirements to Reapportion

Of the 49 states whose constitutions provide for some type of reapportionment of one or both houses of the legislature, 41 require reapportionment every ten years, or after each federal census. In Colorado, reapportionment is required every five years, or after each federal and each state census. In Kansas and Indiana reapportionment is required every five years and six years, respectively. Arizona's is to be conducted after each gubernatorial election. In Maine, it is to take place between minimum and maximum periods of five and ten years. Reapportionment in

Nebraska is to be achieved from time to time but no more often than once every ten years. Ohio's fluctuating membership provisions allow for reapportionment each biennium, in effect, but population ratios are based upon the decennial census. In Rhode Island the General Assembly may reapportion after any presidential election, and in Vermont the senate may be reapportioned after each state census as well as every ten years after each federal census. Since population is the variable factor in reapportionment, the desirability of reapportioning after each federal census is obvious.

In all of the states authorizing reapportionment, except Connecticut, New Mexico, and Rhode Island, reapportionment appears mandatory. Even in Rhode Island where the constitutional provision is written in permissive terms, the Rhode Island Supreme Court has recently ruled that reapportionment is mandatory.[12] Nonetheless, at the time of the decision in *Baker* v. *Carr*, apportionments in effect in 14 states were based upon census figures of 1940 or earlier. In Alabama, Connecticut, and Tennessee there had been no reapportionment for over a half century. Even when some reapportionment statute has been enacted, it is extremely difficult to judge whether there has been compliance with the constitutional criteria. A considerable area of judgment is left to the apportioning agency due to the mixture of population and other criteria. This also results from limitations on the number of legislators and the manner in which district lines may be drawn, which were designed to prevent gerrymandering. For example, if City A has 150,000 population, City B has 100,000 and City C, 80,000 and six seats are to be apportioned on a population basis, giving each city two legislators would result in districts of 75,000, 50,000, and 40,000. If City A is given three seats and City C one seat, we have district populations of 50,000, 50,000, and 80,000. In either case one legislator will represent over one-half as many people as another legislator. If either solution is adopted, it is difficult to conclude that the

---

[12] Sweeney v. Notte, 183 A. 2d (1962).

apportioning agency has not complied with the constitutional mandates.

Furthermore, in some states where reapportionment has occurred more recently, substantial departures from population equality exist even though the predominant criterion for apportionment is equal population for the districts. The 1961 apportionment of the California house, for example, resulted in the largest district having a population of 306,191 and the smallest 72,105. Although the California Constitution requires that districts be "as nearly equal in population as possible," the constitution also specifies that districts should not include parts of more than one county. The ideal district would have a population of 196,465 according to the 1960 census. The "constitutional requirements preserving county lines were almost entirely responsible for these disparities." [13] Discrepancies in size of population of legislative districts where equal populations are prescribed cannot, therefore, be attributed exclusively to refusals to reapportion or to failures to comply with constitutional mandates.

Apportionment Agency

Of the 48 states [14] authorizing reapportionment of one or both houses of the legislature, 41 states impose on the legislature the primary responsibility for conducting reapportionments in accordance with the state constitutional requirements. In seven out of the 41 states an executive official or reapportionment commission may redistrict if the legislature fails to act. [15] In seven states the primary responsibility for reapportionment rests with

---

[13] National Municipal League, *Compendium on Legislative Apportionment* (2d ed., 1962).

[14] The Delaware and Maryland Constitutions fix the districts for both houses of their legislatures, but in Maryland Committee for Fair Representation v. Tawes, 228 Md. 412, 180 A. 2d 656 (1962) the Maryland Supreme Court, after declaring the apportionment of the lower house unconstitutional, indicated that the legislature had the power to reapportion.

[15] California, Illinois, Michigan, North Dakota, Oregon, South Dakota, and Texas.

either an executive official or a constitutional board.[16] Therefore, in only 14 states is it possible for persons other than legislators themselves to conduct reapportionment. As we shall see, the availability of judicial relief is severely circumscribed where the legislature is the exclusive reapportioning agency. In two states, New York and Oklahoma, in which the legislature is assigned the apportionment task, the constitutions specifically authorize the highest court of the state to review judicially any reapportionment under rules prescribed by the legislature. In four states, Alaska, Arkansas, Hawaii, and Oregon, which authorize reapportionment by executive officials, the constitutions also provide for judicial review.

---

[16] Alaska (Apportionment Board with its action reviewable and amendable by governor); Arkansas (Board of Apportionment subject to revision by the supreme court); Arizona (secretary of state allocates to counties; county board divides county into districts); Hawaii (governor); Missouri (house: secretary of state apportions among counties; county courts apportion within counties; senate: commission appointed by governor); New Jersey (governor apportions among counties); Ohio (governor, auditor, and secretary of state).

APPORTIONMENT LITIGATION IN STATE COURTS

ALTHOUGH MOST STATE CONSTITUTIONS require periodic reapportionment to reflect population changes, we have noted that other constitutional restrictions often prohibit the creation of districts having approximately the same population. The typical restrictions are those affording minimal representation to certain political subdivisions, prohibiting districts composed of parts of two or more counties, requiring districts to be composed of contiguous and compact territory, and fixing the total membership of the legislative body. These restrictions, being mandatory in nature, limit the ability of the apportioning agency to establish an apportionment giving equal weight to each citizen when electing legislators. Nevertheless, in most states considerable room for reflecting the population factor remains. In fact, the possible districting schemes available are infinite in number, the typical constitution admonishing only that districts be as equal in population "as possible."

In 34 states only the legislature is specifically directed or authorized to reapportion by the terms of the state constitution. Although some state legislatures have been responsive to the state constitutional directives, others have been notoriously negligent. Some have failed to reapportion for decades; others have enacted reapportionments that do not reflect population to the maximum degree permissible under the constitution. Reasons for this lethargy include the desire to maintain the status quo so as not to imperil re-election of senior legislators, a reluctance to reduce the representation of rural areas in the legislature, and an unwillingness of the party favored by the apportionment to relinquish its advantages.

Naturally, persons adversely affected by the apportionment have turned to the state courts for relief. Interestingly, most state courts have been willing to decide the cases presented to them on their merits rather than holding that the question involved is "political" and therefore not suitable for judicial determination. However, as we shall see, the state courts have not been able to provide any effective judicial relief, particularly where the legislature has failed to act.

The Scope of State Judicial Review

Prior to *Baker* v. *Carr*, allegations of constitutional invalidity were based almost exclusively upon violations of the apportionment provisions of state constitutions. In the few cases where violations of the equal protection clause of the fourteenth amendment to the United States Constitution were alleged, appeals to the United States Supreme Court proved fruitless because of the doctrine of non-justiciability of political questions. Therefore, state courts confined their review to the question of whether or not apportionment complied with the state constitution.

If conformity with the so-called mandatory constitutional provisions leaves few seats to be assigned to populous areas, the scope of discretion in the apportioning agency is narrow. If the mandatory provisions have minimal impact, the scope of discretion is obviously great. Thus in each case the courts must ascertain whether or not the particular exercise of discretion lies within or without the bounds of constitutionality. As Judge Peckham of the New York Court of Appeals stated:

> While it is impossible in the nature of the case, to accurately describe and closely limit the amount of deviation from an equal representation that the practical working of the Constitution may . . . permit, it is on the other hand quite possible to say of a particular example that it does or does not violate the constitutional mandate. We have no trouble whatever in detecting the difference between noon and midnight, but the exact line of separation between the dusk of the evening and the darkness of advancing night is not so easily drawn.[1]

The test to be applied for determining whether the discretion exercised by the apportioning agency falls outside the permissible range has been described variously by the courts. For example, in New York the court has said that there "must be a grave, palpable and unreasonable deviation from the standard, so that when the facts are presented argument would not be necessary to convince a fair man that very great and wholly unnecessary inequality has been intentionally provided for."[2] The Michigan Supreme Court has required that "an honest and fair" discretion be exercised by the legislature.[3] The Illinois Supreme Court apparently has left much more room for the exercise of discretion by requiring that the legislature wholly fail "to have in view and apply" the constitutional standards of equal population and com-

---

[1] Baird v. Kings County, 138 N.Y. 95, 113, 33 N.E. 827 (1893).

[2] *Ibid.*, at 114.

[3] Giddings v. Secretary of State, 93 Mich. 1, 52 N.W. 944 (1892).

pactness of districts.[4] The Minnesota court has required a "clear and palpable violation of the fundamental law," [5] and in Wisconsin the court has indicated that a "wide and bold departure" evincing an intent by the legislature to "utterly ignore and disregard" the constitution is essential before the court will upset an apportionment.[6]

In enunciating these standards for determining the range of permissible legislative discretion, the courts have carefully examined the provisions of the state constitution and have repeatedly emphasized that in some respects the mandatory provisions conflict with the requirement of equal population. Furthermore, they have almost universally agreed that the motives of the legislature in enacting the particular apportionment will not be examined in applying the standard. Finally, although expressing awareness of the delicacy of the questions involved and of the respect due a coordinate branch of government, state courts generally have not refused to decide the constitutional issues. Only in Pennsylvania has the supreme court apparently held the issue to be political in nature and non-justiciable. In an action in 1959 to enjoin elections under a 1921 apportionment, the court, after expressing concern with the possibility that no valid apportionment law would be in effect if the complainants were afforded relief, stated that the issues presented were not justiciable and rested solely within the discretion of the legislature.[7] The precedents relied upon were almost exclusively United States Supreme Court cases which were concerned with the fourteenth amendment in the apportionment context.

As we have seen, the standards formulated by the courts for determining whether or not the legislature has abused its discretion, certainly lack specificity. Some notions of their meaning, however, can be derived from an examination of the statistical

---

[4] People v. Thompson, 155 Ill. 451, 482, 40 N.E. 307 (1895).
[5] State ex rel. Meighan v. Weatherill, 125 Minn. 336, 342, 147 N.W. 105 (1914).
[6] State v. Cunningham, 81 Wis. 440, 484, 51 N.W. 724 (1892).
[7] Butcher v. Rice, 397 Pa. St. 158, 162, 153 A. 2d 869 (1959).

facts of apportionments reviewed by the courts. State courts have held apportionments invalid where the ratio of the largest district to the smallest district in population terms has been slightly less than 1.5 to 1 and up to 9 to 1, with most cases exceeding a 2 to 1 ratio. Apportionments have been held valid where the ratio was slightly in excess of 3.5 to 1, but in most cases the ratio did not exceed 2 to 1.[8] Examination of these statistics without reference to the mandatory constitutional requirements indicates that wherever population is the principal basis for an apportionment, population variations in excess of 2 to 1 seem to fall outside the boundaries of a constitutional exercise of legislative discretion.

Despite the fact that most state courts ruling on the issue have concluded that the courts may review apportionments to determine validity under the state constitution, relatively few courts have had the issue before them. As previously noted, almost every state prescribes periodic reapportionment when population is the variable factor to be considered. Yet less than one-half of the state courts have ruled on the constitutionality of state legislative apportionments. Two reasons may be advanced for the paucity of state judicial review. First, most legislatures in reapportioning have complied with the state constitutional requirements. Second, resort to the courts by adversely affected citizens has been precluded by the inability of state courts to fashion effective judicial relief to correct instances of noncompliance.

The Availability and Effectiveness of State Judicial Relief

Compelling the Apportionment Agency to Reapportion

Malapportionment, in the sense of lack of compliance with state constitutional requirements, often occurs because of the failure of the apportioning agency to exercise its responsibilities.

---

[8] Arthur L. Goldberg, "The Statistics of Malapportionment," 72 *Yale Law Journal* 90, pp. 102-04 (1962).

As we have seen, in the vast majority of states the constitutions grant exclusive authority to reapportion to the legislature.

When complainants have sought a judicial order to require legislative action, the state courts universally have refused the requested relief. In the leading case on the subject, *Fergus* v. *Marks,* the Illinois Supreme Court rejected the petitioner's request that a writ of mandamus be issued commanding the defendant members of the legislature to reapportion.[9] After pointing to the typical state constitutional provisions dividing powers of government among the executive, legislative, and judicial branches, the court observed, "Neither one of these departments can arrogate to itself any control over either one of the other departments in matters which have been solely confided by the Constitution to such other department."[10] The courts' consistent declination to permit mandamus to lie against legislators could be explained on other grounds. Even if the courts were to issue the mandamus, they would have difficulty in enforcing the writ. Contempt citations would not necessarily assure action, and the political disruption of state governmental operations could prove catastrophic. In any event, by concluding that the legislature cannot be compelled to act by judicial order, the state courts severely limited the availability and effectiveness of judicial relief to correct malapportionments arising from legislative inaction.

To correct this situation, the constitutions of 14 states either have given the primary responsibility for reapportionment to another agency or have provided that another agency shall reapportion if the legislature fails to perform its duty. State courts have not hesitated, as a general rule, to issue writs of mandamus against public officers, other than the governor or legislators. Therefore, in those states the judiciary is able to compel some type of action by the apportioning agency. It should be noted, however, that the Missouri Supreme Court in 1912 described an apportioning agency consisting of the governor, secretary of state,

---

[9] 321 Ill. 510, 152 N.E. 557, 46 A.L.R. 960 (1926).
[10] *Ibid.*, at 514.

and attorney general as a "miniature legislature" and indicated that it would be treated in the same manner as the legislature in formulating judicial relief.[11] But wherever redistricting responsibilities are assigned to local governmental bodies or officers, the courts have not hesitated to enter orders compelling action.[12]

Judicial Reapportionment

Given the unwillingness of a state court to order the legislature to act, it is rather surprising to find that few complainants have requested reapportionment by judicial order. The cases, however, are filled with statements that the court may not reapportion. In the few cases where the question has been raised, the state courts have unanimously concluded that they do not have the power. Even in Oklahoma where the constitution specifically authorizes judicial review of apportionments, the court has stated that it may not reapportion because the "duty is legislative in nature." [13] Although the courts have relied exclusively on the separation of powers doctrine in denying judicial reapportionment, practical considerations leading to the same conclusions undoubtedly were significant. For example, the courts do not have at their disposal the necessary tools and resources to conduct primary and general elections which a recalcitrant legislature might fail to provide. Furthermore, to be consistent the courts would be faced with having to provide judicial legislation in other areas where the state constitutions direct the legislature to act. The courts also legitimately are concerned that the assumption of the role of super-legislature could lead to popular disapproval and thereby threaten the court as an institution.

Although it has been described as a "simple, appropriate and

---

[11] State ex rel. Barrett, 241 Mo. 433, 146 S.W. 40 (1912).

[12] See Attorney General v. Suffolk County Apportionment Commissioners, 224 Mass. 598, 113 N.E. 581 (1916); Donovan v. Suffolk County Apportionment Commissioners, 225 Mass. 55, 113 N.E. 740 (1916); People ex rel. Baird v. Brown, 138 N.Y. 95, 33 N.E. 827 (1893).

[13] Jones v. Freeman, 193 Okla. 554, 561, 146 P. 2d 564 (1943).

effective remedy," [14] an order requiring elections-at-large has seldom been sought. In the only case prior to *Baker* v. *Carr* in which a court clearly ruled on the issue, the Supreme Court of Tennessee rejected elections-at-large because there was "no provision of law" for such an election.[15] The reason advanced by the Tennessee court is not very persuasive. However, any court would encounter difficulties in conducting primaries and general elections where 100 or more offices are to be filled if cooperation by legislative and executive officials was not forthcoming.

In 1960 the Supreme Court of New Jersey was asked to consider two additional remedial devices which would have had the same effect as a judicial order reapportioning the assembly. One plan involved court orders restraining county clerks from placing on the ballot either a clearly excessive or an inadequate number of candidates. The other proposed a court order giving different values to the votes of assemblymen depending upon the population represented. The court, although expressing interest in the plans, withheld action until the legislature was afforded an additional opportunity to act.[16] Thereafter the legislature reapportioned so no further judicial action was required.

Prohibiting Election Under Invalid Apportionment

In most state court proceedings contesting the constitutional validity of an apportionment, injunctions or writs of mandamus were sought against election officials to require them to conduct the election under an earlier apportionment because the most recent apportionment was invalid. If the most recent apportionment has been in effect for a considerable number of years, the defendants often have argued successfully that the doctrine of laches should preclude judicial relief because the complainants

---

[14] Anthony Lewis, "Legislative Apportionment and the Federal Court," 71 *Harvard Law Review*, pp. 1057, 1070 (1958).

[15] Kidd v. McCanless, 200 Tenn. 273, 277, 292 S.W. 2d 40 (1956). The Virginia court has ordered elections-at-large of congressmen, Brown v. Saunders, 159 Va. 28, 166 S.E. 105 (1932).

[16] Asbury Park Press, Inc. v. Woolley, 33 N.J. 1, 161 A. 2d 705 (1960).

have acquiesced in the operation of the statute for years. The Kentucky, Missouri, New York, and Washington courts have refused relief where the apportionment had been operative for periods of 13, 21, 5, and 20 years, respectively.[17] In New York the relatively brief period allowed to challenge the apportionment was justified by reference to the constitutional provision for judicial review of apportionment. The New York Court of Appeals stated:

> There are few things in the world in which stability and order are more requisite than in government. . . . This is made plain by the constitutional requirement that every court shall immediately convene and dispose of a litigation involving an apportionment. It would be unreasonable that the utmost speed should be required of the courts . . ., and yet the litigant be not held to any degree of promptness in instituting it.[18]

Even where the New York-type constitutional features are lacking, some courts have suggested that prompt action is necessary. As stated by the Washington court, "No court is required, on a complaint made after this lapse of years, to subject the people of the state to the turmoil such a course would cause." [19] In answer to the claim of laches, however, the New Jersey Supreme Court in 1960 announced, "The point may be disposed of summarily. Acquiescence for no length of time can legalize a clear violation of duty where the people have plainly expressed their will in the Constitution and have appointed judicial tribunals to enforce it." [20]

Another ground which has been advanced by the Minnesota and Wisconsin courts for refusing relief is that a validly enacted

---

[17] Adams v. Bosworth, 126 Ky. 61, 102 S.W. 861 (1907); State ex rel. Lashly v. Becher, 290 Mo. 560, 235 S.W. 1017 (1921); Matter of Reynolds, 202 N.Y. 430, 96 N.E. 87 (1911); State ex rel. Warson v. Howell, 92 Wash. 540, 159 P. 777 (1916).

[18] 202 N.Y. at 439.

[19] 92 Wash. at 545.

[20] Asbury Park Press, Inc. v. Woolley, 33 N.J. 1, 14, 161 A. 2d 705 (1960).

apportionment remains so until replaced by another valid act.[21] The Minnesota court justified its conclusion by stating that because the court cannot compel the legislature to act, it must follow as a corollary that apportionments lawfully enacted continue in force until superseded by a subsequent valid act. The Wisconsin court was also concerned that declaring a once valid enactment invalid because of population changes would leave no source, other than a constitutional convention, to provide another apportionment. The New Jersey Supreme Court, on the other hand, rejected the argument that a once valid apportionment remains valid by stating:

> If by reason of passage of time and changing conditions the reapportionment statute no longer serves its original purpose of securing to the voter the full constitutional value of his franchise, and the legislative branch fails to take appropriate restorative action, the doors of the courts must be open to him. The lawmaking body cannot by inaction alter the constitutional system under which it has its own existence.[22]

The court withheld relief to allow the legislature to act, and the case became moot when the legislature reapportioned.

Where the state courts have found that the most recent apportionment is constitutionally invalid, they have encountered difficulty in providing appropriate relief because the prior apportionment is also most likely to be invalid in view of the most recent population statistics. The Michigan Supreme Court, when asked to require elections under an 1885 act because of the invalidity of the 1891 act, held that the 1885 act was also unconstitutional and then ordered elections under the 1881 act.[23] The court refused to examine the validity of the 1881 statute because it was not in controversy. Other courts have apparently approved elections under the prior apportionment where it has not been placed

---

[21] Smith v. Holm, 220 Minn. 486, 19 N.W. 2d 914 (1945); State ex rel. Martin v. Zimmerman, 249 Wis. 101, 23 N.W. 2d 610 (1946).

[22] Asbury Park Press, Inc. v. Woolley, 33 N.J. 1, 14, 161 A. 2d 705 (1960).

[23] Giddings v. Secretary of State, 93 Mich. 1, 52 N.W. 944 (1892).

in issue by the parties.[24] Presumably those courts which have held that an apportionment originally valid remains so until a subsequent valid apportionment is enacted would order elections under the prior apportionment. Still other courts have not granted any relief because requiring elections under an old apportionment act would result in more striking deviations from the constitutional mandates or would result in no statute under which members of the legislature could be elected. After invalidating the apportionment acts of 1879, 1891, 1893, and 1895 in prior litigation, the Indiana Supreme Court refused to consider the validity of the 1885 apportionment. Asserting the view that the constitutional framers stressed the principle of perpetuity of government, the court stated:

> This court, while free to consider and decide causes . . . can never be authorized to so act as to put an end . . . to the existence of any co-ordinate branch of the State government. Any law, however defective, must stand so long as such law is necessary for the continued movement of the political organization formed by the people.[25]

The Nevada, Oklahoma, and Wyoming courts have refused relief where the only other apportionment available would further diminish representation of underrepresented groups or provide no representation whatsoever for some areas.[26]

The Tennessee and Wisconsin courts have also denied relief on the ground that a declaration of constitutional invalidity would destroy a coordinate branch of government.[27] Their rea-

---

[24] See, for example, Armstrong v. Mitten, 95 Colo. 425, 37 P. 2d 757 (1934); Parker v. State ex rel. Powell, 133 Ind. 178, 32 N.E. 836 (1892); State ex rel. Attorney General v. Cunningham, 81 Wis. 440, 51 N.W. 724 (1892).

[25] Fesler v. Brayton, 145 Ind. 71, 78, 44 N.E. 37 (1896).

[26] State v. Stoddard, 25 Nev. 452, 62 P. 237 (1900); Jones v. Freeman, 193 Okla. 554, 146 P. 2d 564 (1943); State ex rel. Sullivan v. Schnitger, 16 Wyo. 479, 95 P. 698 (1908).

[27] Kidd v. McCanless, 200 Tenn. 273, 292 S.W. 2d 40 (1956), *app. dis.* 352 U.S. 920; State ex rel. Martin v. Zimmerman, 249 Wis. 101, 23 N.W. 2d 610 (1946).

soning has been that such a declaration would render the elections of the current legislature invalid and therefore the legislators could no longer serve. Without a valid legislature no constitutional apportionment could be provided. The conclusions rest upon general principles of law with respect to *de jure* and *de facto* public officials. Under those principles a person may rely upon the acts of a public official as a *de facto* officer even though he does not lawfully hold the office. However, the acts of the *de facto* officer are not valid once his title to office has been adjudged insufficient. The Tennessee Supreme Court, applying the general principles, concluded that

> . . . the *de facto* doctrine cannot be applied to maintain the present members of the General Assembly in office. . . . The ultimate result of holding this Act unconstitutional by reason of the lapse of time would be to deprive us of the present Legislature and the means of electing a new one and ultimately bring about the destruction of the State itself.[28]

Other Judicial Actions

In 1928 an Illinois citizen attempted to enjoin the payment of expenses of the legislature and the salary of its members because of failure to reapportion. The Illinois Supreme Court, although recognizing that the duty of the legislature to reapportion was mandatory and continuing, rejected the indirect attempt to compel reapportionment. The court explained that the duty involved the exercise of legislative power vested solely in the legislature, and therefore "the people have no remedy save to elect a General Assembly which will perform that duty."[29] The court also expressed its opinion that it could enjoin salary payments only if the legislators were not legally holding office and that such a holding would mean that no valid reapportionment could be enacted.

In the following year the Illinois Supreme Court rejected the argument that acts passed by a legislature which has failed to

---

[28] 200 Tenn. at 281-82.
[29] Fergus v. Kinney, 333 Ill. 437, 441, 164 N.E. 665 (1928).

reapportion are unconstitutional. The basis for the conclusion was that the courts are not authorized to declare that the legislature is not a *de jure* body.[30] The Alabama Supreme Court also refused habeas corpus based upon the alleged unconstitutionality of a statute enacted by an allegedly malapportioned legislature. "Probably all governments, at one time or another," the court stated, "have shown breaks from the past in which the theoretical chain of title to sovereignty is broken. Thus, while conquests and revolutions may be wrapped in legalisms, their bases rest on the fact of success. The pragmatic need of avoiding anarchy requires the presumption of legality." [31]

Quo warranto proceedings against the legislators to require them to show by what right and authority they hold office have also proved fruitless. As the Illinois Supreme Court announced: "We have held that this court has no power . . . to compel the legislature to re-apportion. . . . What this court cannot do directly in this respect it cannot do indirectly." [32]

Conclusions

Examination of the state cases involving apportionments which do not conform with the state constitutional provisions reveals that judicial relief is ineffective unless some agency other than the legislature has been given the responsibility for periodic reapportionments. Even where the courts have been willing to state that an existing apportionment is invalid, the judicial relief has been unsatisfactory. To return to an older apportionment may result in even greater departures from the state constitutional standards. Therefore, successful complainants may be in a worse position than under the unconstitutional apportionment.

It should be noted, however, that a mere declaration of unconstitutionality and the retention of jurisdiction has led to legislative apportionments complying with constitutional require-

---

[30] People v. Clardy, 334 Ill. 160, 165 N.E. 638 (1929).
[31] Lindsay v. State, 139 S. 2d 353, 354 (Ala. 1962).
[32] People v. Blackwell, 342 Ill. 232, 225, 173 N.E. 750 (1930).

ments. Nevertheless the conclusion seems inescapable that if the apportionment provisions of the state constitutions are to be made effective, the state constitutions should provide that another agency be empowered to reapportion if the legislature fails to act. The inability of state courts to fashion adequate and effective judicial relief is understandable because state courts derive their powers from the state constitutions. Furthermore, the separation of powers doctrine prohibits judicial interference with a coordinate branch of government.

Finally, we should recognize that exceedingly wide disparities in population among legislative districts often occur because the state constitutions require that result. Consequently, state courts and the apportioning agency, acting exclusively under those constitutions, cannot provide any remedy whatsoever. If the apportionment violates the federal constitution, either the state courts must find some means of giving effective judicial relief or the federal courts must assume the burden.

REAPPORTIONMENT AND THE
FEDERAL CONSTITUTION

Role of The United States Supreme Court

IN EXERCISING ITS FUNCTION as final arbiter of the requirements and limitations imposed by the federal constitution, the United States Supreme Court has developed a number of rules for its own governance. These rules tend to make it possible for the Court to avoid passing upon a number of constitutional questions which are presented to it for decision. Several of these rules have played a significant role in litigation involving apportionment, including the decision of the majority in *Baker* v. *Carr*.[1]

---

[1] 369 U.S. 186 (1962).

Among these rules are: (1) the Court will not decide constitutional questions unless absolutely necessary to the decision in the case; (2) if a non-constitutional ground for decision is available, the constitutional question will be avoided; (3) the Court will not pass upon a constitutional question unless the complainant shows that he has been injured; (4) statutes will be so construed as to avoid raising a constitutional issue, if possible; and (5) legislation and state constitutional provisions are afforded a presumption of constitutionality. In the final analysis, the rules reflect the judicial attitude of the court toward the "gravity and delicacy" of its judicial review function, the comparative finality of its decisions, and the "inherent limitations of the judicial process, arising especially from its largely negative character and limited resources of enforcement."[2] The Court has always been mindful of the fact that the other branches of the government are repositories of constitutional power, that due consideration must be given to their judgment, and that each branch, including the courts, must keep within its proper sphere. Recognition of the division of government powers among the executive, legislative, and judicial branches has led the Court to conclude that certain issues are "non-justiciable." In effect the Court refuses to superimpose its judgment over that of the political departments if the questions involved are "political" in nature, particularly where there is lacking satisfactory criteria for judicial determination.

The Guarantee Clause Cases

From the standpoint of apportionment, the most relevant cases involving "non-justiciability" are those arising under the guarantee clause: "The United States shall guarantee to every State in this Union a Republican Form of Government. . . ."[3] In *Luther* v. *Borden*,[4] a trespass action, the Court was confronted

---

[2] Justice Rutledge in Rescue Army v. Municipal Court of Los Angeles, 331 U.S. 549 (1947).

[3] United States Constitution, article IV, section 4.

[4] 48 U.S. 1 (1849).

with the problem of determining which of two governments was legally constituted in Rhode Island at the time of the political turbulence known historically as Dorr's Rebellion. After noting that the only provision of the Constitution dealing with the problem was the guarantee clause, Chief Justice Taney made clear the Court's view that responsibility for enforcement of the guarantee clause resides with Congress or the President rather than with the courts. He observed that:

> . . . when the senators and representatives of a State are admitted into the councils of the Union, the authority of the government under which they are appointed, as well as its republican character, is recognized by the proper constitutional authority. And its decision is binding on every other department of government and could not be questioned in a judicial tribunal.[5]

The effect of the decision was to remove from judicial consideration the question of whether or not a state has a republican form of government. Over a century has elapsed since that decision, and the Court has consistently adhered to the principles enunciated; namely, that issues raised under the guarantee clause are non-justiciable.

Cogent arguments, both historical and contemporary, have been advanced urging the abandonment of Chief Justice Taney's dicta.[6] During the Reconstruction period the guarantee clause was utilized as a justification for congressional action. However, perhaps partly because the adoption of the fourteenth amendment provided another vehicle for testing the validity of state action in many situations, there has been little additional development of the guarantee clause as a force in American constitutional law. In 1912 the Supreme Court had before it the question of whether or not the initiative and referendum as exercised in Oregon in enacting a tax law were in violation of the republican form guarantee. After indicating that the complaining taxpayers'

---

[5] *Ibid.*, at 42.

[6] See Arthur E. Bonfield, "The Guarantee Clause of Article IV, Section 4: A Study in Constitutional Desuetude," 46 *Minnesota Law Review*, p. 513 (1962).

argument under the fourteenth amendment was spurious, the Supreme Court concluded that the issue was non-justiciable. *Luther* v. *Borden* was considered absolutely controlling in this case.[7] Since then the Supreme Court has continually expanded upon the concepts of due process and equal protection under the fourteenth amendment. It thus has served as a device for settling issues which might have been argued under the guarantee clause. But there are certain issues arguable under the equal protection clause that involve political questions of a nature comparable to those that have led to a holding of non-justiciability under the guarantee clause. The validity of a state legislative apportionment is among these.

Fourteenth Amendment Cases

From the standpoint of judicial precedent the most important case involving apportionment was decided by the Supreme Court in 1946. In *Colegrove* v. *Green*[8] the apportionment of congressional seats in Illinois was alleged to be unconstitutional on a variety of grounds, including the allegation that the apportionment denied equal protection of the laws. The Illinois legislature had failed to reapportion congressional seats since 1901, and on the basis of 1940 census figures the population of the districts varied between 112,116 and 914,053. With only seven Justices participating, four affirmed the lower court's dismissal of the complaint and three dissented. Justice Frankfurter, in an opinion in which two other Justices joined, first indicated that the affirmance could be justified on the basis of statutory provisions, but he then proceeded to explain additional reasons for the holding. Among these was the conclusion that the relief sought was beyond the Court's competence to grant. Characterizing the claim as a demand on "judicial power which cannot be met by verbal fencing," Justice Frankfurter concluded that the issue was "of a

---

[7] Pacific States Telephone & Telegraph Co. v. Oregon, 223 U.S. 118 (1912).

[8] 328 U.S. 549 (1946).

peculiarly political nature and therefore not meet for judicial determination." [9] Reflecting his concern with the inappropriateness of court determination of political issues because of the difficulties involved in affording judicial relief, he observed, "Of course no court can affirmatively re-map the Illinois districts so as to bring them more in conformity with the standards of fairness for a representative system." [10] Pointing to the fact that congressional apportionment is embroiled in politics, he made his position perfectly clear. "Courts ought not to enter this political thicket. . . . The Constitution has many commands that are not enforceable by courts because they clearly fall outside the conditions and purposes that circumscribe judicial action." [11] In other words, if relief is to be afforded, it must be found by resort to political processes. Justice Rutledge concurred in the result but did so only on the basis that the complaint should be dismissed for "want of equity." He specifically drew the Court's attention to the admonition that grave constitutional questions should not be decided if any tenable alternative ground is available.

In the dissenting opinion, Justice Black, with Justices Douglas and Murphy concurring, concluded that equity could and should grant relief. After reviewing the gross inequality in voting power, he unequivocally announced, "The equal protection clause of the Fourteenth Amendment forbids such discrimination." [12] He argued that even though voting is a part of elections and that elections are "political," this was a mere "play upon words," pointing to the cases in which the Supreme Court had dealt with voting-rights questions. On the question of judicial relief he felt that requiring elections-at-large would be appropriate under the circumstances. Finally, because of its significance in recent litigation, we should note Justice Black's observation that "no one would deny that the equal protection clause would also prohibit

---

[9] *Ibid.,* at 552.

[10] *Ibid.,* at 553.

[11] *Ibid.,* at 556.

[12]*Ibid.,* at 569.

a law that would expressly give certain citizens a half-vote and others a full vote." [13]

Colegrove v. *Green,* involving as it did a truncated court and a precarious majority, would hardly alone be considered as authoritative by constitutional scholars. In *Colegrove* v. *Barrett* [14] the Court in a per curiam decision dismissed an appeal "for want of a substantial federal question," citing *Colegrove* v. *Green.* The litigants in the later case sought to test the state legislative apportionment in Illinois under the equal protection clause, alleging a failure to reapportion for over 45 years. In a series of subsequent cases involving other state legislative apportionments, the Georgia county-unit system, and a city council apportionment, the Court dismissed appeals largely by per curiam opinions with Justices Black and Douglas often stating that probable jurisdiction should be noted.[15] In *MacDougall* v. *Green* [16] the complainant sought to invalidate an Illinois statute because it required—as a condition for placing a new political party on the ballot—petitions having at least 200 voter signatures from each of at least 50 counties. In another per curiam opinion, five Justices joining, the Court announced:

> To assume that political power is a function exclusively of numbers is to disregard the practicalities of government. Thus the Constitution protects the interests of the smaller against the greater by giving in the Senate entirely unequal representation to populations. It would be strange indeed, and doctrinaire, for this Court, applying such broad constitutional concepts as due process and equal protection of the laws, to deny a State the power to assure a proper diffusion of political initiative as between its thinly populated counties and those having concentrated masses, in view of the fact that the latter have practical opportunities for exerting their political weight at the polls not available to the former.[17]

---

[13] *Ibid.*

[14] 330 U.S. 804 (1947).

[15] For a collection of the cases, see Baker v. Carr, 369 U.S. 186, 270, n. 1 (1962).

[16] 335 U.S. 281 (1948).

[17] *Ibid.,* at 283-84, citing Colegrove v. Green and Colegrove v. Barrett.

Again Justice Rutledge thought merely that the Court should decline to exercise its equity jurisdiction because of the short time before the election. Justices Black, Douglas, and Murphy dissented stating their belief that the fourteenth amendment was violated by such legislation. Justice Douglas, writing for the dissenters, categorically stated, "None would deny that a state law giving some citizens twice the vote in either the primary or general election would lack that equality which the Fourteenth Amendment guarantees." [18] However he noted that federal courts should enjoin state elections only when such action would be satisfactory and effective, although he felt that in the particular case no "futile or ineffective" judicial action was involved.

Although legal arguments could be advanced that these cases did not establish precedent for the proposition that the fourteenth amendment was unavailable as a vehicle for obtaining relief in cases of malapportionment, the conclusion seemed inescapable, for most legal commentators, that the Supreme Court had precluded relief, particularly in light of the statements contained in the opinions.

Meanwhile the Supreme Court's expansion of due process and equal protection concepts as limitations upon state action culminated in the unanimous opinion declaring segregation in public schools unconstitutional.[19] Interestingly, the Supreme Court was confronted in that case with problems involving the nature, appropriateness, and effectiveness of judicial relief. Nonetheless, the Court did not hesitate to find a denial of equal protection of the law. Consequently, it placed upon lower federal courts the duty of formulating adequate relief as specific factual situations demanded. Subsequent events have revealed the difficulties encountered in enforcing the judicial orders, but generally speaking the experience has indicated that court decrees can be made effective despite highly tense political and social environments. Therefore the school segregation case seemed to undercut the effectiveness of the argument that the difficulties in devising

---

[18] *Ibid.*, at 288.

[19] Brown v. Board of Education, 347 U.S. 483 (1954).

effective judicial relief in apportionment cases should be a weighty consideration in holding them non-justiciable.

Fifteenth Amendment Cases

In *Gomillion* v. *Lightfoot* [20] Negro complainants alleged that an Alabama statute redefining the boundaries of the city of Tuskegee violated the fourteenth amendment and denied them the right to vote in defiance of the fifteenth amendment. The statute removed from the city all but four or five of its 400 Negro voters. The lower court dismissed the case on grounds utilized in the apportionment cases; namely, failure to state a claim upon which relief could be granted as well as lack of jurisdiction. In overruling the dismissal Justice Frankfurter writing for the majority concluded that *Colegrove* v. *Green* did not preclude judicial action because the racial character of the legislation lifted the "controversy out of the so-called 'political' arena and into the conventional sphere of constitutional litigation." [21] Justice Douglas concurred on the basis of his dissents in the apportionment cases. Necessarily, the racial discrimination involved makes this case distinguishable from the apportionment cases because of the specificity of the fifteenth amendment with respect to voting rights. Again, however, it should be noted that judicial relief involved striking down a state law defining a political boundary, and some slight erosion of the non-justiciability doctrine was involved.

---

[20] 364 U.S. 339 (1960).

[21] *Ibid.*, at 347.

CONCLUSIONS

THE 1950 AND 1960 FEDERAL censuses revealed major population shifts in many states, particularly in the growth of urban
areas and the continued relative decline of rural population.
Instances of malapportionment became more severe, and it was
inevitable that relief would continue to be sought by resort to the
judiciary. As we have seen, in many states the possibility of
obtaining state court relief where the apportionment did not
comply with the state constitutional provisions was indeed
minimal. Reliance on the equal protection clause, although certainly not promising, appeared feasible for a number of reasons.

First, many of the Supreme Court cases denying relief could be differentiated on a factual basis, particularly by reference to the state constitutional requirements. Second, the Supreme Court's expansion of due process and equal protection concepts made more cogent the argument that malapportionment denied equal protection of the laws. Third, failure of state legislatures to reapportion made the inequities even more pronounced. Fourth, the willingness of the Supreme Court to provide judicial relief in somewhat comparable situations indicated that less reliance would be placed on this factor in determining the justiciability question. Fifth, the lack of unanimity in prior cases coupled with rather strong dissenting views and changes in Court personnel made it possible for complainants to hope that the Supreme Court would hear arguments in a new apportionment case involving somewhat different facts.

As expected, the litigation received a mixed acceptance in the federal district courts. In one case a motion was denied to dismiss a complaint alleging a denial of equal protection because of failure to reapportion the Hawaii Territorial Legislature. After pointing to the school segregation and Negro voting cases, the district court announced:

> The time has come, and the Supreme Court has marked the way, when serious consideration should be given to a reversal of the traditional reluctance of judicial intervention in legislative apportionment. The whole thrust of today's legal climate is to end unconstitutional discrimination. It is ludicrous to preclude judicial relief when a mainspring of representative government is impaired.[1]

In Minnesota, a three-judge district court took jurisdiction but declined to provide judicial relief until the state legislature had a further opportunity to act.[2] Thereafter the case was dismissed as moot, the legislature meanwhile having reapportioned.[3] Contrariwise, in Michigan, New York, and Tennessee the courts

[1] Dyer v. Kazuhisa Abe, 138 F. Supp. 220, 236 (1956).
[2] Macgraw v. Donovan, 163 F. Supp. 184 (1958).
[3] 177 F. Supp. 803 (1959).

dismissed actions apparently on the basis of the Supreme Court's decisions in the Colegrove case and its progeny.[4] On appeal the decision of the Supreme Court in the Tennessee case of *Baker* v. *Carr* [5] marked the turning point in apportionment litigation. Both the Michigan and New York cases were remanded for review in light of the Tennessee decision. Unquestionably the legal setting was materially altered, but as we shall see, the ramifications of the decision in both the legal and practical senses remain conjectural.

---

[4] Scholle v. Hare, 360 Mich. 1, 184 N.E. 2d 63 (1960); W.M.C.A. Inc. v. Simon, 202 F. Supp. 741 (S.D.N.Y. 1962); Baker v. Carr, 179 F. Supp. 824 (M.D. Tenn. 1959).
[5] 369 U.S. 186 (1962).

APPENDIX

APPORTIONMENT OF LEGISLATURES

As of December 1962

State or other jurisdiction	Citation: article and section of constitution	Basis of apportionment		Frequency of required reapportionment		Apportioning agency	Dates of last two apportionments	
		Senate	House	Required every 10 years*	Other schedules for reapportioning			
Alabama	IV, 50; IX, 197-203; XVIII, 284	Population, except no district more than one member.	Population, but each county at least one member.	X	......	Legislature.	1962	1901
Alaska	VI, XIV	Area, with population factors; combination of house districts into four at-large districts and a varying number of minor districts.	Population (civilian) 19 districts.	X	......	Apportionment board; its recommendations are reviewed, and confirmed or changed by the Governor.	1956	1953
Arizona	IV, 2, 1 (1)	Districts specifically established by constitution.	Votes cast for Governor at last preceding general election, but not less than if computed on basis of election of 1930.	..	After every gubernatorial election (every 2 years).	No provision for Senate; redistricting for House by County Boards of Supervisors.	1958	1956

APPORTIONMENT OF LEGISLATURES

As of December 1962

State or other jurisdiction	Citation: article and section of constitution	Basis of apportionment		Frequency of required reapportionment		Apportioning agency	Dates of last two apportionments
		Senate	House	Required every 10 years*	Other schedules for reapportioning		
Arkansas ... VIII, 1-5; Amndt. XLV		Senate is fixed. (a)	Each county at least one member; remaining members distributed among more populous counties according to population.	X	......	Board of Apportionment (Governor, Secretary of State, and Attorney General). Subject to revision by State Supreme Court.	1961 1951
California .. IV, 6		Population, exclusive of persons ineligible to naturalization. No county, or city and county, to have more than one member; no more than three counties in any district.	Population, exclusive of persons ineligible to naturalization.	X	......	Legislature or, if it fails, a reapportionment commission (Lieutenant Governor, Controller, Attorney General, Secretary of State, and Superintendent of Public Instruction). In either case, subject to a referendum.	1961 1951
Colorado ... V, 45-47		Population ratios.	Population ratios.	..	Every 5 years(b)	General Assembly.	1953 1933

State	House	Senate	Senate		Body which reapportions			
Connecticut .III, 3, 4, 5	Population, but each county at least one member.	Two members from each town having over 5,000 population; others, same number as in 1874.	.....	.....	General Assembly for Senate, no provision for House.	.....	H-1876 S-1903	1818 .....
Delaware ..II, 2	Districts specifically established by constitution.	Districts specifically established by constitution.	:	.....	No provision.	.....	1897	.....
Florida ....VII, 3, 4	Population, but no county more than one member.	3 to each of 5 largest counties, 2 to each of next 18, 1 each to others.	X	.....	Legislature.	.....	H-1955	1945
Georgia ...III, 2; (Par. 1), 3 (Pars. 1, 2)	Territory, but no senatorial district more than one member.	Population, i.e., 3 to each of 8 largest counties, 2 to each of next 30, 1 each to others.	X	.....	General Assembly "may" change senatorial districts. Shall change House apportionment at first session after each U.S. census.	.....	1961	1953
Hawaii ....III, 2, 4	Districts specified by constitution.	Population, but each county at least one.	X	.....	Governor.	.....	1959	1958

41

APPORTIONMENT OF LEGISLATURES

As of December 1962

State or other jurisdiction	Citation: article and section of constitution	Basis of apportionment — Senate	Basis of apportionment — House	Frequency of required reapportionment — Required every 10 years*	Frequency of required reapportionment — Other schedules for reapportioning	Apportioning agency	Dates of last two apportionments
Idaho	III, 2, 4, 5; XIX, 1, 2	One member from each county.	Total House not to exceed 3 times Senate. Each county entitled to at least one representative, apportioned as provided by law.	X	......	Legislature.	1951 1941
Illinois	IV, 6, 7, 8	Fixed districts based on area.	Population.	House	Senate is fixed.	General Assembly or, if it fails, a reapportionment commission appointed by the Governor.	1955 1901
Indiana	IV, 4, 5, 6	Male inhabitants over 21 years of age.	Male inhabitants over 21 years of age.	..	Every 6 years.	General Assembly.	1921 1915

State	Constitutional Reference	Basis (Lower House)	Basis (Senate)			Body	Years
Iowa	III, 34, 35	Population, but no county more than one member.	One to each county, and one additional to each of the nine most populous counties.	X	......	General Assembly.	H-1927 1921 / S-1911 1906
Kansas	II, 2; X, 1-3	Population.	Population, but each county at least one.	..	Every 5 years.	Legislature.	H-1961 1959 / S-1947 1933
Kentucky	Sec. 33	Population.	Population, but no more than two counties to be joined in a district.	X	......	General Assembly.	1942 1918
Louisiana	III, 2-6	Population.	Population, but each parish and each ward of New Orleans at least one member.	X	......	Legislature.	1921 1902
Maine	IV, Pt. 1, 2, 3; IV, Pt. II, 1	Population, exclusive of aliens and Indians not taxed. No county less than one nor more than five.	Population, exclusive of aliens. No town more than seven members, unless a consolidated town.	House(c)	......	Legislature.	H-1961 1955 / S-1961 1951

APPORTIONMENT OF LEGISLATURES

As of December 1962

State or other jurisdiction	Citation: article and section of constitution	Basis of apportionment		Frequency of required reapportionment		Apportioning agency	Dates of last two apportionments
		Senate	House	Required every 10 years*	Other schedules for reapportioning		
Maryland ..III, 2, 5		One from each county and from each of six districts constituting Baltimore City.	Population, but minimum of two and maximum of six per county. Each of Baltimore districts as many members as largest county.(d)	:	......	Membership frozen for House; no provision for Senate.	1962 1943
Massachusetts ..Amdt. LXXI		Legal voters.	Legal voters.	X	......	General Court.	H-1947 1939 S-1960 1948
Michigan ..V, 2-4		Districts specifically prescribed by constitution.	Population.(e)	House	Senate is fixed.	Legislature or, if it fails, State Board of Canvassers apportions House. Senate is fixed.	1953 1943
Minnesota ..IV, 2, 23, 24		Population, exclusive of nontaxable Indians.(f)	Population, exclusive of nontaxable Indians.(f)	X	And after each state census.	Legislature "shall have power."	1959(g)1913

State	Apportionment of lower house	Apportionment of upper house		When reapportioned	Body		
Mississippi .. XIII, 254-256	Prescribed by constitution.	Prescribed by constitution, each county at least one. Counties grouped into three divisions, each division to have at least 44 members.	X	.....	Legislature "may."	1916	1904
Missouri ...III, 2-11	Population.	Population, but each county at least one member.	X	.....	House: Secretary of State apportions among counties; county courts apportion within counties. Senate: by commission appointed by Governor.	1961	1951
Montana ...V, 4; VI, 2-6	One member from each county.	Population, but at least one member from each county.	X	Session following federal census.	Legislative Assembly.	1961	1951
Nebraska ...III, 5	Unicameral legislature—population excluding aliens.	Unicameral legislature—population	..	From time to time, but no oftener than once every 10 years.	Legislature "may."	1935	1920
Nevada ....I, 13; IV, 5	One member for each county.	Population.	X	.....	Legislature.	1961	1951
New Hampshire Pt. II, 9, 11, 26	Direct taxes paid.	Population. (h)	House	Senate—from time to time.	General Court.	H-1961 S-1961	1951 1915

APPORTIONMENT OF LEGISLATURES

As of December 1962

State or other jurisdiction	Citation: article and section of constitution	Basis of apportionment		Frequency of required reapportionment		Apportioning agency	Dates of last two apportionments
		Senate	House	Required every 10 years*	Other schedules for reapportioning		
New Jersey. IV, ii, 1; IV, iii, 1		One member from each county.	Population, but at least one member from each county.	X	.....	For lower house, Governor apportions among counties; Secretary of State certifies to county clerks.	1961 1941
New Mexico IV, 3		One member from each county.	At least one member for each county and additional representatives for more populous counties.	X	.....	Legislature "may."	1955 1949
New York.. III, 3-5		Population, excluding aliens. No county more than 1/3 membership, nor more than 1/2 membership to two adjoining counties.	Population, excluding aliens each county (except Hamilton) at least one member.	X	.....	Legislature. Subject to review by courts.	1954 1944

State						
North Carolina . II, 4-6	Population, excluding aliens and Indians not taxed.	Population, excluding aliens and Indians not taxed, but each county at least one member.	X	......	General Assembly.	H-1961 1941 S-1941 1921
North Dakota .. II, 26, 29, 32, 35	Set by constitution, but somewhat reflects population.	Population, but each county or district entitled to one member.	X	......	Legislative Assembly, or if it fails, a special board composed of Chief Justice of Supreme Court, Attorney General, Secretary of State, and Majority and Minority Leaders of House shall reapportion House.	1961 1931
Ohio ...... XI, 1-11		Population, but each county at least one member.	X(i)	Each biennium(i).	Governor, Auditor, and Secretary of State, or any two of them.	1961 1951
Oklahoma ..V, 9-16	Population	Population, but no county to have more than seven members.(j)	X	......	Legislature.	1961 1951

APPORTIONMENT OF LEGISLATURES

As of December 1962

State or other jurisdiction	Citation: article and section of constitution	Basis of apportionment		Frequency of required reapportionment		Apportioning agency	Dates of last two apportionments
		Senate	House	Required every 10 years*	Other schedules for reapportioning		
Oregon	IV, 6, 7	Population.	Population.	X	......	Legislative Assembly, or failing that, Secretary of State. Reapportionment subject to Supreme Court review.	1961 1954
Pennsylvania	II, 16-18	Population, but no city or county to have more than 1/6 of membership.	Population, but each county at least one member.	X	......	General Assembly.	H-1953 1921 S-1921 1906
Rhode Island ...	XIII; Amdt. XIX	Qualified voters, but minimum of 1 and maximum of 6 per city or town.	Population, but at least one member from each town or city, and no town or city more than 1/4 of total, i.e., 25.	..	......	General Assembly "may" after any Presidential election.	H-1930 .... S-1940 ....

State	Basis of apportionment (Senate)	Basis of apportionment (House)			Apportioning body		
South Carolina ..III, 1-8	One member from each county.	Population, but at least one member from each county.	X	.....	General Assembly.	1961	1952
South Dakota ..III, 5	Population.	Population.	X	.....	Legislature, or failing that, Governor, Superintendent of Public Instruction, Presiding Judge of Supreme Court, Attorney General, and Secretary of State.	1961	1951
Tennessee ..II, 4-6	Qualified voters.	Qualified voters.	X	.....	General Assembly.	1962	1901(k)
Texas ......III, 25-26a, 28	Qualified electors, but no county more than one member.	Population, but no county more than 7 representatives unless population greater than 700,000, then 1 additional representative for each 100,000.	X	.....	Legislature or, if it fails, Legislative Redistricting Board (Lieutenant Governor, Speaker of House, Attorney General, Comptroller of Public Accounts, and Commissioner of General Land Office).	1961	1951
Utah ......IX, 2, 4	Population.	Population. Each county at least one member, with additional representatives on a population ratio.	X	.....	Legislature.	1955	1931

APPORTIONMENT OF LEGISLATURES

As of December 1962

State or other jurisdiction	Citation: article and section of constitution	Basis of apportionment		Frequency of required reapportionment		Apportioning agency	Dates of last two apportionments
		Senate	House	Required every 10 years*	Other schedules for reapportionment		
Vermont .. II, 13, 18, 37		Population, but each county at least one member.	One member from each inhabited town.	Senate	Senate—or after each state census.	Legislature apportions Senate; no provision for House.	H-1793(1) 1962 1941
Virginia .. IV, 43		Population.	Population.	X	.....	General Assembly.	1962 1958
Washington. II, 3, 6; XXII, 1, 2		Population, excluding Indians not taxed and soldiers, sailors, and officers of U.S. Army and Navy in active service.	Population, excluding Indians not taxed and soldiers, sailors and officers of U. S. Army and Navy in active service.	X	.....	Legislature, or by initiative.	1957 1931
West Virginia .. VI, 4-10, 50		Population, but no two members from any county, unless one county constitutes a district.	Population, but each county at least one member.	X	.....	Legislature.	1950 1940

State & Citation	House	Senate		Body			
Wisconsin ..IV, 3-5	Population.	Population.	....	Legislature.	X	1951	1921
Wyoming ..III, 3; III, 2-4	Population, but each county at least one member.	Population, but each county at least one member.	....	Legislature.	X	1931	1921
Guam .....Organic Act: 1950 (2d), Sec. 512	Legislature elected at large.	....	....	....	..	....	....
Puerto Rico. III, 3, 4, 7	Two senators for each of eight senatorial districts, and eleven at large.	One representative for each of 40 representative districts and eleven at large.	....	Board composed of Chief Justice and two additional members representing different political parties, appointed by Governor with Senate consent.	X	1952	1917

* Every ten years, or after each federal census.

Abbreviations: H—House; S—Senate.

(a) Amendment adopted November, 1956, "froze" the senatorial districts as then established. Future apportionment of the Senate will not be made.

(b) Required every five years, after each federal and each state census.

(c) Constitutional provision "at most ten years and at least five."

(d) In 1948, membership in House frozen at then existing levels.

(e) Any county with a moiety of ratio of population is entitled to separate representation.

(f) Section on Indiana is still in constitution but is ineffective due to federal legislation.

(g) Effective in 1962.

(h) Amendment adopted in November, 1942, sets the membership of the House of Representatives at not more than 400 and not less than 375. It requires, for each representative additional to the first, twice the number of inhabitants required for the first, with the provision that a town or ward which is not entitled to a representative all of the time may send one a proportionate part of the time, and at least once in every 10 years.

(i) At the reapportionment following the decennial census, a ratio is established to provide for fractional representation during the succeeding decade. Any county or senatorial district with a population larger than the minimum requirement for Representative or Senator, but not as large as required for an additional full Representative or Senator, is allotted fractional additional representation by adding a Representative or Senator for one to four of the legislative sessions during the decade.

(j) In practice no county has less than one member.

(k) In 1945 a flotorial district was changed to eliminate one county.

(l) Apportionment plan for House is provided in the constitution with no provisions for reapportionment. House apportionment thus dates from adoption of constitution in 1793.

Source: *Book of the States*, as amended to December 1, 1962

LEGAL SETTING:
POST-BAKER v. CARR

By William J. Pierce

THE DECISION IN *BAKER* V. *CARR*

ALTHOUGH THE DECISION in *Baker* v. *Carr* has been heralded as "one of the most important of the century," [1] its ultimate significance in terms of a solution to malapportionment problems remains conjectural. This uncertainty arises mainly from the fact that the majority opinion in which six Justices joined did not decide the merits of the claim involved, namely, whether the Tennessee apportionment scheme violated the equal protection clause of the fourteenth amendment. The majority opinion

---

[1] Thomas Emerson, "Malapportionment and Judicial Power," 72 *Yale Law Journal*, p. 64 (1962).

written by Justice Brennan carefully confined the decision by stating:

> . . . we hold today only (a) that the court possessed jurisdiction of the subject matter; (b) that a justiciable cause of action is stated upon which appellants would be entitled to appropriate relief; and (c) . . . that appellants have standing to challenge the Tennessee apportionment statute.[2]

The limited nature of the holding was emphasized by Justice Stewart in his separate concurring opinion.[3] Despite this, the Supreme Court, by remanding the case for trial and decision, has definitely laid the groundwork for a further expansion of equal protection guarantees accorded judicial protection. Furthermore, the majority opinion did provide some slight, but exceedingly general, guidance to the lower court as regards the tests to be applied in determining the validity of the Tennessee apportionment under the equal protection clause. "Judicial standards under the Equal Protection Clause are well developed and familiar," Justice Brennan wrote, "and it has been open to the courts since the enactment of the Fourteenth Amendment to determine, if on the particular facts they must, that a discrimination reflects *no* policy, but simply arbitrary and capricious action."[4] Finally, in answer to the problem of providing appropriate relief by judicial order, the majority merely noted ". . . we have no cause at this stage to doubt the District Court will be able to fashion relief if violations of constitutional rights are found. . . ."[5]

Only Justice Clark was willing to decide the case on its merits. Pointing to the fact that 37 percent of the voters of Tennessee elect 20 of the 33 senators and that 40 percent of the voters elect 63 of the 99 members of the house, he concluded that the "frequency and magnitude of the inequalities in the present districting admit of no policy whatever" and that the "apportionment

---

[2] 369 U.S. 186, 197-98 (1962).

[3] *Ibid.,* at 265.

[4] *Ibid.,* at 226.

[5] *Ibid.,* at 198.

picture in Tennessee is a topsy-turvical of gigantic proportions." [6] However, Justice Clark indicated that he would not favor intervention by the Supreme Court into "so delicate a field if there were any other relief available to the people of Tennessee." [7]

In Tennessee the initiative and referendum are not available, and even the call of a constitutional convention requires legislative approval. As we shall see, the availability of relief through political devices has been pointed to by some courts in more recent litigation as a basis for rejecting attacks upon the apportionment patterns in other states.

It remained for Justice Frankfurter in his dissenting opinion (in which Justice Harlan concurred) to assert perhaps the ultimate significance of the decision. Characterizing the majority position as a "massive repudiation of the experience of our whole past," [8] he concluded that "the case is of that class of political controversy which by the nature of its subject, is unfit for federal judicial action." [9] Although the majority opinion concluded that the claim involved did not rest upon or implicate the guarantee clause ("The United States shall guarantee to every State in this Union a Republican Form of Government. . . .") [10] and also distinguished the guarantee clause cases, Justice Frankfurter opined that the claim was "in effect, a Guarantee Clause claim masquerading under a different label." [11]

Finally, in explaining his reasons for believing that the claim should be held non-justiciable, Justice Frankfurter stated that considerable weight should be given to the "difficulty or impossibility of devising judicial remedies in this class of case." [12] He felt that an injunction to restrain general elections would paralyze a state's political system, that a declaration devoid of compulsion

---

[6] *Ibid.*, at 254.
[7] *Ibid.*, at 258.
[8] *Ibid.*, at 267.
[9] *Ibid.*, at 330.
[10] United States Constitution, article IV, section 4.
[11] 369 U.S. 186, *op. cit.*, at 297.
[12] *Ibid.*, at 327.

was an idle threat, that elections-at-large had too sweeping political implications, and that a state might be deprived of an effective "law-based" legislature under its own constitution.

In general, however, Justice Frankfurter's opinion reflects his basic philosophy concerning the proper role of the judiciary in constitutional litigation.

> Disregard of inherent limits in the effective exercise of the Court's "judicial Power" not only presages the futility of judicial intervention in the essentially political conflict of forces by which the relation between population and representation has time out of mind been and now is determined. It may well impair the Court's position as the ultimate organ of "the supreme Law of the Land" in that vast range of legal problems, often strongly entangled in popular feeling, on which this Court must pronounce.[13]

Emphasizing this concern, he asserted that the majority's failure to provide guidance to the lower courts "manifests an odd—indeed an esoteric—conception of judicial propriety." [14] Pointing to Justice Clark's concurring opinion, he claimed that it afforded a "disheartening preview of the mathematical quagmire (apart from divers judicially inappropriate and elusive determinants) into which this Court today catapults the lower courts of the country without so much as adumbrating the basis for a legal calculus as a means of extrication." [15]

. Justice Harlan in his dissenting opinion, which Justice Frankfurter joined, examined the merits of the claim and concluded that the "allegations, accepting all of them as true, do not, parsed down or as a whole, show an infringement by Tennessee of any rights assured by the Fourteenth Amendment." [16] "I can find nothing in the Equal Protection Clause or elsewhere in the Federal Constitution which expressly or impliedly supports the view that state legislatures must be so structured as to reflect

---

[13] *Ibid.*, at 267.

[14] *Ibid.*, at 268.

[15] *Ibid.*

[16] *Ibid.*, at 331.

with approximate equality the voice of every voter." [17]   In a separate appendix entitled "The Inadequacy of Arithmetical Formulas as Measures of the Rationality of Tennessee's Apportionment," Justice Harlan argued that Tennessee's apportionment could be found to possess rationality by maintaining rigidity and preserving the electoral strength of rural areas.[18]

[17] *Ibid.*, at 332.
[18] *Ibid.*, at 340.

SUBSEQUENT FEDERAL AND
STATE COURT LITIGATION

Apportionment and the Fourteenth Amendment

IT MIGHT BE ARGUED that "invidious discrimination" proscribed
by the equal protection clause was the implicit finding of the
majority in the Tennessee apportionment scheme. The better
view, however, and that which apparently has been accepted by
most state and federal courts in subsequent apportionment litigation, would seem to be that the *Baker* v. *Carr* decision did not
provide any standards for determining the validity of apportionment schemes even by reference to the specific facts of the

Tennessee situation.[1] In legal terms, therefore, the effect of *Baker* v. *Carr* on the malapportionment problem remains uncertain. This uncertainty will undoubtedly persist until the Supreme Court reviews the Alabama, Maryland, Michigan, and New York cases which now are pending.

Meanwhile we may receive some guidance as to the standards which eventually may evolve by an examination of the lower court opinions rendered since *Baker* v. *Carr*. Perhaps in the final analysis these opinions reflect basic differences of opinion as to the function of representative government.

On the one hand, some stress, in effect, the "one-man, one-vote" principle. In other words, each representative district should contain the same population (or an equivalent, such as registered voters, eligible voters, or voters participating in a preceding election). Any significant variation from this standard—recognizing that some minor inequalities may exist because of the difficulty in drawing boundary lines of election districts—is considered to be constitutionally invalid. This approach recently has been endorsed by the majority report of the Advisory Commission on Intergovernmental Relations. It categorically states, " 'Equal protection of the laws' would seem to presume, and considerations of political equity demand, that the apportionment of both houses in the State legislature, be based strictly on population." [2]

Others believe that departures from numerical equality are valid if they have any "rational" justifications. This approach would permit a much wider range of valid apportionment schemes. However, it may vary depending upon premises adopted by those utilizing its flexible nature. Some might start, for example, with the proposition that numerical equality is the rule from which rational departures are permissible. Others would

---

[1] Jerrold Israel, "On Charting a Course Through the Mathematical Quagmire: The Future of *Baker* v. *Carr*," 61 *Michigan Law Review*, pp. 107, 112 (1962).

[2] Advisory Commission on Intergovernmental Relations, *Apportionment of State Legislatures*, December 1962, p. 67.

frankly assume that different basic apportionment rules may be valid, at least with respect to one house of a bicameral legislature (such as apportionment of seats among local governmental units) from which rational departures may be made, including recognition of the population factor.

In addition to these variations in attitude, one must not lose sight of the fact that the attitude toward the propriety and nature of judicial remedies also may have important ramifications. If one feels that the possible judicial remedies available are inadequate or impractical, then he may well reach the conclusion that the range of constitutional apportionment standards is relatively broad. Another underlying factor may well be the attitude toward the role of the states, as governmental institutions, in the last half of the 20th century. The majority report of the Advisory Commission on Intergovernmental Relations emphasized the federal-state relationship problems in endorsing the one-man, one-vote approach by stating:

> If minority interests are permitted to control the legislative branch of State government so as to defeat the wishes of the majority, the nation is faced with one of three alternatives: (1) the eclipse of State government because the people will turn to a more broadly responsive National Government to obtain their needs; (2) the perpetuation of tyranny of a minority over the affairs of State government; or (3) the resort to precipitous or illegal means by the majority of the people whose desires have been frustrated.[3]

These and many other considerations of minor and major significance undoubtedly affect the conclusions of responsible officials and others who are called upon to define the standards to be applied in determining the constitutionality of legislative apportionment schemes. Unfortunately, or fortunately if you prefer, these underlying considerations often do not find expression in judicial utterances. Nevertheless, we should recognize their presence even though, in the legal context, we must make evalua-

---

[3] *Ibid.*, p. 7.

tions of judicial opinions only on the basis of strict analysis of the written words emanating from the judges.

Many of the recent opinions are difficult to appraise, however, because statements in the opinions are often ambiguous and reasonable readers may draw different conclusions. Yet, some classification of the recent cases as interpreted by the author may be useful in delineating the major trends that have appeared.

One-Man, One-Vote Principle

Although many commentators have endorsed the numerical equality principle,[4] at least four of the eight Justices participating in the *Baker* v. *Carr* decision indicated that this was not the only standard which would be constitutionally valid under the equal protection clause. The two dissenters, Frankfurter and Harlan, found no invalidity in the Tennessee apportionment statutes. In addition Justice Clark indicated that he would apply the law as stated in *MacDougall* v. *Green*: [5]

> It would be strange indeed, and doctrinaire, for this Court, applying such broad constitutional concepts as due process and equal protection of the laws, to deny a State the power to assure a proper diffusion of political initiative as between its thinly populated counties and those having concentrated masses, *in view of the fact that the latter have practical opportunities for exerting their political weight at the polls not available to the former.*[6]

Furthermore, Justice Stewart in his concurring opinion even more explicitly indicated that he did not believe that the decision of the majority should be read as requiring numerical equality. "Contrary to the suggestion of my Brother Harlan," he wrote, "the Court does not say or imply that 'state legislatures must be so structured as to reflect with approximate equality the voice

---

[4] Twentieth Century Fund, *One Man-One Vote* (1962); Advisory Commission on Intergovernmental Relations Report, *op. cit.*

[5] 335 U.S. 281 (1948).

[6] Baker v. Carr, 369 U.S. 186, 252, emphasis supplied by Justice Clark quoting MacDougall v. Green, 335 U.S. at 284.

of every voter' . . . and contrary to the suggestion of my Brother Douglas, the Court most assuredly does not decide the question 'may a State weight the vote of one county or one district more heavily than it weights the vote in another?' " [7] He also cited language from a prior equal protection case [8] to the effect that "the Fourteenth Amendment permits the States a wide scope of discretion in enacting laws which affect some groups of citizens differently than others." [9]

In subsequent litigation, the Michigan Supreme Court, among others, has placed considerable emphasis on the numerical equality test as the standard for determining constitutional validity of an apportionment scheme. After the Supreme Court remanded the Scholle case [10] to the Michigan Supreme Court for reconsideration in light of its decision in the Tennessee case, the Michigan court declared the apportionment of the Michigan senate invalid. In 1952 the voters of Michigan had frozen, in effect, the then existing senate apportionment by adopting a constitutional amendment. In a majority opinion in which, however, only one other justice concurred, Justice Kavanaugh concluded:

> When a legislative apportionment provides districts having more than double the population of others, the constitutional range of discretion is violated. This is not to say that less than such 2 to 1 ratio is constitutionally good. It is to say only that peril ends and disaster occurs when that line is crossed.[11]

The majority opinion of Justice Souris, concurred in by one other justice, apparently recognized the possibility of some variation from the numerical equality principle by stating, "The lesson . . . is that the Fourteenth Amendment requires substantial equality between citizens except where there exist differences justifying the classification of citizens, in which event there must

---

[7] Baker v. Carr, 369 U.S. 186, 265.

[8] McGowan v. Maryland, 366 U.S. 420 (1961).

[9] 369 U.S. at 266.

[10] Scholle v. Hare, 369 U.S. 429, remanding 360 Mich. 1, 104 N.W. 2d 63 (1960).

[11] 367 Mich. 176, 189, 116 N.W. 2d at 355 (1962).

be equality within the classes."[12] However, he added, "Beyond the objective of according to citizens effective representation in the legislature, it is difficult for me to conceive of any other legitimate State purpose for classification of citizens in their participation in the electoral process, a process inherently the right of each individual citizen. Perhaps there are such other legitimate objectives of classification which would constitutionally justify State denial of the citizen's right to a free and undiluted ballot, but if there are such, none has been suggested nor can be imagined by me which would save the 1952 amendments from constitutional invalidity."[13]

Another decision, in Oklahoma, which may be considered as utilizing the numerical equality test is that of the federal district court in *Moss* v. *Burkhart*.[14] The opinion apparently left room for some other standard by stating:

> While mere numerical disparity in voting strength is not, per se, invidiously discriminatory, it is, to be sure, cogent evidence of it and . . . may be sufficiently disproportionate to constitute a prima facie showing. This is so, we think, because under our democratic institutions and republican form of government, the suffrage right of the individual is, and must be, the keystone—the common denominator, of self-government.[15]

More specifically, in its later per curiam order the court established the following standard:

> The Oklahoma Legislature will be reapportioned on the general principle of substantial numerical equality, to the end that each voter shall have approximately the same power and influence in the election of members of the two houses, which is in consonance with the intent and spirit of the Oklahoma Constitution and the equal protection clause of the Fourteenth Amendment. . . .[16]

---

[12] 367 Mich. at 240, 116 N.W. 2d at 388.
[13] 367 Mich. at 243, 116 N.W. 2d at 381-82.
[14] 207 F. Supp. 885 (1962).
[15] *Ibid.*, at 893.
[16] *Ibid.*, at 898.

Furthermore, the court struck down the provision of the Oklahoma Constitution which placed a seven-member ceiling on the number of representatives from any county. The decree also specifically stated that Oklahoma and Tulsa Counties, the most populous, are entitled to 19 and 15 legislative seats, respectively. The court retained jurisdiction, however, until March 1963 in order to allow the legislature to act. It indicated that if reapportionment was not effected by the legislature, it would be achieved by judicial order in conformity with the guidance offered by the court. Therefore, in formulating its standard the Oklahoma district court apparently attached primary significance to the numerical equality standard. It should be emphasized, however, that the Oklahoma Constitution, like the Tennessee Constitution, generally required apportionment of both houses upon the basis of population.

The Rhode Island Supreme Court also has indicated that the numerical equality test should be followed in apportioning at least one house of the legislature. After observing that apportionment along municipal and county lines does not necessarily constitute a denial of equal protection, the court stated, "The dilution of the vote of a majority of electors to one-fourth of that enjoyed by others is, in our opinion, so unjust as to be invidiously discriminatory." [17] In suggesting possible reapportionment plans the court indicated that no greater than a 2 to 1 discrepancy in the population of assembly districts should be permitted. Because the validity of the senate apportionment was not contested, the court did not express its views concerning the applicability of the numerical equality test to that body as well.

Rational Departures From One-Man, One-Vote Principle

The Solicitor General of the United States, Archibald Cox, is a major advocate of a standard which predominantly requires numerical equality but allows "rational" departures.[18] In explain-

---

[17] Sweeney v. Notte, 183A. 2d 296 (1962).

[18] See Brief for the United States as Amicus Curiae, p. 25, Baker v. Carr, 369 U.S. 186 (1962).

ing the position taken by the Federal Government in the Tennessee case, he has written:

> An apportionment which produces extreme and capricious divergencies in voting power without any evident reason or justification will be held to violate the Fourteenth Amendment. In *Baker* v. *Carr* we argued as *amicus curiae* that the existing apportionment in Tennessee . . . was invalid under this constitutional principle. . . .

> In *Baker* v. *Carr* we also argued that the starting point in determining the constitutionality of any apportionment should be per capita equality of representation and that any serious departure from the standard is invalid unless shown to have rational justification. Both points were largely based on history, for history is a powerful influence in constitutional law. State constitutions reflect the extent to which the idea of equality of voting power is imbedded in our political heritage. . . . They also suggest some of the justifications for diverging from exact numerical equality—the claims of historically separate units such as towns and counties to have equal recognition, the desirability of distributing political power geographically, the need to prevent a a single large city or two from dominating an entire state. . . .[19]

The solicitor general, however, also expressed one possibly noteworthy limitation in the totality of departure from numerical equality that he felt was permissible. This was that numerical equality should be required in at least one house of a bicameral legislature. He wrote,

> . . . [It] would not surprise me greatly if the Supreme Court were ultimately to hold that if seats in one branch are apportioned in direct ratio to population, the allocation of seats in the upper branch may recognize historical, political and geographical subdivisions *provided that the departure from equal representation in proportion to the population is not too extreme.*[20]

---

[19] Archibald Cox, "Current Constitutional Issues," 48 *American Bar Association Journal*, pp. 711, 712 (1962).

[20] *Ibid.*

This corollary proposition, of course, limits the departure from the numerical equality standard to one house of a bicameral legislature.

A standard which would allow departure from the numerical equality principle if rational justifications exist has been utilized by the majority of courts deciding the issue since *Baker* v. *Carr*. One of the more significant of these decisions is that of the Maryland court. It sustained the apportionment of the Maryland senate after the legislature had reapportioned the house of delegates according to population. The court quoted the solicitor general on the validity of departures from numerical equality in one branch of a legislature. It then held that the Maryland senate constitutionally could be based on area and geographical location because the system (1) protects minorities and prevents hasty legislation, (2) preserves checks and balances and the republican form of government, and (3) is based on history, tradition, and reason.[21]

In the Georgia case, the federal district court concluded that so long as at least one house is not based on population, the apportionment failed to meet constitutional requirements.[22] In subsequent litigation in the same case, the district court approved a plan which allowed representation in one house on a county basis if the other house was based on population. Judge Tuttle, however, dissented, stating that the plan in his opinion violated fourteenth amendment standards because the plan based on geographical areas was too disproportionate in terms of population.[23]

In both the Maryland and Georgia cases the courts approved departures from numerical equality in one branch of the legislature. In part, this was based on an analogy to the Federal Congress, where representation in the Senate obviously results in

---

[21] Maryland Committee for Fair Representation v. Tawes, 1 National Municipal League, *Court Decisions on Legislative Apportionment*, Anne Arundel County Circuit Court, *affd.* 182 A. 2d 877 (Md. 1962).

[22] Toombs v. Fortson, 205 F. Supp. 248 (N.D. Ga. 1962).

[23] *Ibid.*

marked departures from any numerical equality standard. Reliance on the federal analogy has been criticized on the grounds that the states, as sovereign entities, created the Federal Government while the counties and other local governmental subdivisions are mere creatures of the states.[24]

The basic question, however, would seem to be: Is a scheme which allows apportionment of one house on the basis of political subdivisions rational, thereby meeting constitutional requirements? In the Alabama case, which dealt with the constitutional validity of a proposed constitutional amendment affording each county one senator, the federal district court stated:

> The only conceivable rationalization of this provision is that it is based on political units of the State and is analogous [to the United States Senate]. . . . The analogy cannot survive the most superficial examination into the history of the requirement of the Federal Constitution and the diametrically opposing history of the requirement of the Alabama Constitution that representation shall be based on population. Nor can it survive a comparison of the different political natures of states and counties.[25]

Pointing to the fact that, although the Alabama Constitution employs a population standard, it also requires that each county have at least one member in the house and limits membership to 105, the court concluded: "The result may well be that representation according to population *to some extent* must be required in *both* Houses if invidious discrimination in the legislative systems as a whole is to be avoided." [26]

In the Virginia apportionment case the federal district court formulated the following standard for invidious discrimination:

> While predominant, population is not in our opinion the sole or definitive measure of districts. . . . Compactness and contiguity of the territory, community of interests of the people, observance

---

[24] See Israel, *op. cit.*, p. 121.

[25] Sims v. Frink, 208 F. Supp. 431, 438 (M.D. Ala. 1962).

[26] *Ibid.*, at 439.

of natural lines, and conformity to historical divisions, such as county lines, for example, are all to be noticed in assaying the justness of the apportionment.[27]

The court, however, concluded that once numerical inequality is shown, the burden of proof shifted to the party defending the apportionment. Rejecting the analogy of the United States Senate the court observed, "The bicameral system is a creature of history and many of the reasons for its creation no longer obtain." [28] The court enjoined further elections under the Virginia statute where a 2 to 1 numerical discrepancy prevailed in the senate and a 4 to 1 discrepancy in the lower chamber. However, it stayed the order to allow legislative action or an appeal to the United States Supreme Court.

Other cases, in which the courts have indicated that the predominant consideration is numerical equality apparently with allowable rational departures, have involved the validity of apportionments in Colorado,[29] Idaho,[30] Kansas,[31] and Mississippi.[32] Finally, it is significant to note that the federal district court in the further proceedings in the Tennessee case indicated its approval of a scheme allowing representation to counties or flotorial districts having two-thirds of the population ratio. However, in indicating its disapproval of the entire reapportionment plan,

---

[27] Mann v. Davis, 577 F. Supp. 548 (E.D. Va. 1962), U.S.L. Week, p. 2263 (1962).

[28] *Ibid.* The court further declared: "The chief justification for bicameralism in State government now seems to be thought that it insures against precipitate action—imposing greater deliberation—upon proposed legislation."

[29] Lisco v. McNichols, 208 F. Supp. 471 (1962).

[30] Caesar v. Williams, 371 F. 2d 241 (Idaho 1962).

[31] Harris v. Shanahan, 2 National Municipal League, *Court Decisions in Legislative Apportionment*, Shawnee County District Court (1962), approving minimum of one representative per county, but requiring utilization of numerical equality otherwise as provided by the Kansas Constitution.

[32] Fortner v. Barnett, 1 National Municipal League, *Court Decisions on Legislative Apportionment*, Chancery Court of Hinds County (1962), allowing representative from one county in house but requiring population basis in senate.

the court concluded that "equal protection requires . . . that apportionment in at least one house shall be based, fully and in good faith, on numbers of qualified voters without regard to any other factor." [33]

If one accepts the proposition that the equal protection clause not only requires adherence to the one-man, one-vote principle but also justifies rational departures, the extent of the departure which is permissible becomes the crucial issue. If a 4 to 1 discrepancy is invalid, is a 3 to 1 discrepancy valid? This question is representative of the difficulties involved in applying the standard. Perhaps this difficulty underlies the tendency of most courts which have given this standard at least some lip-service. That tendency is to emphasize also that numerical equality should be followed in apportioning at least one house of the legislature. They then indicate approval of other possible standards for apportioning the other house even though some major discrepancies in population may occur. Particularly is this true where the apportionment scheme is designed to represent political subdivisions.

Other Apportionment Principles

Another approach to resolving the question of a particular apportionment's constitutional validity is exemplified by the New York apportionment case which has been appealed to the United States Supreme Court.[34] The New York Constitution provides for legislative apportionment based on population. It also provides that each county shall have at least one assemblyman and requires a "full ratio" for each senator in excess of three for a district.

Starting with the principle that legislative acts are presumed to be constitutional and that violations must be clear before a federal equity court will disrupt state election processes, the

---

[33] Baker v. Carr, 206 F. Supp. 341, 349 (M.D. Tenn. 1962).
[34] 31 U.S.L. Week, p. 3132 (1962).

federal district court posed the following tests for "invidious discrimination":

(1) Rationality of state policy and whether the system is arbitrary.

(2) Whether or not the present complexion of the legislature has a historical basis.

(3) Whether there lies within the electorate of the State of New York any possible remedy (if gross inequalities exist).

(4) Geography, including accessibility of legislative representatives to their electors.

(5) Whether the Court is called upon to invalidate solemnly enacted State Constitutions and laws.[35]

In applying these tests, the court concluded that the New York constitutional provisions are not arbitrary because rural and urban counties are not classified differently. Also, the "net result is that assemblymen, subject to the minimum provision per county, like the minimum provision for members in the Federal House of Representatives are in fact substantially based on citizen pouplation." [36] With respect to the senate provisions, the court found no irrationality or arbitrariness because they were "designed to effectuate administration of the senatorial electorate, and designed to meet accessibility, and practicability." [37] Turning to his historical test, the court recited the significance of county governments in New York and the recognition of counties in selecting legislative representatives since the 1777 Constitution. With respect to the test of availability of a political remedy, the court noted that (1) the electorate in 1957 had voted down the call of a constitutional convention although the governor had emphasized the apportionment issue, and (2) the constitution requires a vote on the call of a constitutional convention every 20 years. Applying the geographical discrimination test, the

[35] W.M.C.A., Inc. v. Simon, 208 F. Supp. 368, 374 (1962), citing for these tests Toombs v. Fortson, 205 F. Supp. 248 (N.D. Ga. 1962), Sanders v. Gray, 203 F. Supp. 158 (N.D. Ga. 1962), Baker v. Carr, 369 U.S. 186, 258, 259 (1962), Justice Clark's concurring opinion.

[36] *Ibid.*, at 375.

[37] *Ibid.*, at 376.

court noted that "geography, accessibility, proper diffusion of political initiative as between a state's thinly populated counties and those having concentrated masses, have not been cast out as proper factors in apportionment methods." [38] The court also felt that the interests of "upstate" counties may be diverse while city districts may be united. After noting that some senatorial districts were greater in size than the states of Connecticut and Delaware, the court also approved of geographical variation because "Economic and social matters, extensive resources and their developments, roads, school systems, welfare and other matters emphasize the necessity of some geographic consideration in a state the size and character of New York." [39] Finally, with respect to the invalidation of duly adopted state constitutions, the court expressed its reluctance to overthrow "the choice of the electors."

From the standpoint of standards to be applied to determine whether the equal protection clause has been violated by an apportionment scheme, the New York case presents a number of interesting features. In one sense it may be described as a legalistic approach, particularly since the court concluded that "the plaintiffs have not shown by a fair preponderance of the relevant evidence that 'invidious discrimination' exists." [40] The court, however, did not indicate what evidence would be necessary to override the presumption of constitutionality. The decision might also be described as political in the sense that the court has recognized the kinds of arguments that appear in constitutional deliberations and that are recognized in the political compromises that underlie state constitutional provisions governing the apportionment of legislatures. Finally, the decision is notable because the opinion does not place any emphasis whatsoever on discrepancies in population represented by legislators, even though the Appendices to the opinion indicate that the population of senatorial districts would vary from 190,343 to

[38] *Ibid.*, at 379.
[39] *Ibid.*
[40] *Ibid.*

425,267 and assembly districts from 14,974 to 216,704,[41] if the legislature was reapportioned on the basis of the 1960 census according to the constitutional formula. By contrast, for the courts which have utilized the numerical equality test, these statistics have been of utmost importance. Inferentially, however, the New York district court seems to have considered a somewhat different numerical test, one that may be described as the "majority control" test. In its recitation of facts, the court noted:

> New York City with a population of 7,781,984 or 46.0% of the state's population of 16,782,304, has 65 assemblymen or 43.3% of the total assembly, and 25 senators or 43.1% of the total number of senators, while the counties other than those in New York City, with 54.0% of the population, have 56.7% of the total assembly and 56.9% of the senate seats.[42]

The court also emphasized that the ten most heavily populated counties having 73.5 percent of the population would have 64.9 percent of the senate seats and 61.3 percent of the assembly seats under apportionment according to the 1960 census figures.[43] If one takes the approach of adding the population in the smallest districts listed in order of size up to a majority of seats and compares that total with the state population, the result is that 36.9 percent of the population can elect a majority of the senate and 38.2 percent a majority of the Assembly.[44] Therefore, if the decision can be described as placing any emphasis on a "majority control" test, the test also incorporated a measuring of rural vs. urban interests in order to define the majority, other than in terms of population. This may, in part, have been considered significant because, according to a concurring opinion, the plaintiffs alleged that the method of apportionment "is unconstitutional because it discriminates against the urban residents

---

[41] *Ibid.*, at 380-82.

[42] *Ibid.*, at 370.

[43] *Ibid.*, at 378-79.

[44] National Municipal League, *Compendium on Legislative Apportionment* (2d ed. 1962).

of the state. . . ." [45] Noteworthy in this connection is the fact that the concurring opinion of Judge Ryan is replete with references to rural and area considerations. He concluded:

> If population were to be made the sole criterion of apportionment, the area per representative in certain districts would increase even further. Representatives might not adequately represent localities which were not their homes and, correspondingly, the residents of these localities might lose the benefit of the democratic governmental process.[46]

Therefore, although the opinions are not explicit on the point, there is at least some indication that an apportionment can be validated under the equal protection clause if the predominantly urban counties are able to control the legislature. This would hold true even though there are numerical inequalities in the size of legislative districts, rural areas are overrepresented in terms of population, and less than a majority of the population can control both houses of the legislature.

In the Florida apportionment case, a federal district court adopted as its standard for determining whether or not invidious discrimination exists, merely the requirement that the plan be rational. More specifically, it apparently approved as a rational scheme an apportionment plan based on representation of local governmental units with rational departures allowed providing additional representation for more populous areas. Expressing its rejection of any numerical equality concept, the court stated:

> It is our considered view that the rationality of a legislative apportionment may include a number of factors in addition to population. Certainly it cannot be said that the proposed apportionment . . . reaches approximate equality on a strict basis of population.[47]

Some recognition of population is involved in the composition of the house but each county is afforded at least one representa-

---

[45] 208 F. Supp. 384.
[46] *Ibid.*, at 385.
[47] Sobel v. Adams, 208 F. Supp. 316, 321 (S.D. Fla. 1962).

tive. Under the proposed plan five counties having 50.42 percent of the total population would have 32.6 percent of the members of the lower chamber and 10.9 percent of the members of the senate.

Nevertheless, after pointing to the fact that from the inception of statehood each county has had at least one representative, the court explained its reasons for holding the scheme to be rational. Of particular significance to the court was Florida's system for handling the affairs of local government. Most of the law relating to county and municipal government is in the form of special legislative acts because only Dade County has a home rule charter. During the 1961 legislative session, 1,266 special acts were passed by the legislature affecting 64 of the 67 counties and over 100 municipalities. The court, after reciting these facts, presented the best explanation for permitting representation of local governmental units yet to appear in the apportionment cases.

> The enactment of the special acts is procured by the legislative delegations from the affected areas with the heavier burden resting upon the members of the House of Representatives from those counties which are joined with another or others in senatorial districts. The measures included in these special acts are of vast importance to the people of the respective counties or municipalities to which they apply. We are not convinced that this phase of sovereignty could be adequately carried out if a substantial number of the less populous counties . . . were deprived of representation in the Legislature. The way of the State of Florida in providing for the government of its counties and municipalities may not be the best of possible methods but we are not willing and doubt that we are able to require that it be changed. We do not think it would be reasonable to render unworkable the system by which a very large part of the State's legislative function is exercised.[48]

Under the proposed plan the Florida senate was to be apportioned on a district basis with no more than one senator per

---

[48] *Ibid.*, at 322.

county. In approving this scheme, the court, without perhaps any considerable accuracy, stated that the house would be so composed that population would be heavily weighted and therefore "population need not be a major factor in the apportionment of the other House." [49] The court, however, proceeded to find the senate apportionment rational because the scheme afforded "not only common geographical locations and contiguous areas, but a somewhat general unity of economic interests which result in the combinations being desirable for the purpose of legislative representation." [50]

Turning to the argument advanced by the plaintiffs that the rural areas have a strangle hold on the Florida legislature, the court expressed its difficulty in determining what is urban and what is rural and cited the changing nature of the counties because of the growth in the mining and tourist industries and the activities of the Federal Government at Cape Canaveral. But the court felt that if there had been any strangle hold, the "proposed plan will result in the breaking of it." [51] This conclusion seems to be difficult to justify in view of continued underrepresentation of populous areas in both houses of the legislature. Interestingly, the Florida electorate rejected the proposed amendment, and the court retained jurisdiction if this eventuality did occur.

Although the specific questions involved in the Florida case have now become moot, the court's approval of representation of local governmental units is noteworthy because it is one of the common features of state legislative apportionment schemes. In states which handle local affairs by special legislative acts, the argument that counties should be given representation, even though marked departures from numerical equality result, seems particularly persuasive. Even in states where considerable local autonomy exists, the complexities of modern society and the

---

[49] *Ibid.*, at 323.
[50] *Ibid.*
[51] *Ibid.*, at 324.

continued expansion of governmental services are leading to the enactment of a multitude of statutes by the state legislatures. Even where general in nature, these acts are often, as a practical matter, special because they are utilized only by a single local governmental unit. If the premise is that specific local governmental needs demand local representation, the conclusion would be that an apportionment scheme which is based upon representation of local government, in and of itself, is rational. Furthermore, it may be argued, departures from the numerical equality standard can be substantial if the departure is based upon representation of local governments in the state legislative processes.

Another apportionment standard that has received judicial approval since *Baker* v. *Carr* is the unique system employed in New Hampshire for apportioning its 24 senatorial seats. Under the New Hampshire Constitution the legislature is directed to apportion the senate on the basis of the "proportion of direct taxes paid." [52] Significantly, studies of this system indicate it closely parallels population distribution. Although senatorial districting according to the equal valuation formula is not mathematically perfect (the maximum variation of the highest being 4.67 percent and the lowest 4.2 percent), the New Hampshire Supreme Court found that there was no evidence that the apportionment act "produced an impermissible or an invidious discrimination." [53] It should be noted that the lower house of the legislature is apportioned on a population basis, but the court apparently attached no significance to this fact. In its conclusion that no violation of the fourteenth amendment existed, the court noted: "Some leeway in the political process is inevitable since '. . . the machinery of government would not work if there were not allowed a little play in its joints.'" [54] Despite the fact that the New Hampshire apportionment contains elements which

---

[52] New Hampshire Constitution, part II, article 26.

[53] Levitt v. Maynard, 182 A. 2d 897, 900 (N.H. 1962).

[54] *Ibid.*, quoting Justice Holmes in Bain Peanut Co. of Texas v. Pinson, 282 U.S. 499, 501 (1931).

result in limited departures from a numerical equality standard, the decision is representative of the approach of those courts which have approved other rational schemes as being constitutionally valid without placing emphasis upon population as the single or predominant relevant factor.

Appropriateness of Judicial Relief as a Consideration

The majority opinion in *Baker* v. *Carr*, since it did not deal with the merits of the case, also avoided indicating the nature of the relief which could be afforded. The opinion merely noted that "we have no cause at this stage to doubt the District Court will be able to fashion relief if violations of constitutional rights are found." [55] In typical litigation it is only after a finding of illegality that the courts turn to a consideration of the relief to be afforded an injured party. However, as Justice Frankfurter emphatically announced, the appropriateness and effectiveness of judicial relief is an omnipresent factor in determining whether or not malapportionment allegations present a "justiciable" issue.

> We were soothingly told at the bar of this Court that we need not worry about the kind of remedy a court could effectively fashion once the abstract constitutional right to have courts pass on a statewide system of electoral districting is recognized as a matter of judicial rhetoric, because legislatures would heed the Court's admonition. This is not only a euphoric hope. It implies a sorry confession of judicial impotence in place of a frank acknowledgment that there is not under our Constitution a judicial remedy for every political mischief, for every undesirable exercise of legislative power. The Framers carefully and with deliberate forethought refused so to enthrone the judiciary. In this situation, as in others of like nature, appeal for relief does not belong here. Appeal must be to an informed, civically militant electorate. In a democratic society like ours, relief must come through an aroused popular conscience that sears the conscience of the people's representatives. In any event there is nothing judicially more unseemly nor more self-defeating than for this

---

[55] 369 U.S. 186, 198 (1962).

Court to make *in terrorem* pronouncements, to indulge in merely empty rhetoric, sounding a word of promise to the ear, sure to be disappointing to the hope.[56]

On the other hand, Justice Clark in his concurring opinion, while recognizing that a lack of effective judicial remedies was relevant, expressed his belief that some minor redistricting in Tennessee by judicial order would be appropriate.

> Finally, we must consider if there are any appropriate modes of effective judicial relief. The federal courts are of course not forums for political debate, nor should they resolve themselves into state constitutional conventions or legislative assemblies. Nor should their jurisdiction be exercised in the hope that such a declaration as is made today may have the direct effect of bringing on legislative action and relieving the courts of the problem of fashioning relief. To my mind this would be nothing less than blackjacking the Assembly into reapportioning the State. If judicial competence were lacking to fashion an effective decree, I would dismiss this appeal. However, like the Solicitor General of the United States, I see no such difficulty in the position of this case. One plan might be to start with the existing assembly districts, consolidate some of them, and award the seats thus released to those counties suffering the most egregious discrimination. Other possibilities are present and might be more effective. But the plan here suggested would at least release the strangle hold now on the Assembly and permit it to redistrict itself.[57]

As in the case of determining whether malapportionment presents a "justiciable" issue, the adequacy and effectiveness of judicial relief seems to have been a relevant consideration in the formulation of the standard for ascertaining constitutional validity of a particular apportionment scheme. The numerical equality test obviously is easier to apply to determine the constitutional issue, but it may be more difficult for the courts to provide a judicial remedy which will result in compliance with the standard. On the other hand, a flexible standard involves

[56] *Ibid.*, at 269-70.
[57] *Ibid.*, at 259-60.

less certainty in the determining of the constitutional issue, but the types of relief which the court may grant are perhaps more flexible. For example, the consolidation of a few overrepresented districts, as suggested by Justice Clark, may release the current strangle hold on the legislature, but it would not effectuate necessarily an apportionment which would meet a strict numerical equality standard. Furthermore, the possible occasions for utilizing judicial relief of a drastic nature are reduced in number if the standard of constitutionality allows considerable leeway.

To what extent the appropriateness and adequacy of judicial relief has been a factor in the formulation of a constitutional standard by the courts is difficult to appraise. It is significant, for example, that Justice Clark on the one hand stressed that no political avenues, by initiative or referendum, were available under the Tennessee Constitution, while on the other hand, the New York federal district court emphasized the availability of a political remedy. Even where the Alabama federal district court found constitutional invalidity, the court observed that "a federal court, in the light of its delicate relationships with a state legislature, should, so far as possible, accept such parts of the Acts of the Legislature as have any merit in framing the order of the Court." [58] And in the Georgia apportionment case, in which the court concluded that the federal constitution does not require the apportionment of both houses of a state legislature on a population basis, the court specifically mentioned that the judiciary should refrain from interference if rationality is found. The inference here is that problems of formulating judicial relief lead to the conclusion that the courts should exercise considerable forbearance before applying a standard which would require judicial intervention. [59]

Finally, it should be noted that in a considerable number of cases the courts have not formulated any specific judicial relief when unconstitutionality has been found. Rather they have

---

[58] Sims v. Frink, 208 F. Supp. 431, 441 (M.D. Ala. 1962).
[59] Toombs v. Fortson, 205 F. Supp. 248 (N.D. Ga. 1962).

withheld affirmative relief in order to allow the legislature or the people through the constitutional amendment device to reapportion, a process which Justice Clark described as "blackjacking" the legislature. Once the political organs have acted, the tendency, in all likelihood, would be to approve that action by employing a standard which either would allow rational departures from the numerical equality principle or frankly recognize other rational bases for apportionment of state legislatures. Striking down a new apportionment by strict application of the numerical equality principle, particularly if the strangle hold on the legislature has been released, would appear at that juncture to place the courts in an extremely difficult, if not politically unpopular, posture. Therefore, the inherent difficulties involved in the judicial reapportionment—the court in effect acting as a super-legislature—would seem to lead to the conclusion that the standard of constitutional validity should be flexible in nature.

Compliance with State Constitution as a Consideration

One of the salient features of *Baker* v. *Carr* was the fact that the Tennessee legislature had failed to reapportion since 1901 with the result that there was no compliance with the requirements of the Tennessee Constitution. According to Justice Frankfurter, the appellants argued

> . . . that although the same or greater disparities of electoral strength may be suffered to exist immune from federal judicial review *in States where they result from apportionment legislation consistent with state constitutions,* the Tennessee Legislature may not abridge the rights which, on its face, its own constitution appears to give, without by that act denying equal protection of the laws.[60]

The argument continued that because Tennessee's Constitution made the choice of apportionment principles, the legislature could not use others. Justice Frankfurter forcefully demonstrated that this type of argument is not persuasive in constitu-

---

[60] 369 U.S. 186, 325 (1962), emphasis added.

tional litigation involving the fourteenth amendment. Pointing to prior cases in which this type of argument has been rejected, he maintained that the Tennessee statute must be considered on the same footing as a constitutional provision and that the statute was "unaffected by its supposed repugnance" to the state constitution. As he indicated, the argument of the appellants does not warrant analysis because the courts, in applying federal constitutional limitations, must consider the state law not necessarily as it is written but as it is applied in fact. "Tennessee's law and its policy respecting apportionment are what 60 years of practice show them to be, not what appellants cull from the unenforced and, according to its own judiciary, unenforceable words of its Constitution." [61] Nevertheless it may be argued, perhaps with some effectiveness, that a denial of rights created by a state constitution constitutes a separate and distinct violation of the equal protection clause. If the fourteenth amendment protection extends only to cases where there has been non-compliance with the state constitution, its effect on apportionment will be severely limited.

Despite the conclusion that, legally speaking, compliance or lack of compliance with the provisions of a state constitution should have no relevance in determining whether a particular apportionment is valid under the fourteenth amendment, these considerations as a practical matter have had some significance in recent litigation. For example, in the New York case the Alabama, Idaho, Maryland, Oklahoma, Rhode Island, and Tennessee cases were distinguished because they "involved substantial discrepancies between existing legislative apportionments and pre-existing state constitutional provisions." [62]

Failure over an extended period of time to comply with a state constitutional provision which gives any weight to population seems to make it easier for the court to find a "crazy quilt" which amounts to invidious discrimination. Three reasons might be

---

[61] *Ibid.*, at 327.
[62] W.M.C.A., Inc. v. Simon, 208 F. Supp. 368, 374 (S.D. N.Y. 1962).

advanced for this observation. First, inaction over an extended period of years leaves the court little evidence upon which to base a finding of rationality. Second, the "rational justifications" which might exist are unarticulated and undocumented whereas the principles enunciated in a state constitution reflect the deliberations of a political instrumentality. In some instances the records of a constitutional convention may assist in divulging the underlying reasons for adoption of the particular apportionment scheme, thereby making it easier for the court to discover "rationality." Third, compliance with state constitutional provisions apparently makes more difficult the burden of proof that must be sustained to overcome the presumption of constitutionality afforded state acts.

Nature of Judicial Relief

Where the courts to date have concluded that the present apportionment is unconstitutional, in the vast majority of cases they temporarily have withheld specific relief. Three factors apparently have been prominent in the courts' refusing to order reapportionment. First, and perhaps of primary importance, is the traditional reluctance of the courts to interfere with political processes; they universally recognize that the responsibility for reapportionment resides with the legislature. Second, coterminously with judicial action, the legislatures have undertaken to revise the existing apportionment structure either by statute or by promulgating a proposed constitutional amendment. Third, because the litigation reached the courts during the 1962 election year, the courts have particularly hesitated to interfere with the selection of state officials where various primary machinery has already been utilized or a court order would place undue burdens upon the election machinery on the eve of election. In Colorado, Florida, Georgia, Maryland, Mississippi, North Dakota, Oklahoma, Rhode Island, Tennessee, and Vermont the courts, although expressing views indicating that the existing apportionment was invalid, refused to reapportion by judicial order or allow other affirmative relief. In each instance the courts were of the opinion that the legislature should be afforded an additional opportunity to comply with constitutional requirements.

In some cases the legislature, such as in Tennessee, had taken some action; in others such as Colorado and Florida constitutional amendments had been submitted to the electorate for ratification. In each instance the courts retained jurisdiction until after the election or after the next legislative session. This approach had proved successful in both Minnesota and New Jersey prior to the decision in *Baker* v. *Carr.* It will be recalled, however, that Justice Clark thought that mere declarations of unconstitutionality were "nothing less than blackjacking" the legislatures to reapportion. And Justice Frankfurter thought that reliance on judicial rhetoric was a "euphoric hope." Nonetheless a number of courts have apparently found temporary solace by avoiding the framing of a specific order reapportioning the particular legislature involved. Often they have expressed views that ordering elections-at-large would cause practical problems in primary and general elections that should be avoided if at all possible. For example, they have pointed to the fact that voting machines could not be utilized when 100 or more candidates are to be elected. A system of weighted voting, each legislator voting the number of persons represented, has been rejected as impractical or as possibly violating other state constitutional directives. Some have indicated that they would, if necessary, consolidate some overrepresented areas by judicial order and assign the released seats to the more populous areas. Nevertheless, the courts have indicated that they would not hesitate to frame specific reapportionment orders if all other remedial avenues fail.

Only in Alabama, Kansas, and Michigan have the courts provided specific relief. In Alabama, the federal district court undertook to reapportion the legislature by accepting the features of a proposed constitutional amendment with respect to the lower chamber and features of a statutory reapportionment of the senate. It declared the proposed constitutional amendment unconstitutional as regards the senate.[63] The case has been appealed to the United States Supreme Court.[64] The Michigan Supreme Court, although allowing a very brief period for legislative action, ordered elections-at-large on rehearing the Scholle case, but Justice Stewart stayed the order pending further proceedings before the United States Supreme Court.[65] A Kansas lower court ordered elections-at-large of senators when next elected in 1965 if reapportionment was not effectuated earlier. It also ordered election-at-large of multi-member representative districts immediately.[66]

Certainly, in the apportionment area, the courts are plowing new ground, and a cautious attitude toward the relief problem is to be commended. Moreover, the Supreme Court traditionally has been reluctant to circumscribe judicial relief formulated by the lower courts, so it is doubtful that any definitive guidance will be forthcoming in the near future.

Just as the nature and appropriateness of judicial relief have been important factors in determining justiciability, and less directly in determining the constitutional validity of a particular apportionment, the standard employed to test validity under the fourteenth amendment plays an important role in deciding the nature of the judicial relief to be awarded. If the standard requires numerical equality, then elections-at-large or weighted voting in the legislature carry out the principle. If, however, the standard allows rational departures from numerical equality, elections-at-large are not constitutionally required and the range of permissible districting schemes available to the court may become infinitely great.

Assuming that the standard requires apportionment by population of only one house and that both houses currently depart

---

[63] Sims v. Frink, 208 F. Supp. 431 (M.D. Ala. 1962).

[64] 31 U.S.L. Week, p. 3147 (1962).

[65] Petition for certiorari filed October 1962; 31 U.S.L. Week, p. 3147 (1962).

[66] Harris v. Shanahan, 2 National Municipal League, *Court Decision on Legislative Apportionment* (1962).

from the numerical equality concept, the court is faced with the task of selecting the house to be reapportioned. The task of prescribing specific relief obviously becomes easier if compliance with the state constitution would result in valid apportionment. But if the constitution is being followed and the resulting apportionment is invalid, the courts apparently are faced with providing by judicial decree either an apportionment that is valid or an apportionment that does not meet constitutional standards but may break a strangle hold on the legislature so that it can carry out constitutional mandates. The federal district court in Alabama took the latter course in ordering reapportionment. The court, retaining jurisdiction, explained:

> The Court hopes that the moderate steps taken by this order may be enough to break the strangle hold. They certainly will not suffice as any permanent reapportionment. If they should prove insufficient . . ., the Court remains under the solemn duty to relieve the plaintiffs . . . from further denial of the equal protection of the laws.[67]

Therefore the court not only gave affirmative relief but also relied upon the legislature to effectuate a permanent constitutional apportionment. Inherently apportionment involves political compromise and practical difficulties. Even where the numerical equality principle is followed, the drawing of geographical boundaries for legislative districts places the supposedly non-political judiciary in a difficult position. Therefore, ordering elections-at-large has considerable appeal for the courts. Elections-at-large tend to be opposed by political organizations because of the practical handicaps they create for conducting political campaigns. Because of this opposition, ordering elections-at-large may hasten political action in the reapportioning processes. Furthermore, merely requiring elections-at-large avoids the creation of districts which may tend to be treated as fixed when the legislature considers further action either to comply fully with constitutional requirements or to reflect changing population distributions.

---

[67] Sims v. Frink, 208 F. Supp. 431, 442 (M.D. Ala. 1962).

A recalcitrant legislature poses the most serious problem for the courts. If the legislature fails to adopt a constitutional apportionment, the courts either must engage in political remapping or order elections-at-large. Redistricting schemes, being highly controversial, are not an attractive alternative to the courts which necessarily must rely upon public support because their powers are largely negative in character. On the other hand, elections-at-large may result in political control of the legislature by a group which could not capture control if any compact and contiguous districting scheme was established. For example, assume a state population of 2,000,000 with County A having a population of 800,000. Assume, further, that in County A 700,000 belong to one political party and in the remainder of the state 400,000 belong to that same party and are evenly distributed. A legislature of 100 indicates an ideal legislative district size of 20,000 population. By districting, 40 seats would go to County A and 60 to the rest of the state. Under a districting arrangement one party would have 60 percent of the seats although they have less than a majority of the electorate. Elections-at-large would result in the other party having 100 percent of the seats. The chances that the party in power after elections-at-large would redistrict are materially reduced in this type of situation. Therefore, ordering elections-at-large might substitute one strangle hold for another. If elections-at-large are ordered, it would appear that the court should retain jurisdiction until such time as the newly elected legislature provides a constitutional apportionment.

Obviously, the process of framing orders giving effective, affirmative judicial relief is a difficult one. Understandably the majority of courts have avoided the difficulty, at least temporarily, by providing the legislature an additional opportunity to act. Another consideration also has been relevant. The legislatures have had no judicial guidance concerning the bounds of constitutional apportionment. This stems primarily from the fact that the standards for determining constitutional validity under the fourteenth amendment had not been enunciated previously, even by the lower courts. Furthermore, the United States Supreme Court's position remains unknown. Once rules are established, the legislatures have some concrete concepts of the constitutional methods that may be employed to carry out their responsibilities. Therefore with due respect for the legislative branch, the majority of courts have provided them the initial opportunity to provide a constitutional apportionment. The record indicates that the approach has been successful, particularly where compliance with the state constitutional provisions apparently would not violate the equal protection clause.

CONSTITUTIONAL AMENDMENTS AND
LEGISLATIVE ACTION

THE DECISION IN *Baker* v. *Carr* led not only to a rash of litigation in the courts (70 cases in 33 states, 39 in state courts, and 31 in federal courts).[1] Five state legislatures also have been reapportioned. In response to specific court declarations of unconstitutionality either under the fourteenth amendment or the state constitution, new apportionment legislation has been adopted in Alabama, Georgia, Maryland, Tennessee, and Vermont. In Delaware the legislature adopted a constitutional reapportionment

---

[1] *The New York Times,* October 21, 1962, p. 71, col. 1.

plan in 1962 which became effective upon its approval by the legislature in 1963. This action corrected some of the more egregious malapportionment situations but substantial deviations from population persist. In 11 states (California, Colorado, Florida, Georgia, Mississippi, Nebraska, North Carolina, Oklahoma, Oregor., Tennessee, and West Virginia) proposed constitutional amendments appeared on the November ballot. In Washington the voters had an opportunity to vote on a proposed statutory reapportionment. Considering the fact that few state legislatures hold regular sessions during election years, the record of response by the legislatures is impressive. Legislative reapportionment in a number of states can be expected during 1963, particularly in those states where federal and state courts refused to provide relief on the eve of elections and retained jurisdiction to allow further action either by the people or the legislature.

In Colorado, Georgia, Nebraska, North Carolina, and Oklahoma the voters approved the apportionment proposals. The Colorado proposal increased the number of senate seats and froze senatorial districts. Georgia voters approved a redistricted state senate previously adopted by the legislature in response to court litigation. The Nebraska electorate adopted an amendment allowing redistricting of its unicameral legislature on other than county lines with primary emphasis on population. North Carolina's new constitutional provision provides for a 120-member house with each of the 100 counties having a minimum of one member. It also provides for apportionment by population standards of the remaining 20 seats every ten years by the speaker of the house. In Oklahoma a reapportionment agency was established to enforce the state constitution's apportionment provisions. The Colorado and North Carolina actions result in apportionment schemes of dubious constitutionality if numerical equality is required in apportioning both houses of a bicameral legislature. In California, Florida, and Mississippi the voters rejected plans which would have provided some relief to underrepresented areas. In both Florida and Mississippi where the courts retained jurisdiction if the legislature failed to act, the governors convened the legislatures in special sessions after the election. Thus, reapportionment is being effectuated in a number of states even though the United States Supreme Court has not determined what, if any, apportionment schemes violate the equal protection clause.

Wherever the courts have not ruled on the constitutional validity of the current apportionment but have retained jurisdiction, the legislatures are in the awkward position of having to choose between reapportionment by court order, including a possibility of elections-at-large, or enactment of a reapportionment statute without knowing whether or not the existing apportionment is invalid. No state legislature has reapportioned on a basis incompatible with the state constitution, except where the court has declared that the apportionment thereunder violates the fourteenth amendment. Legislatures probably will not enact apportionment statutes which do not comply with their own state constitutions if the provisions of the state constitution are not clearly invalid. Unless the standards for equal protection of the laws developed by the Supreme Court are precise, an eventuality that appears remote, we can expect that legislatures will not reapportion in violation of their state constitutions in the absence of a specific judicial decision.

UNRESOLVED LEGAL ISSUES BEFORE U.S. SUPREME COURT

Requirements of Equal Protection Clause

SINCE BAKER V. CARR both state and lower federal courts have grappled with the problem of defining what the equal protection clause requires in the area of state legislative apportionment. As we have seen, three different basic principles of constitutional apportionment have been developed: (1) numerical equality; (2) numerical equality with departures that can be rationally justified; and (3) other reasoned apportionment principles, such as representation of political subdivisions, with rational departures. Various corollaries have also developed such as: (1) only one house of a bicameral legislature must be apportioned according to the numerical equality principle; (2) compliance with state constitutional requirements demonstrates a lack of invidious discrimination; (3) if urban areas having a majority of a state's population are able to control both houses of the legislature, numerical inequalities are not as significant.

The variety of inferior court pronouncements and their admixture even in a single opinion indicate the lack of unanimity among the courts in applying the equal protection clause in the apportionment field. Obviously the situation is ripe for further Supreme Court pronouncements, and the Court already has further proceedings pending before it arising out of litigation in Alabama, Maryland, Michigan, and New York.

Predicting Supreme Court decisions is a hazardous occupation at best, but it is probably even more hazardous in this particular case. First, the Supreme Court has not developed any constitutional doctrine which can be described as eminently relevant to the problem of formulating the requirements for valid apportionment arising under the equal protection clause. Second, the apportionment issue involves a number of political considerations, such as federal-state relationships, not typically encountered in litigation under the equal protection clause. Third, Justices Goldberg and White have been appointed since the decision in *Baker* v. *Carr* so the opinions of two members of the Court with respect to the non-justiciability doctrine are unknown.

At present, there appear to be three options open to the Supreme Court. The first is to leave the states considerable leeway in effecting apportionments compatible with constitutional requirements. The second would be to restrict the scope of apportionments essentially to the numerical equality principle. The third would fall somewhere between the first two, adopting the majority control test, a test that takes cognizance of the numerical equality principle while permitting rational departure from it.

Among the arguments designed to persuade the Supreme Court that a wide range of factors may be utilized by the states in effectuating an apportionment compatible with constitutional requirements are: (1) the historical development of the United States since colonial times reflects a considerable variety of apportionments; (2) bicameralism loses its *raison d'être* if both houses of the legislature are apportioned on the same basis; (3) representative government validly may include recognition of minorities as well as the majority; (4) local governmental units require representation, particularly in states where local autonomy is minimal; (5) in a modern society representation of various economic and social groups is desirable if the legislatures are to be responsive to developing needs; (6) in many states a majority of the people not only have approved the state constitutional apportionment provisions, but through the initiative and referendum, the people may change the apportionment by constitutional amendment or by direct legislation; (7) the courts should not disrupt validly adopted constitutions and legislation unless violations of the United States Constitution are clearly evident; (8) apportionment involves political factors that are not satisfactory criteria for judicial application; (9) any rigid numerical equality test would involve the Court in a continuous process of reviewing apportionments because the practicalities of districting preclude the achievement of a goal under which each district has the same population as all other districts; and (10) apportionment according to population is always imprecise because of population movements before and after the apportionment. (In other words, why should an apportionment which was based on the 1960 census statistics be valid in 1966 when other population statistics reveal significant population changes?)

Among the arguments designed to persuade the Supreme Court to conclude that the equal protection clause rigidly limits the scope of permissible constitutional apportionment are: (1) representative government in the mid-20th century requires as close adherence to numerical equality as possible if it is to be responsive to the needs of the people; (2) numerical equality will not prevent representation of various minority interests because they tend to be reflected by operation of political processes wherever the numerical equality principle is followed; (3) the majority should be able to control the organs of state government, at least in theory; (4) urban areas must have a numerically fair hearing in state capitols if the states are to continue to play a significant role in governmental affairs; (5) the initiative and referendum processes are not, as a practical matter, effective remedial devices; (6) electorate approval of an apportionment is not relevant to a determination of the protection afforded citizens under the fourteenth amendment; (7) flexible criteria which would allow room for justifying gross discrepancies in the population included within representative districts would give constitutional sanction to a basically unfair system even where the legislature has failed to carry out the mandates of its own state constitution; and (8) the finding of justiciability in *Baker* v. *Carr* would be rendered largely meaningless if every type of apportionment can be rationalized, thereby leaving adversely affected citizens a day in court but giving no hope for judicial relief.

The third option that appears to be open to the Supreme Court would favor the proposition that equal protection of the laws restricts the area of permissible apportionment and limits departures from the numerical equality principle. A fairly wide range of permissible types of apportionment would still remain, but to the extent that other principles of apportionment are recognized they would fall within the overriding principle of numerical equality. The scope of permissible deviations well might vary depending upon their total effect in a bicameral legislature. Accordingly, under this test, if one house of the legislature is apportioned exclusively on a population basis, a wider range of rational departure might be permitted in apportioning the other house. If neither house is apportioned exclusively on a population basis, the deviations permitted in each house might be more limited.

One possible test of determining whether or not the departures exceed constitutional bounds is the ability of a majority of the people to have an effective voice in the legislature. If 50 percent of the people can elect only 10 percent of the membership of a house, the departures from numerical equality of districts probably would not *be considered rational*. If, however, 50 percent can elect 40 percent of the membership, the departures may be judged rational. The difficulty with this test is that it requires the drawing of some arbitrary lines. However, the numerical equality principle has this inherent difficulty when divergencies in populations of the smallest and largest districts are examined. For example, if the ideal district would include 30,000 people and the size of the smallest is 20,000 and the largest 40,000, the decision must be made as to whether a 2 to 1 discrepancy is too great. If so, is a 1.5 to 1 discrepancy valid? Because of the practical impossibility of having each district absolutely equal in population, the courts will have to draw some rather arbitrary lines if numerical equality is to be established as the major principle of apportionment. On the other hand, a test requiring that a *majority have an effective voice* in the legislature—a more flexible test than the strict numerical equality rule—would allow greater leeway to the apportionment agency to reflect other apportionment factors by departures from numerical equality among districts. At the same time, however, it could be more effective in achieving greater representation of the majority. The 2 to 1 test, which the Michigan Supreme Court has indicated is the outer boundary of constitutionality, would permit theoretically one-third of the population to control the legislature. The two tests might be joined so that the population of any single district should not exceed twice the population of the smallest district and 50 percent of the population should be able to elect 40 percent of the legislators in each house. Of course, it might be argued that the majority of the population should be able to elect a majority of the legislators, but its achievement as a practical matter is difficult. Some room would remain for the exercise of judgment in drawing district boundaries even though the variations do not exceed 10 percent.

British experience has indicated that as much as a 25 percent variable seems to be demanded because of the practical problems one encounters in making district lines somewhat understandable to the voting population who also vote on local issues and elect local officers often at the same election. Furthermore any districting scheme may thwart majority control in the political party sense. Even if all districts were numerically equal, one party may receive a majority of all votes cast but still have substantially less than a majority of the legislators because of the unequal distribution of its supporters among the districts. Districting also may prevent the majority from achieving its goals on a specific legislative proposal for the same reason. Therefore, under the majority control test, the only achievable goal would seem to be that the majority of the people have a voice in the legislature roughly equivalent to its numerical strength within the total population.

The New York case may provide the Supreme Court with an opportunity to consider the majority control test. There, it will be recalled, the district court pointed to the fact that New York City received nearly the representation in the legislature to which it would be entitled on a population basis. Moreover, the district court indicated that the urban counties were able to control both houses of the legislature. However, in New York 36.9 percent of the population can elect a majority of the senators and 38.2 percent a majority of the assemblymen.

In the Michigan case the apportionment of the house was not contested, but 44 percent of the population may elect a majority and the population of the districts ranges between 34,006 and 135,268, far exceeding the 2 to 1 test. In the senate apportionment, which the Michigan Supreme Court declared unconstitutional, 29 percent of the population can elect a majority with the population ranging in the districts between 55,806 and

690,259.[1] The Michigan case involves two significant facts which differentiate it from the Tennessee case. First, the senate apportionment resulted from a constitutional amendment adopted by the people in 1952 and the legislature had complied with the state constitutional requirements. Second, one house of the legislature is apportioned on a population basis. The Michigan case affords the Supreme Court the opportunity to rule on the question of whether the equal protection clause requires that both houses be apportioned on a population basis and the extent of the departures, if any, from numerical equality which will be permitted.

The Michigan case has become moot, however, because the people of Michigan approved the adoption of a new constitution on April 1, 1963. The new constitution continues apportionment of the house on a population basis, but the senate is to be apportioned by a formula which gives 80-20 weight to population and area factors, respectively. Interestingly, this provision if adopted will be the only state constitutional apportionment rule which frankly recognizes area in terms of square miles as a basis of apportionment. Other states undoubtedly recognize area but this recognition, which might be justified for other reasons, evolves from the fixing of districts in the constitution or the giving of minimal representation to each county. The only justifications for area as an apportionment factor would seem to be that districts should not be so large that effective campaigning is precluded and that area tends to reflect different economic and geographical interests. These justifications do not seem to be as cogent as those which are advanced for minimal representation of political subdivisions, but the courts have often pointed to economic, social, and geographical factors as relevant to the issue of permissible classification under the equal protection clause.

The use of area in some states having large uninhabited areas in the public domain could lead to ridiculous results with the

---

[1] National Municipal League, *Compendium on Legislative Apportionment* (2d ed., 1962).

magnitude of the discrepancy in terms of population being inordinately large. If numerical equality in terms of variation in the population of the districts is the standard adopted, the Michigan plan would not be constitutional in a number of states. However, under the plan in Michigan 40.2 percent of the population would be necessary to elect a majority of the senate and the population of the senatorial districts would range between 82,962 and 363,187, slightly greater than a 4 to 1 ratio. Again, the 2 to 1 test would render the plan unconstitutional, but the test of substantial majority representation would render it constitutional. The application of the latter test to the Michigan situation demonstrates its flexibility in permitting some discrepancies in population within individual districts. At the same time, however, it requires greater representation of the majority than a numerical test that only takes into account the population variables between the smallest and largest districts. Similarly, the majority control test would allow apportionment based upon minimal representation of political subdivisions if a majority could elect 40 percent of the legislators even with substantial population variations in individual districts. At the same time, however, it requires greater representation of the majority than a numerical test that only takes into account the population variables between the smallest and largest districts. Similarly, the majority control test would allow apportionment based upon minimal representation of political subdivisions if a majority could elect 40 percent of the legislators even with substantial population variations in individual districts.

One measure of the efficacy of any particular test would be its effect upon existing legislative apportionments. *A test which would preclude any district having a population more than twice that of any other district would render unconstitutional every senate apportionment except those in Missouri and Ohio and every lower house apportionment. A test which would require 40 percent or more to elect a majority would leave only 13 senate and 13 lower chamber apportionments constitutional.* If only one house was required to be so apportioned, apportionments in

20 states would be preserved. If the test required only that one-third of the population be able to elect a majority, 10 additional senate and 17 additional lower chamber apportionments could be validated. If only one house had to meet this test, the apportionments in Alabama, Colorado, Delaware, Florida, Georgia, Idaho, Kansas, Maryland (prior to reapportionment of lower chamber), New Mexico, Oklahoma, and Tennessee (prior to reapportionment) would be declared invalid. Significantly, in seven of these 11 states the apportionments have been declared invalid by state or federal courts and only in Idaho has a state court found the apportionment constitutional. In Delaware the legislature has adopted a constitutional amendment which is being contested in the courts. In Colorado the state court has withheld action to allow the 1963 legislature an opportunity to reapportion on the basis of the 1960 census. Only in New Mexico, apparently, has there been no action.

One major question remains. If the test to be applied under the equal protection clause requires that the majority have substantial representation, must that test be applied to the apportionments of both houses of a state legislature? Obviously it is rather difficult to conclude that the federal constitution requires some equality in the election of one set of state officials but not with respect to another. However, historical facts have always played an important role in constitutional interpretation, and historically states have often apportioned one house on bases other than population, such as representation of political subdivisions, geographical areas, and economic interests. Furthermore, bicameralism in itself reflects the desire of the constitutional framers to have some internal checks upon the exercise of legislative powers. Within the Federal Government it has always been thought that deliberation of legislative measures by both the Senate and House of Representatives, which have different apportionment bases, materially improves the legislative product. If the states were denied the possibility of having different bases of apportionment, the value of bicameralism as a check on hasty, ill-conceived, although popular, legislation would be diminished. As the Solicitor General of the United States has observed, if the apportionment of one house is on a population basis, the other house might well reflect different apportionment factors provided that the departure from equal representation is not too extreme.

Again, it would appear appropriate to examine the population required to elect a majority rather than the discrepancies in population of the individual districts. Assume that the basis of apportionment is rational, such as representation of political subdivisions with perhaps additional representation for more populous counties or municipalities. Assume further that 20 percent of the population is required to elect a majority. Then one may well conclude that the departure from equal representation is not so extreme that the apportionment must be invalidated. Once more, the courts would be faced with drawing a line in terms of minimal percentages necessary to control a state legislative body, but this approach seems preferable to any test which only measures discrepancies in size of population within districts. If minimal representation of political subdivisions is a sound principle in apportioning at least one house, the 2 to 1 discrepancy test would preclude its availability in most states unless the number of members of the particular legislative body was increased to unmanageable proportions. The approach outlined here would assure that sparsely settled areas, such as the upper peninsula of Michigan, had some representation in the legislature. At the same time, however, the majority would not be so underrepresented that it could not obtain passage of intensely demanded legislation because its probable control is limited to one house of the legislature and the executive branch.

In conclusion we can only speculate on the meaning the Supreme Court will give to the equal protection clause in state legislative apportionment cases. State and lower federal courts have enunciated a plentitude of standards; perhaps other approaches to formulating the standards are within the realm of possibility. It is most doubtful that the Court will develop a constitutional standard which would sanction almost any apportionment scheme now used by the states. Nor is it likely that it will become almost impossible for complainants to prove the existence either of invidious discrimination or of arbitrary and capricious state action. Neither of these approaches would solve the malapportionment problem.

Formulation of a standard that would leave the states some latitude in establishing legislative districts would seem to be required by practical, political, governmental, social, and economic considerations. But the principle of majority control in a democracy should not constitute the price of that latitude. A standard that would require an effective and substantial voice for the majority in one house of a state legislature and, at least, an effective voice in the other would provide flexibility. At the same time, it would give fair assurances of a legislature responsive to majority interests. A rigid numerical equality standard, on the other hand, which measures only the value of votes in each district would not necessarily give any greater assurances of a responsive legislature. It also would tend to preclude any effective representation of underpopulated and isolated areas of a state even where a single metropolitan area is able to elect a majority of both houses. A standard permitting flexibility in the apportioning processes has the major disadvantage of constitutional uncertainty, necessitating litigation. Its overall advantages, however, seem to predominate.

The Guarantee Clause

In *Baker* v. *Carr* the majority opinion dealt at some length with the guarantee clause cases which have held that claims arising thereunder are non-justiciable. Three reasons were advanced for non-justiciability: (1) political questions cannot be resolved by the courts; (2) sufficient criteria are not available for judicial action; and (3) the actions of coordinate branches of government should be respected by the judiciary. Although comparable arguments could be advanced for concluding that state legislative apportionment questions are not justiciable under the equal protection clause, the majority concluded that "it is the relationship between the judiciary and the coordinate branches of the Federal Government, and not the federal judiciary's relationship to the States, which gives rise to the 'political question.'" [2] Justice Frankfurter vigorously disagreed and asserted that the case involved a "Guarantee Clause claim masquerading under a different label." [3] By holding that apportionments may be challenged under the equal protection clause, the Court has placed in question the relevancy of two of the three reasons previously advanced for holding the guarantee clause to be non-justicable; namely, the "political question" doctrine and the lack of satisfactory criteria for judicial action. It may well be that the Supreme Court will eventually re-examine the role of the guarantee clause in constitutional litigation. [4]

Aside from the fact that the decision in *Baker* v. *Carr* tended to make doubtful the foundations of the non-justiciability doctrine in guarantee clause cases, the guarantee clause would appear to be relevant to determining the limitations imposed by the equal protection clause on state legislative apportionment. If we conclude that equal protection of the laws requires equal representation in some degree, our conclusion must necessarily be based upon our concepts of representative democracy. The only definition supplied in the Constitution is that which guarantees to each state a "republican" form of government.

However, as noted previously, the Supreme Court has refused to provide any guidance as to what is considered "republican" by holding that the guarantee clause is non-justiciable. If the Supreme Court were to establish meaningful criteria for what constitutes a "republican" form of government, the limitations imposed by the equal protection clause could be formulated

---

[2] 369 U.S. 186, 210 (1962).

[3] *Ibid.*, at 297.

[4] For a persuasive argument of the view that the guarantee clause should be made effective by the judiciary, see Arthur E. Bonfield, "*Baker* v. *Carr*: New Light on the Constitutional Guarantee of Republican Government," 50 *California Law Review* (1962).

with greater specificity. For example, if "republican" means a popular democracy, then equal protection would require equal population districts in both houses of the legislature. If a "republican" form of government was satisfied by a representative system comparable to that in the Congress, and certainly few would deny that it is "republican," then only one house of a legislature would have to be based upon a numerical equality principle. A majority of the United States senators can be elected by 16.5 percent of the population. If this standard was required of state legislative apportionments as a minimal basis for having a "republican" form of government, a departure from equal representation principles in at least one house of a state legislature would seem to be more justifiable than if equal protection concepts are applied without reference to the guarantee clause. Whether or not the Supreme Court will interpret and apply the equal protection clause in apportionment cases by reference to the guarantee clause remains problematical. The approach certainly has considerable appeal because it provides a framework, not otherwise available, for determining the limitations of the equal protection clause on state apportionment schemes. Interestingly, the apportionment of the New Hampshire senate on the basis of direct taxes paid might be found "non-republican" although 43.3 percent of the population is required to elect a majority.

There exists the slight possibility that *Baker* v. *Carr* will be limited to its facts, and the equal protection clause will be available to attack state legislative apportionments only where the state legislature has failed to reapportion in accordance with state constitutional requirements. The only ground then remaining for attacking apportionments which comply with the state constitutional provisions would be the guarantee clause. The majority opinion indicates that some recession from the non-justiciability doctrine under the guarantee clause is within the realm of possibility. In some respects the guarantee clause presents more attractive possibilities than the equal protection clause as the foundation upon which to build constitutional standards for state legislative apportionment.

Availability of Judicial Remedies

In apportionment litigation before the Supreme Court prior to *Baker* v. *Carr* one of the grounds of decision was that federal equity courts, although they had jurisdiction, should decline to act. This conclusion often was based largely on the belief that the courts could not provide adequate and appropriate relief. The non-justiciability of political questions doctrine also was partially explained by reference to the problem of the potential ineffectiveness of judicial relief. In *Baker* v. *Carr*, the majority opinion merely noted that if a constitutional violation was found, there was no reason to doubt that the district court would be able to fashion relief. Justice Clark in his concurring opinion expressed the view that the courts should not become legislative assemblies and forums for political debate. However, he did feel that in the particular case appropriate judicial relief could be provided. He suggested as a possibility the consolidating of some overrepresented areas. Justice Clark also stressed his view that judicial relief in malapportionment cases should be confined only to those cases where other means were not available.

Four questions involving the availability and appropriateness of judicial relief are presented by cases now pending before the Supreme Court: (1) Does a district court have the power to redistrict a state? (2) If the district court has power, is it an abuse of discretion to redistrict? (3) Is it an abuse of discretion to order elections-at-large? (4) If other political remedies are available, should the courts provide judicial relief?

The Alabama district court was the first to reapportion a state legislature by judicial decree, and the Michigan Supreme Court ordered elections-at-large of the state senators. In the exercise of their equity powers courts usually may fashion relief appropriate to the rights of the complaining party. Although the courts will not provide extraordinary relief except in unusual circumstances, the Supreme Court has given the lower federal courts considerable latitude in deciding the relief to be afforded under the circumstances. In the apportionment setting, since no precedents exist, almost all affirmative relief could be considered unusual. It is extremely doubtful that the Court, if it sustains a finding of unconstitutionality, would hold either that a district or state court may not order elections-at-large or reapportion a legislature at least sufficiently to break the existing strangle hold on the legislature. In the school segregation cases, the Supreme Court left considerable discretion in the trial courts to implement school integration. A similar attitude on the relief in apportionment cases can undoubtedly be expected once a deprivation of constitutionally guaranteed rights has been established.

Both the Michigan and New York cases raise the issue of whether judicial relief should be given if other remedies are theoretically available. In both states, the people are periodically afforded an opportunity to vote on the question of calling a constitutional convention. In Michigan the initiative is available, and in 1952 the electorate adopted the senate apportionment held unconstitutional by the Michigan Supreme Court. Justice Clark indicated that the availability of other remedial devices would cause him to conclude that the courts should not provide judicial relief. As a practical matter the initiative is a time-consuming and costly remedy, and therefore it appears doubtful that the Court will deny relief merely because of the availability of the initiative. If the Court should wish to extricate itself from the hazards and burden of apportionment litigation, however, it could find that dismissals should have been ordered on the ground that the courts should only provide relief where no other method for rectifying malapportionment is available.

IMPACT OF *BAKER V. CARR* AND ITS PROGENY ON LOCAL GOVERNMENT APPORTIONMENT PROBLEMS

LOCAL LEGISLATIVE BODIES, such as city councils and county boards of supervisors, are often composed of members elected on a district basis. The districts also reflect major discrepancies if judged exclusively on the basis of the population residing in the districts. These districts were established either by action of the local electorate in approving a city charter or by state legislative action establishing the particular local government. The first is comparable to the establishment of state legislative districts by the people adopting a constitutional provision, and the second is comparable to state legislation establishing the legislative districts. There is no apparent reason for treating the situations differently when making a determination of whether or not the requirements of the fourteenth amendment have been met.

If the Supreme Court decides that equal protection of the laws demands substantial numerical equality among state legislative districts, the same requirement logically should be imposed on local legislative districts. Both situations involve state action and similar dilutions of voting strength of adversely affected citizens. Therefore the constitutional standards under the fourteenth amendment evolved by the courts may result not only in political remapping of state legislatures but also in sweeping revisions of a substantial number of local governmental bodies within the United States.

The following conceivable but unpersuasive argument might be made for the proposition that the equal protection clause is inapplicable to local legislative apportionments. Under traditional concepts local governments are creatures of the state and may be abolished by the legislature.[1] Because the state has absolute control over local affairs, the legislature could provide for the appointment by the governor of local officials in the same manner in which administrative agencies having quasi-legislative functions are established. If a person as a member of one group of citizens is given the privilege, as contrasted to the right, to vote for a local official, he cannot complain that another smaller group of citizens can name another local official.* The argument is not strictly applicable where the state constitutions afford local autonomy, but in terms of federal constitutional concepts, the municipalities and *counties* may be considered mere creatures of the state. The argument obviously stresses the relevancy of basic concepts of representative democracy. If election of local legislative bodies is not a constituent of representative democracy, and if only concepts of representative democracy alone lead to the conclusion that some numerical equality is required, the fourteenth amendment is unavailable as a ground upon which to

[1] See, for example, Hunter v. City of Pittsburgh, 207 U.S. 161 (1907).

upset local legislative apportionments. The argument might continue that the fourteenth amendment should be given meaning in light of the guarantee to the states, not local governments, of a "republican" form of government. Or alternatively, the Supreme Court should handle state legislative apportionment problems exclusively under the guarantee clause because the guarantee clause also would not prospectively place in jeopardy methods of selecting judicial officers. In some states supreme court justices are appointed, in other states they are elected at large, and in other states they are elected from districts which do not contain equal populations. Certainly none would argue that any of these groups of states lack a "republican" form of government because of the method employed for the selection of supreme court justices. The argument would also emphasize that if the equal protection clause requires substantial numerical equality in voting without any reference to the guarantee clause, then a whole host of existing schemes for the election of various village, town, city, county, and state officials will be found wanting.

The argument should be rejected because the Supreme Court has not differentiated between actions at the state level and local level in other litigation under the fourteenth amendment. In 1950 the Supreme Court considered an appeal of a Louisiana decision involving the city council districts of New Orleans. The complainant alleged that the commission form of government violated the fourteenth amendment because he could not vote for six of the eight commissioners who were assigned administrative duties and because nearly one-half the population of New Orleans could elect only two-sevenths of the city council. District voter populations varied between 8,508 and 48,020. The Supreme Court dismissed the appeal, per curiam, "for want of a substantial federal question." [2] Justice Brennan in the majority opinion in *Baker* v. *Carr* did not distinguish the case on the ground that local governmental districting was involved. In fact he intimated that local districting involves the same ques-

---

[2] Tedesco v. Board of Elections, 339 U.S. 940 (1950).

tion as state legislative districting by distinguishing the New Orleans case because "it was urged that there was a rational justification for the challenged districting." [3] And Justice Frankfurter in his dissent treated the New Orleans case as involving the same questions as are posed in congressional and state legislative apportionment litigation. Furthermore, in voiding under the fifteenth amendment the statute redistricting the city of Tuskegee in a manner to exclude Negro voting, the Supreme Court did not indicate that arguments based upon state supremacy over local units would in any way affect constitutional limitations upon discrimination. Thus the Supreme Court's treatment of local legislative districting in prior cases does not lend support to the argument that local districting does not come within the sphere of protection against invidious discrimination afforded by the equal protection clause.

In fact, it could be argued that state legislative apportionment should be judicially reviewed only under the guarantee clause and that all local districting should be reviewed under the equal protection clause. Conceivably the guarantee clause would permit greater deviations from the numerical equality principle than would be permitted under the fourteenth amendment. It is most unlikely, however, that the Supreme Court would devise different tests. Because most local legislative bodies are unicameral, fairly strict adherence to equal representation would seem to be required unless the court decides that all reasoned departures are justifiable in both state and local legislative apportionments. In the municipal context it would appear even more difficult to justify departures from numerical equality by reference to other factors, such as economic and geographical interests, and the principle of representing political subdivisions is completely unavailable.

The conclusion seems inescapable that if citizens are given the right to vote for particular local officials, the limitations of the fourteenth amendment apply. For example, a city need not

---

[3] 369 U.S. 186, 235.

build a municipal swimming pool, but if it does, use cannot be confined to citizens having incomes of over $25,000 since the classification would amount to invidious discrimination. Similarly, any invidious discrimination in the electon of public officials will be voided under the equal protection clause. Once again, a test which *merely requires that a majority of the people have an effective voice in the legislative body would probably be less disruptive of existing apportionments than any test which is based solely on the discrepancy between the largest and smallest district in terms of population.* Of course the mere specter of having to hear hundreds of local apportionment cases may lead the Court to conclude either that the fourteenth amendment places practically no restraints on apportionment or that the standards of numerical equality are so precise that no further Supreme Court elucidation of the standards will be warranted.

In the local governmental setting not only is the fourteenth amendment available as a ground upon which to attack apportionments, but also the equal protection clauses of the several state constitutions may be available. For example, in Michigan the supreme court has concluded that discrepancies greater than 2-1 among districts are invalid under the fourteenth amendment. Regardless of whether or not the United States Supreme Court agrees, the Michigan Supreme Court may interpret the state's equal protection clause similarly when any municipal apportionment is challenged. As long as the state provides protection at least as great as that afforded under the fourteenth amendment the state court's interpretation of its own constitution will be conclusive in the litigation. Therefore, those state courts which have enunciated the numerical equality test under the fourteenth amendment have cast doubt upon the constitutional validity of apportionments within local governmental units under the state equal protection clause.

CONCLUSIONS

THE UNITED STATES SUPREME COURT now has the task of determining the applicability and meaning of the fourteenth amendment in relation to the problem of legislative apportionment. The Court assigned this task to itself by holding that federal courts had jurisdiction and that apportionment presented a justiciable issue under the equal protection clause in *Baker* v. *Carr*. The conceivable range of future judicial action is broad in terms of both constitutional and legal principles. The fourteenth amendment may be so interpreted as to render most existing apportionments unconstitutional or to affect very few apportionments. If equal protection of the laws requires numerical equality in populations of legislative districts, reapportionments of almost all legislative bodies will be required. If the fourteenth amendment permits rational departures from numerical equality or other rational apportionment schemes, its effect on existing apportionment will be minimal. Similarly its effect will be minimal if a denial of equal protection occurs only when the apportionment does not comply with state constitutional directives. In between these extremes lie many possibilities. One would be a standard of equal protection that requires an effective voice for the majority in one house and that permits rational schemes in the apportionment of the other house if the representation afforded the majority of the population is reasonable.

In our constitutional system we have assigned the Supreme Court the responsibility of interpretation. The gravity of this responsibility is especially evident in apportionment litigation. Apportionment inevitably involves the foundations of representative government and the art of politics. Apportionment even under relatively clear state constitutional provisions is an exceedingly complex task, and the ways in which district lines may be drawn are infinite in number. If the complexities of apportionment and its political nature are to lead the Supreme Court to conclude that the fourteenth amendment places no practical limitations on apportionment, the Court will have given constitutional sanction to systems of apportionment which all would concede are grossly unfair. At the other extreme, any rigid formula for determining compliance with the requirements of equal protection of the laws faces the hazards of unpopularity and unreasonable interference with state and local governmental structures having historical foundations and popular acceptance. The middle road appears preferable. It has proved workable and acceptable in apportioning the Senate and House of Representatives of the United States; it has historical meaning in most state constitutions. It provides a basis for correcting the most egregious malapportionment situations. It is the road that many federal and state courts have followed in recent months.

The Supreme Court also has available various approaches which would avoid the establishment of any specific standards for apportionment under the equal protection clause. As suggested previously, the Supreme Court could confine the applicability of the equal protection clause only to those apportionments which violate state constitutional mandates. Although feasible, the distinction has not been employed recently by the Supreme Court in other constitutional litigation. It has the advantage of specificity in the sense that a state cannot argue that its apportionment is rational if it does not comply with the state constitution. It has the disadvantage of placing the Supreme Court in the position of having to review state supreme court determinations of compliance, and under strict concepts the state supreme court is the final arbiter of the state constitution.

Another approach available is that suggested by Justice Clark; namely, that the Supreme Court and federal courts should not exercise equity jurisdiction in apportionment cases if other remedial devices are available. The adequacy and nature of the other remedial devices would have to be ascertained. The initiative and periodic opportunities to vote upon the call of a constitutional convention are available in less than one-half of the states so that approach would not make it possible for the Court to avoid the constitutional issue in all cases. Furthermore, the practicability of these devices is subject to serious question.

Another possible legal approach would be to place a heavy burden of proof on complainants to show that they are adversely affected by the existing apportionment. In recent litigation, except perhaps in New York, the courts have assumed that the complainants have suffered damage. However, if some actual damage must be shown, it is difficult to see just how it could be proved. Therefore, although the Supreme Court has available conceivable methods of avoiding the necessity of handling the constitutional questions involved, it is most unlikely that the Court will resort to them.

Whatever the Court's disposition of the apportionment cases may be, we can be assured that it will be favorably received in some quarters and condemned in others. Whether its immediate effect on existing state and local legislative apportionments is maximal or minimal, the decisions will have lasting effects on the body politic and the course of American history.

LEGISLATIVE APPORTIONMENT UNDER THREE MICHIGAN CONSTITUTIONS

By John P. White

AT THE OUTSET of this brief historical review of legislative apportionment in Michigan, one might note that certain aspects of the Michigan experience should be familiar to students of and participants in the present-day debate and discussion on apportionment and representation.

The basic conflict over legislative apportionment that is raging today throughout the United States centers on the question: should the apportionment system promote control by a state-wide majority or should this goal be subordinated to the effective representation of smaller communities? This is not a new issue.

The debate in 1850 over the proposed legislative apportionment system for Michigan, for example, was on this very same issue. Present-day supporters of "one man, one vote" would have felt at home had they been by the side of Delegate Hanscom at the Michigan Constitutional Convention in 1850. Likewise, opponents of "one man, one vote" would have applauded Delegate Sutherland in his rebuttal to Hanscom. In short, the debate of 1850 in Michigan has a familiar ring today, not only in Michigan, but probably in many other states as well.

THE TERRITORIAL PERIOD

MICHIGAN'S FIRST FUNDAMENTAL law was written before the United States Constitution. On July 13, 1787, the unicameral Congress provided for in the Articles of Confederation adopted "An Ordinance for the government of the territory of the United States, northwest of the river Ohio." At the time, Michigan was still under British rule, and did not come under American control until 1796.

The provisions of the Northwest Ordinance had a definite and important effect on the development of the legislative representation system in Michigan. The ordinance provided in its bill of rights that "The inhabitants of the said territory shall always be entitled to . . . a proportionate representation of the people in the legislature."[1]

The ordinance also provided for a unicameral legislative assembly, apportioned on a basis of one representative for every 500 free, male inhabitants, until the number of representatives should reach 25, after which "the number and proportion of representatives shall be regulated by the legislature."[2]

The district assembly contemplated in the Northwest Ordinance was never organized in Michigan, but it seems to have served as the model for the territorial legislature established after Congress organized the Michigan Territory in 1805.[3]

It was not until 1827 that the voters of the state were given authority to elect members of the territorial legislature directly. Prior to that time, 26 nominees for the 13 seats were selected by the voters but final selection was made by the governor.[4]

The language of the congressional act authorizing the direct election of members of the Michigan Legislative Council is interesting. It specifies that:

> For the purpose of securing an equal representation the Governor and Legislative Council of said Territory are hereby authorized and required to apportion the representatives so to be elected as aforesaid among the several counties or districts in the said territory in proportion as near as may be to the whole number of inhabitants in each county or district exclusive of Indians not taxed.[5]

The territorial legislature was evidently somewhat handicapped in carrying out this congressional mandate because of uncertainty regarding the actual population of many counties which were little more than lines on the map although settlers were

---

[1] Northwest Ordinance, article II.

[2] *Ibid.*, article I, section 9.

[3] 2 Stat. 309, 1 Mich. Stat. Ann. 119n.

[4] 2 Terr. Laws, pp. 259-60.

[5] Act of January 29, 1827.

arriving in increasing numbers. Contingent provisions were written into the Apportionment Act of 1827 to account for various possibilities which might arise when population data became available.[6]

---

[6] 2 Terr. Laws, pp. 645-46 (Act of April 13, 1827).

THE CONSTITUTION OF 1835

BETWEEN MAY 11 AND JUNE 24, 1835, Michigan's first constitutional convention sat in Detroit. The document it produced is a model of brevity and conciseness. There were some spirited debates in the convention, especially on the question of suffrage: whether aliens and/or Negroes or Indians should be granted the right to vote. But apportionment was not a controversial subject. The principle that apportionment should be based on population was carried over from territorial practice into the new state constitution. However, the concept of representation according to population, as understood in 1835, did not require the precise mathematical near equality often insisted on today by the "one man, one vote" school of thought.

The first Michigan constitution allowed a house as small as 48 members or as large as 100. The size of the senate was always to be one-third that of the house. The senate was to be apportioned into no less than four nor more than eight multi-member districts, with each district electing an equal number of senators, as nearly as possible.[1]

A limitation on the principle of equal-district populations was the proviso that:

> Each organized county shall be entitled to at least one representative; but no county hereafter organized shall be entitled to a separate representative, until it shall have attained a population equal to the ratio of representation hereafter established.[2]

The principle that county lines should be respected, i.e., that no county should be divided in the formation of legislative districts, unless entitled to more than one seat, was explicitly stated in Michigan's first state constitution, although only in regard to the senate.[3] No such language is found regarding the house, but the phrase "the several counties or districts into which the state shall be divided for that purpose" (i.e., for the election of representatives)[4] was apparently felt to mean the same thing. The term "districts" seems to have been intended to refer to the groupings of counties not large enough to receive separate representation. In any event, under the first and all subsequent apportionments under the 1835 constitution, county lines were uniformly respected, thus setting a pattern which has persisted to the present.

The legislature was apportioned three times under the original state constitution: in 1838, 1841, and 1845. The problem confronting the legislature in those years would appear familiar to

---

[1] Constitution of 1835, article IV, sections 3 and 4.
[2] *Ibid.*, section 4.
[3] *Ibid.*, section 6.
[4] *Ibid.*, section 4.

a modern legislator, torn between the conflicting demands of a population equality standard on the one hand and a demand for effective representation of sparsely populated areas on the other. In 1837, the entire upper peninsula of Michigan contained barely 1,000 white inhabitants: 366 in Chippewa County and 644 in Mackinac County. Neither of these counties was then organized,[5] and thus neither was entitled to separate representation under the 1835 constitution, and even if the entire upper peninsula had been merged into one representative district, its population would have been far below the average district population of 3,251. Yet all three apportionments under the constitution of 1835 granted separate representation to these counties. At the same time, stringent efforts were made to adhere to population equality in the senate apportionment. This is well illustrated by the map of the 1841 senate apportionment in Figure 1. The sixth senatorial district extended from Oakland County to the farthest reaches of the upper peninsula, and district populations were remarkably close to equality with each other, considering the vastly uneven distribution of population.

We can conclude that legislative apportionment under Michigan's first state constitution was characterized by relative population equality in the senate, with such equality being facilitated by the multi-member senate district system provided for in the constitution, and by a fairly close adherence to the population standard in the lower house, somewhat modified by the creation of a small number of very sparsely populated districts.

---

[5] Chippewa was organized in 1843, Mackinac in 1849 (*Michigan Manual, 1959-1960*, pp. 9 and 11). However, there may well have been some confusion as to the meaning of the term "organized," since it was not uncommon for unorganized counties to organize themselves by electing county officers without benefit of legislative authorization. Delegates to the 1850 constitutional convention apparently were quite uncertain as to which counties were and were not organized. See *Report of the Proceedings and Debates in the Convention to Revise the Constitution of the State of Michigan, 1850* (Lansing: R. W. Ingalls, State Printer, 1850), p. 366 *passim.* (Hereafter cited as *Proceedings and Debates, 1850.*)

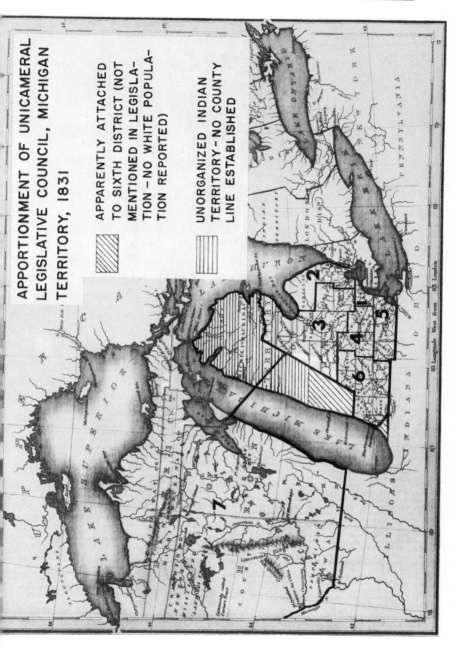

Figure 1

THE CONSTITUTION OF 1850

LEGISLATIVE APPORTIONMENT was an important issue in the convention of 1850. The multi-member senate districts of the 1835 constitution were opposed by many delegates as being too large for effective representation of the people. The committee on the legislative department recommended a compromise which would have created 16 senatorial districts, each electing two members.[1] However, an amendment was moved from the floor, providing for single-member districts. A major reason advanced for the change

---

[1] *Proceedings and Debates, 1850*, p. 111.

was that if each district were to include two and only two seats, and if, as the committee draft provided, no county should be divided in the formation of senate districts, a large county might be underrepresented if it had a population entitling it to three senators. It would be too small for two districts and too large for one district.[2] There was some opposition to the change to single-member districts. A Wayne County delegate insisted that single districts would overemphasize the role and importance of particularistic local interests, to the detriment of the majority:

> Sir, it is a sacred principle in our government, that majorities shall govern, unawed by dollars or any influences. Happily, the democracy of the State has been triumphant. It is the banner State, and every man has been proud of it. But divide up its people and where will be the predominancy of the masses. These local divisions will necessarily create laws to correspond with them. . . . Nothing can be calculated so disadvantageous to the masses as the district system.[3]

This line of argument illustrates the durability of the basic conflict over legislative apportionment: should the apportionment system promote control by a state-wide majority or should this goal be subordinated to the effective representation of smaller communities? Delegate Bagg was arguing that "the democracy of the state" (i.e., the Democratic party, in the usage of that day) enjoyed the support of a majority of Michigan voters, and that its control of the legislature should not be put in jeopardy by the creation of multiple senate districts, which might well produce a senate of a different complexion from that of the state-wide majority. But although the Democratic party dominated the state at that time, Delegate Bagg's position was a minority view of the rights of a majority.

The district system was adopted by voice vote, and the convention went on to a more controversial question: whether each organized county should be granted at least one seat in the house of representatives. As noted above, the constitution of 1835 had

---

[2] Remarks of Delegate Fralick, *ibid.*, pp. 113-14.
[3] Remarks of Delegate Bagg, *ibid.*, p. 118.

allowed a representative to every county then organized, but specified that no county subsequently organized should have separate representation until "it shall have attained a population equal to the ratio of representation hereafter established." [4] The committee on the legislative department brought in a draft article which omitted the requirement of separate representation for each county.[5]

Delegate J. G. Sutherland, of Saginaw County (then one of the smaller counties, with a population in 1850 of only 2,112) moved to amend the draft article by inserting the words "each organized county shall be entitled to at least one representative." This language would have gone beyond the 1835 constitution in favoring newly settled counties, since the old constitution had required that counties organized after 1835 would not automatically receive representation, but would be represented only when possessed of a full population ratio.

The Sutherland amendment precipitated a debate in which many of the arguments on both sides have a familiar sound to those who have followed the recent apportionment controversy. Delegate Hanscom, of Oakland County (then as now one of the most populous counties) invoked what would today be called the "one man, one vote" argument:

> A moment's reflection would convince anyone that the most gross injustice would be done to the population of Michigan by the adoption of the amendment. It is not geographical territory we seek to have represented, but individuals—numbers. . . . From what information he could get . . . a ratio may be fixed, by which one-fourth of the population would have at least one-half of the representation. Such a proposition as this must be unjust; it would practically disfranchise the more populous counties.[6]

The proponents of the Sutherland amendment, for the most part, did not appear to quarrel with the basic premise that population should be the fundamental basis of representation. Suther-

---

[4] Constitution of 1835, article IV, section 4.
[5] *Proceedings and Debates, 1850,* p. 111.
[6] *Ibid.,* p. 119.

land himself, in replying to the speech of Hanscom quoted above, denied that he had any intention of disfavoring the more populous counties:

> The proposition is not to do injustice to the old counties but justice to the new. . . . If the ratio be fixed so as not to give the old counties a sufficient number, increase that number. Allow the new counties one vote—one member—and the others a multitude.[7]

The great inequality of population size among the counties in 1850 would have made for a very large house of representatives, if Sutherland's words had been applied literally, and this must have been immediately evident. No attempt was made to frame an amendment combining guaranteed county representation with strict adherence to a population standard.

A majority of the 1850 convention understood apportionment by population in a different sense than the contemporary advocates of "one man, one vote." The notion that mathematical equality is required for an apportionment based on population found some expression, as we have seen, even in 1850. But it was decidedly a minority view, even among those who believed in population as the basic standard of apportionment.

One other feature of the 1850 apportionment system should be noted. The responsibility of districting counties entitled to more than one house seat was delegated to the Board of Supervisors of each such county, with the proviso that any city or township entitled to more than one representative should elect the requisite number on a general ticket, i.e., at large.[8]

The local autonomy in house districting was somewhat limited in its effect, however, by a further provision that the Board of Supervisors in multi-seat counties should only assemble and act on redistricting when and as directed by the legislature. Thus, the county boards were not in a position to act independently to redistrict the counties.

---

[7] *Ibid.*

[8] Constitution of 1850, article IV, section 3.

THE CONSTITUTION OF 1908

THE CONSTITUTION of 1908 was not a new document, but only a moderate revision of the 1850 constitution. No fundamental changes were made in legislative apportionment. The most significant change was the abolition of the state census, and the accompanying requirement that reapportionment take place following both the federal and state censuses. The 1908 constitution required reapportionment in the year 1913 and every tenth year thereafter, with the last preceding federal census forming the basis for the reapportionment.

The authority of the county board of supervisors to draw district boundaries for house seats in multi-district counties was retained, but again the county board lacked the power to redistrict the county in the absence of a state reapportionment. That such a construction should be placed on the 1908 constitution was established by an opinion of the attorney general in 1915.[1]

The clear intent of the 1908 constitution was that one and only one reapportionment should take place in each decennial period. This was established beyond all doubt by the language which specified that:

> Each apportionment so made, and the division of any county into representative districts by its board of supervisors, made thereunder, shall not be altered until the tenth year thereafter.[2]

---

[1] Op. Att'y. Gen., 1915, p. 103.
[2] Constitution of 1908, article V, section 4.

THE "BALANCED LEGISLATURE" AMENDMENT OF 1952

THE ONLY MAJOR CHANGE in the apportionment provisions of the 1908 constitution was made in 1952. In that year, Michigan voters approved the so-called "balanced legislature" plan of apportionment, which guaranteed the decennial reapportionment of the house of representatives substantially on a population basis, and fixed senate districts permanently in the constitution, with no provision for reapportionment. As we shall see in our analysis of past apportionments of the Michigan legislature, the constitutions of 1835 and 1850 were, in general, complied with rather closely by the legislature in that periodic apportionments demanded by those constitutions were made, and were made in reasonable compliance with the standards set forth in the first two constitutions. The apportionment provisions of the 1908 constitution, however, were much more honored in the breach than in the observance. The senate was in fact never apportioned according to the terms of the 1908 constitution, insofar as that constitution required apportionment on a periodic basis according to population.

The senate was reapportioned nominally in 1917, but this was actually only a re-enactment of the Apportionment Act of 1907, and in 1925, after a considerable struggle, a reshuffling of districts took place, but hardly a reapportionment according to population. The house was reapportioned in 1913, but this act was held unconstitutional by the state supreme court in *Stevens v. Secretary of State*,[1] and under the legal doctrine of that day the house reverted to the last previous apportionment, that of 1905 (itself a re-enactment of the apportionment of 1901). In 1925 and again in 1943, the house was reapportioned, but with scant adherence to the standard of population.

The sharp difference between the observation of the 1835 and 1850 apportionment provisions on the one hand and those of the 1908 constitution on the other was obviously not due to any important difference between the older and the newer apportionment provisions. As we have noted, the 1908 constitution made no material change in the apportionment system provided by the 1850 document, other than the abolition of the state census and the accompanying intra-decennial reapportionment. The impasse that finally culminated in the 1952 amendment arose because the rapid urbanization and industrialization of the state had created political cleavages between a rising urban majority and a dwindling rural population that felt its interests threatened by the reapportionment of both houses on a population basis.

---

[1] 181 Mich. 199. Interestingly, the court did not void this apportionment primarily because of any failure to adhere to population, but because of failure to grant separate representation in the house of representative to counties having a moiety of the representative quota.

There had been a very rapid growth in Michigan's population during the life of the 1850 constitution. From 1850 to 1900, the total state population increased by 608.8 percent, from 397,654 to 2,420,982. Throughout this period of rapid growth, the constitutional system of periodic apportionment according to population was carried out with remarkable fidelity, whereas the system broke down completely about the time of the adoption of the 1908 constitution. While it would be easy to ascribe this failure of a well-established system to a decline in the civic virtue of the legislature, it would be most unwise. The population growth prior to the turn of the century, while quite large, was rather evenly distributed, and the periodic reapportionments of the legislature did not result in any sudden or dramatic shifts in political power. But in the 20th century, the city of Detroit and Wayne County grew at an unprecedented rate, while the growth of many rural counties slowed down or stopped, and some parts of the state began to experience an absolute decline in population.[2]

Wayne County, whose legislative representation was to be the major bone of contention in the many struggles over apportionment in the 20th century, maintained a 19th century growth rate very closely parallel to that of the state as a whole. As indicated in Table 1, Wayne had 10.8 percent of the state population in 1850, and as late as 1885 this percentage was slightly less, at 10.2. Thereafter, a steady growth in the relative percentage took place, but even by 1900, only 14.4 percent of the state's population resided in the largest county. But by 1930, Wayne had no less than 39.0 percent of the people of Michigan.

Thus it was only in the 20th century that the disproportionate population growth of Wayne County and the city of Detroit

---

[2] For example, Keweenaw County, in the copper county of the upper peninsula, reached its maximum population in 1874, and has been declining ever since. Generally speaking, northern Michigan was never suited to extensive farming, and when the natural resources of copper, iron, and timber were depleted, there was little basis for population growth.

presented the possibility of a legislature dominated by a single metropolitan area. There can be no doubt that this population change caused the breakdown of an apportionment system that, in its basic outlines, had been successfully applied from the beginning of the state's history.

Table 1

REPRESENTATION OF WAYNE COUNTY UNDER THE CONSTITUTION OF 1850

Apportion-ment	County population	Pct. of state population	Senate seats	Repres. index	House seats	Repres. index
1851	42,756	10.8	3	93	7	90
1855	64,709	12.8	4	96	9	88
1861	75,547	10.1	3	94	9	90
1865	83,292	10.4	3	91	9	87
1871	119,038	10.1	3	93	9	89
1875	144,903	10.9	3	86	10	92
1881	166,444	10.2	3	92	10	100
1885	188,966	10.2	3	92	10	98
1891	237,114	12.3	4	102	12	98
1895	292,461	13.0	4	96	12	92
1901	348,793	14.4	4	87	14	97
1905	386,827	15.3	4	82	14	92

It is significant that from the beginning of this troubled period, the people of the state as a whole had within their grasp the means of restoring population as the basic criterion of apportionment. The constitution could be amended directly by the people of the state to provide for any system of legislative apportionment consistent with the Constitution of the United States. The refusal of the legislature to abide by the apportionment provisions of the constitution gave rise to several attempts to amend the constitution to provide for compulsory reapportionment.

In 1924, following the very limited reapportionment of the senate which took place in that year, a proposal known as the Corliss amendment was placed before the people. This amendment would have taken legislative apportionment out of the hands of the legislators and given it to an ex officio board composed of the lieutenant governor, the secretary of state, and the attorney general. This board would have reapportioned the legislature every eight years and, instead of basing the apportionment on population as revealed by the United States census, it would have been based on the number of qualified voters reported by the various county, city, and township clerks. In both houses, the board would create single-member districts containing as nearly as possible equal numbers of qualified electors. The amendment further provided that county, city, and township lines should be followed in the creation of both senatorial and representative districts.[3]

The Corliss amendment apparently satisfied very few people in the state. Most of the Wayne County legislators opposed it, although it would presumably have benefitted the Wayne County area. The innovation of counting registered voters rather than the total population was no doubt a contributory factor in the overwhelming defeat of this amendment, which received only 216,437 votes while being disapproved by 781,351 voters.[4]

The issue of apportionment according to population was placed squarely before the voters in 1930. An amendment placed before the people in that year would have required the legislature to reapportion both houses of the legislature in the first regular session following each United States census, and if the legislature failed to act the secretary of state would have assumed the duty of reapportionment. In either case the apportionment would be based on population. This amendment was successful enough in Wayne County, but was snowed under by out-state votes, and was rejected, 292,659—411,043.[5]

The 1930 vote made it rather clear that there was no state-wide majority in favor of apportioning both houses strictly on a population basis. Accordingly, an attempt was made in 1932 to

---

[3] *The Detroit News*, November 2, 1924.
[4] *Michigan Manual*, 1937, p. 58.
[5] *Ibid.*

arrive at a compromise solution. An amendment backed by the Wayne County board of supervisors would have provided for the decennial reapportionment of the house on a strict population basis, but in return senate districts would be permanently frozen into the constitution. As in the 1930 proposal, the secretary of state would be empowered to reapportion if the legislature failed to act. Senate terms would have been increased to four years. While this amendment fared better than either the 1924 or the 1930 amendments, it was still decisively defeated, 520,740–665,766. The affirmative margin of close to 100,000 votes in Wayne County was overwhelmed by the massive out-state opposition.

In 1952, voters at the same election which saw the approval of the "balanced legislature" amendment rejected still another proposal to guarantee apportionment on a population basis. This plan, supported by organized labor, resembled the 1930 proposal in that both houses would have been reapportioned every ten years on a strict population basis. Only two of the 83 counties voted for it (Wayne and adjacent Macomb), and it was defeated 924,242–1,415,355.[6]

The "balanced legislature" amendment of 1952 was very similar to the 1932 amendment in that it attempted to compromise the issue of apportionment by guaranteeing periodic reapportionment of the lower house while freezing the senate districts. The major differences between the two were that the 1952 amendment preserved the ancient moiety clause, which would have been eliminated in the 1932 proposal, and in the fact that the 1952 amendment retained two-year terms for senators. But while the 1932 amendment had been supported in Wayne County and heavily opposed out-state, the 1952 amendment was disapproved 293,975–543,286 in Wayne County but carried the state by a healthy, 1,269,807–975,518 margin.

During the 1950's, Michigan's legislative apportionment was in accordance with the state constitution for the first time since

---

[6] *Michigan Manual*, 1953-54, pp. 460-61.

the beginning of the century. But the decision of the United States Supreme Court in *Baker* v. *Carr* opened up the possibility that it might not continue to be within the province of the people of a state to accept any apportionment system not based closely on population.

As we shall see in our analysis of the apportionment provisions of the new constitution, the system adopted by the people of the state will insure a closer approximation to apportionment of both houses by population than has been achieved in Michigan for many years, and closer than the legislative apportionment system of almost all of the other states. Whether this approximation of apportionment according to population is within the competence of a majority of the electorate to adopt is a major question of constitutional law, not only for Michigan but for the entire nation.

APPORTIONMENT OF THE MICHIGAN LEGISLATURE, 1838-1953: A SUMMARY VIEW

WHILE IT IS NOT the purpose of the present publication to present a complete history of Michigan apportionment, it is necessary to place the present controversy in a proper historical perspective. In connection with our study of apportionment in Michigan, we examined every apportionment made in the state from territorial days to the present. Limitations of space do not permit the presentation of complete data on all these apportionments. However, two master tables were constructed, showing the most pertinent statistics on each apportionment. These are presented in Tables 2 and 3, for the senate and house respectively.

Since attorneys, judges, and scholars have used various measuring devices to evaluate apportionment statistics, these tables utilize some of the more commonly employed devices. The range between the largest and smallest districts has been widely employed, despite certain crucial statistical problems.[1] Although a maximum range of 2-1 in district population sizes has sometimes been suggested,[2] our tables show that even under the constitutions of 1835 and 1850 these limits were seldom maintained in the senate, and never in the house. Since one of the difficulties with the range is that it compares only two districts, the largest and the smallest in a given apportionment, it is significant to know how many districts fall outside the 2-1 limits. Our tables show there has been a wide variation in such deviations.

Another possible measure of closeness to population as an apportionment standard is the number of districts that are either 25 percent under or over the average population size. The percentage of such seats has usually been a considerable portion of the total, rising to a peak in the apportionments of the 20th century.

The Dauer-Kelsay index, which measures the percentage of the population necessary to elect a legislative majority, has also been widely employed. Again, like all such measures, it presents some problems, which are discussed at length during our analysis of the new Michigan apportionment system.[3] It is perhaps significant that the Dauer-Kelsay score for most past Michigan apportionments was in the low forties.[4]

Finally, the David-Eisenberg index of the "value of the right to vote" has come into prominence in recent discussions of apportionment. This index assigns a figure of 100 to a district which has a population exactly equal to the state-wide average. A

---

[1] See "An Analysis of the Michigan Plan of Legislative Apportionment," by the present author, pp. 233-361, below.

[2] See Scholle v. Hare.

[3] See below, pp. 275, 278-79.

[4] Some users of the Dauer-Kelsay scale have suggested a 45 percent minimum limit.

district with twice the average population would cause, according to the logic of the David-Eisenberg system, a dilution of the "right to vote" by one-half, and therefore such a district would have an index of 50. Conversely, a district with only half the average population would, in effect, multiply the vote value of the inhabitants of that district by two, and such a district would receive an index number of 200.

Tables 2 and 3 present the mean deviations of the David-Eisenberg indices for past Michigan apportionments. The mean deviation is the average of the deviation of district indices from the hypothetical ideal of 100. Thus, a district index of 90 would deviate by ten points, and so also would an index of 110. The purpose of the mean deviation is to illustrate the degree of dispersion of the David-Eisenberg indices.

The measures presented in these tables are utilized in the later chapter which evaluates the new Michigan apportionment system, and thus may be useful in comparing the new system to past Michigan apportionments.

The Appendix immediately following contains maps illustrating selected Michigan apportionments of the past. These maps may be useful in comparing present problems of district construction with those of the past.

Table 2

Apportionment of the Michigan Senate, 1838-1952

Year	No. seats	State pop.	Avg. pop. per seat	Largest dist.	Smallest dist.	Range	Seats outside 2-1 range No.	Pct.	Seats outside +25% range No.	Pct.	Dauer-Kelsay index	David-Eisenberg index (Mean deviation)
1838	17	169,056	9,944	12,121	4,758	2.5	14	82	2	12	51.8	21
1841	18	212,267	11,793	12,832	10,334	1.2	0	0	0	0	53.6	5
1846	22	302,521	13,752	14,892	13,036	1.1	0	0	0	0	52.7	4
1851	32	397,654	12,427	16,159	4,745	3.4	30	94	4	13	45.7	16
1861	32	749,970	23,437	31,447	8,959	3.5	30	94	6	19	44.8	21
1865	32	803,661	25,168	34,048	13,842	2.5	15	47	5	16	44.6	20
1871	32	1,184,282	37,009	50,410	22,132	2.3	7	22	7	22	44.5	18
1875	32	1,334,031	41,688	62,671	26,605	2.4	6	19	8	25	43.7	20
1881	32	1,636,937	51,154	73,252	31,167	2.4	6	19	8	25	42.8	20
1885	32	1,853,658	57,927	84,600	31,617	2.7	15	47	8	25	44.2	21
1891	32	2,093,889	65,434	88,678	40,033	2.2	15	47	9	28	44.3	20
1892	32	2,093,889	65,434	87,241	47,629	1.8	0	0	3	9	46.1	13
1895	32	2,241,641	70,051	90,044	49,400	1.8	0	0	2	6	46.8	13
1901	32	2,420,982	75,656	99,006	54,182	1.8	0	0	2	6	47.2	13
1905	32	2,530,016	79,063	116,033	52,731	2.2	5	16	3	9	46.2	15
1907	32	2,503,016	79,063	97,564	61,402	1.6	0	0	1	3	48.3	9
1917	32	2,810,172	87,818	131,365	60,946	2.2	2	6	3	9	46.6	11
1925	32	3,668,412	114,638	223,891	78,146	2.9	26	81	14	44	41.8	24
1952	34	6,372,009	187,412	396,001	61,008	6.5	20	59	26	76	32.3	63

Table 3

APPORTIONMENT OF THE MICHIGAN HOUSE, 1838-1953

Year	No. seats	State pop.	Avg. pop. per seat	Largest dist.	Smallest dist.	Range	Seats outside 2-1 range		Seats outside +25% range		Dauer-Kelsay index	Mean deviation David-Eisenberg index
							No.	Pct.	No.	Pct.		
1838	52	169,056	3,251	4,863	366	13.3	52	100	6	12	43.8	37
1841	53	212,267	4,005	5,715	534	10.7	53	100	26	49	43.8	34
1846	66	302,521	4,584	5,608	1,017	5.5	66	100	6	9	44.1	26
1851	72	397,654	5,523	8,631	891	9.7	72	100	11	15	42.3	40
1855	79	507,521	6,424	9,704	1,504	6.5	79	100	10	13	46.8	32
1861	100	749,970	7,500	9,252	2,981	3.1	95	95	10	10	45.4	15
1865	100	803,661	8,062	10,163	3,961	2.6	92	92	10	10	45.3	14
1871	100	1,184,282	11,843	15,820	6,025	2.6	55	55	12	12	44.4	16
1875	100	1,334,031	13,340	20,815	7,174	2.9	66	66	20	20	42.4	20
1881	100	1,636,937	16,369	25,394	8,689	2.9	36	36	16	16	43.9	15
1885	100	1,853,658	18,537	27,661	9,982	2.8	30	30	16	16	43.9	27
1891	100	2,093,889	20,918	33,639	11,224	3.0	24	24	23	23	46.6	14
1892	100	2,093,889	20,939	33,639	15,698	2.3	15	15	26	26	45.1	13
1895	100	2,241,641	22,416	35,150	16,194	2.2	15	15	22	22	43.9	15
1901	100	2,420,982	24,210	37,036	14,439	2.6	29	29	25	25	43.1	17
1905	100	2,530,016	25,300	37,373	14,636	2.6	22	22	25	25	42.9	17
1913	100	2,810,172	28,102	40,577	17,736	2.3	11	11	14	14	44.0	16
1925	100	3,668,412	36,684	56,078	17,522	3.2	79	79	53	53	37.8	29
1943	100	5,256,106	52,561	74,981	26,502	2.8	66	66	57	57	38.4	30
1953	110	6,372,009	63,720	88,461	32,469	2.7	38	35	28	25	43.6	19

Figure 2

HOUSE APPORTIONMENT 1841

Figure 3

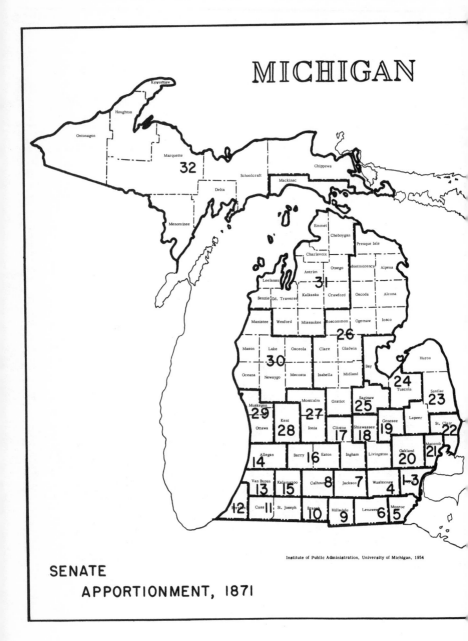

SENATE
APPORTIONMENT, 1871

Figure 4

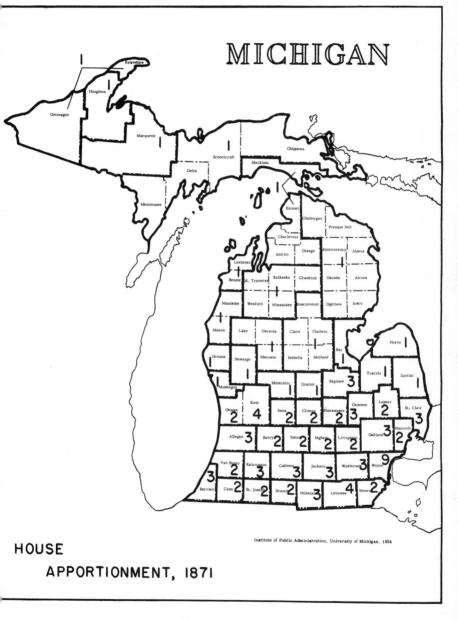

HOUSE

APPORTIONMENT, 1871

Figure 5

HOUSE
APPORTIONMENT, 1891

Figure 6

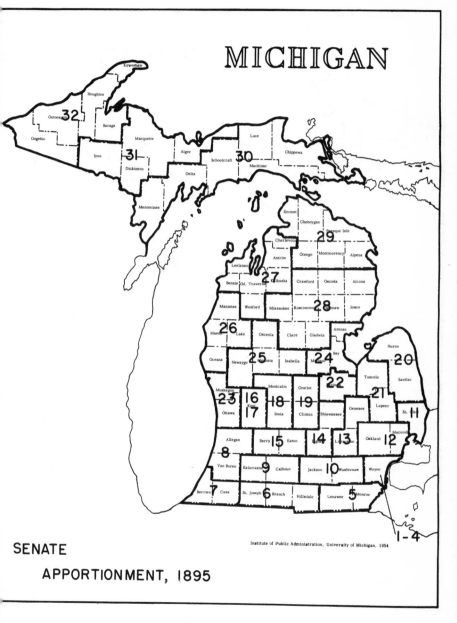

SENATE

APPORTIONMENT, 1895

Figure 7

MICHIGAN

HOUSE

APPORTIONMENT, 1901

Institute of Public Administration, University of Michigan, 1954

Figure 8

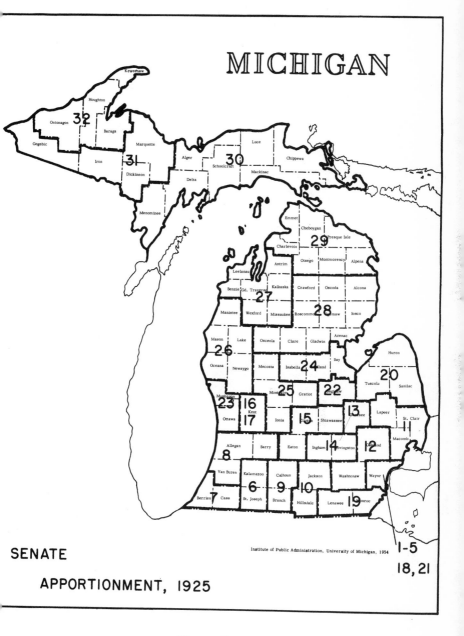

SENATE

APPORTIONMENT, 1925

Figure 9

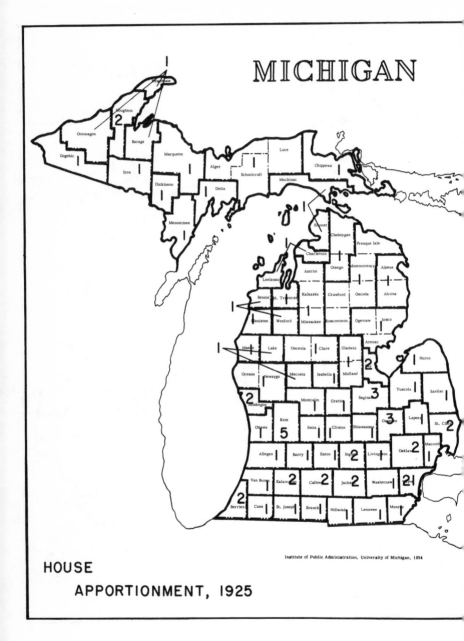

HOUSE
APPORTIONMENT, 1925

Figure 10

THE POLITICAL EVOLUTION OF THE MICHIGAN APPORTIONMENT FORMULA

By Karl A. Lamb

THE PROBLEM OF LEGISLATIVE apportionment was the central issue of the Michigan Constitutional Convention of 1961-62. This issue received more attention than any other during the campaign for the election of delegates; the proposed apportionment formula affected the attitudes of convention delegates on many other issues which came before the convention; and legislative apportionment remained the question most discussed in the debate over the adoption of the proposed constitution.

Legislative apportionment was a political issue in the sense that its resolution would determine the relative power of each

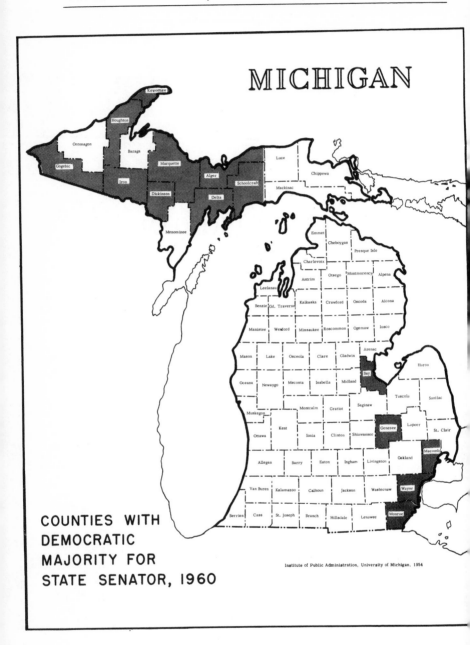

COUNTIES WITH
DEMOCRATIC
MAJORITY FOR
STATE SENATOR, 1960

Institute of Public Administration, University of Michigan, 1954

Figure 1

Figure 2

party in forming governmental policies for years to come; it was also a political issue in the sense that it has been a perennial source of conflict in Michigan and, in fact, antedates the development of a two-party political system.

The burgeoning growth of the Detroit area began with the centralization of the automobile industry in the second decade of this century. There have been sporadic attempts by the growing urban areas to obtain increased legislative representation. Political organizations and interest groups in Michigan have formulated rigid attitudes on the question. There was an open clash between such interests as recently as 1952, when a constitutional amendment calling for population-based representation in both houses of the legislature, supported by organized labor and by liberal groups, was defeated. A conservative counterproposal was adopted which provided periodic reapportionment of the lower house but froze the existing senate districts into the constitution permanently. The hostility between the Republican legislature constituted on that basis and the Democratic governor brought the state to the brink of insolvency by 1959 and inspired citizens' groups to launch a movement for constitutional revision.[1]

Because of the importance of the issue and the real power stakes involved, the apportionment formula proposed by the Michigan Constitutional Convention can be understood only as the outcome of a political process characterized by the clash of competing interests, rather than the calm study of the principles of political theory. To be complete, such an analysis must consider at least the following aspects of political conflict:

(1) The nature of the interests involved and their stake in the existing legislative districts or in a proposed new allocation

---

[1] The 1952 experience also apparently convinced Michigan labor leaders that the issue of legislative apportionment should be taken to the courts rather than to the people. The legal issue is analyzed by William Pierce on pages 1-114 in this volume. The history of legislative apportionment and the impact of apportionment systems upon contemporary Michigan politics are analyzed by John P. White on pages 115-139 of this volume.

of representatives. "Interests," as used here, includes not only organized pressure groups, but also political parties and the factions within them.

(2) The system through which these interests were directly represented in the political institution involved, the Michigan Constitutional Convention.

(3) Characteristics of that institution making it more or less responsive to the expression of constituency attitudes.

(4) The procedures used by the institution to resolve the issues before it. Such procedures include the gathering of research data, the use of public hearings, the structure of committee membership, the rules of debate, and the influence of organizations outside the official convention structure, such as party caucuses.

(5) The relation of the issue of legislative apportionment to other issues in the convention. The apportionment formula became, in fact, only one of the items on the agenda for compromise between contesting factions in the convention.

(6) The impact of events within or outside the convention process which changed the expectations of delegates concerning the usefulness of convention procedures for achieving their desired purposes.

The single most important event in the last category was the decision of the United States Supreme Court which held, in *Baker* v. *Carr*, that the question of state legislative apportionment is a justiciable matter. This decision was rendered at a crucial point during the convention. It came after the relevant committee reported a proposed apportionment formula which became a major part of an agreement between the feuding factions of the majority party, but before that proposal had been debated by the Committee of the Whole. *Baker* v. *Carr* resulted in crucial changes in the expectations of the delegates. Republican delegates, who authored the original proposal, realized that it could not escape a judicial examination according to a federal standard which had yet to be carefully defined; and Democratic delegates became convinced of the possibility of obtaining a more satisfactory resolution of the problem through legal action.

The *Baker* v. *Carr* decision, therefore, became one of the most important determinants of the final nature of the apportionment proposal in Michigan. The decision of the Michigan court in *Scholle* v. *Hare*, dealing with the pre-convention Michigan legislature, came near the end of the convention process and exerted a lesser influence. But neither decision changed the nature of the Constitutional Convention, which was a political institution that reflected the division of political forces in Michigan and operated in an atmosphere highly charged with partisanship.

THE CONSTITUTIONAL CONVENTION
AS A REPRESENTATIVE INSTITUTION

THE CONSTITUTIONAL CONVENTION was made possible by the "gateway amendment," which included a compromise system of representation worked out by the citizens' groups. It provided that one delegate be elected for each senator and one for each representative. The 110 seats in the lower house combined with the 34 of the upper house resulted in a convention with 144 delegates, elected from overlapping districts. If the sole standard for judging the effectiveness of a representative system is the standard of population distribution, then the convention reflected population distribution imperfectly, but within limits that would be considered tolerable in most states. The residents of urban areas (accepting the Census Bureau definition of urbanity) constituted a majority of the convention, just as they constituted a majority of the state's population and elected the majority of members of both houses of the existing legislature. If the conflicts to be resolved by the convention were viewed simply as conflicts between an urban population majority and a rural population minority, the urban majority would have no reason to fear tyrannical behavior by rural delegates who represented both a minority of the people and of the convention.

But political conflict in Michigan is not simply a matter of statistically urban areas arrayed against statistically rural areas. It is, in fact, a conflict between the cities and villages of out-state Michigan and the populous Detroit metropolitan area, where racial minorities are concentrated, labor unions constitute a major political force, and the Democratic party rolls up overwhelming majorities. It was precisely this area of the state which approved the calling of the Constitutional Convention, voting heavily enough to give a 51 percent state-wide majority to the proponents of constitutional revision. Four counties in southeastern Michigan favored the Constitutional Convention (or Con-Con) and the remaining 79 counties opposed it.

Paradoxically, constitutional revision carried by a substantial majority in those four counties in spite of the nearly unanimous opposition of the Democratic party. Such opposition was based on the general claim that even the compromise method of selecting delegates to the Constitutional Convention would provide a convention so weighted in favor of out-state Michigan that no satisfactory solution to the problems of the southeastern area could be expected. There was also the specific fear that such a convention would make no meaningful change in senate apportionment.

For evidence as to the accuracy of this charge, it is interesting to compare the percentage of Michigan's population found in those four counties approving Con-Con to the proportion of the total convention delegation elected by those counties. As Table 1 shows, Wayne, the most densely populated county of the state, containing Detroit and its nearest suburbs, in the 1960 census had 34.08 percent of the state's population and in 1961 over 31 percent of the delegation at the Constitutional Convention. Washtenaw County, which is on the fringe of the Detroit metropolitan area and has not been a principal beneficiary of the rush to the suburbs, won almost exactly the same representation at the convention as a population apportionment would have provided. In percentage terms, the most underrepresented counties were Oakland and Macomb, which have grown dramatically in recent years with the development of Detroit suburbs. This growth, has not been reflected in increased legislative representation, particularly in the state senate. Yet these suburbs are less Democratic in their voting habits than the central city.

As a result, although a slender majority of the state's voters approved the calling of a constitutional convention, 58 percent of the delegates to that convention would represent areas which had voted against constitutional revision. The conclusion does not follow that the majority of the delegates were hostile to constitutional revision and worked to frustrate any change in the 1908 document. Such a conclusion would be based on the assumption that both the voters and the candidates for the delegate positions in the out-state areas refused to accept the majority decision of the April 1961 election and conspired to frustrate it. There is no method which could prove or disprove the assertion concerning voter opinion at that time; but one may examine the proposed constitution, which contains many new provisions which were adopted without a division along either sectional or party lines, and conclude that the majority of the delegates did, in fact, favor a thorough revision of the old document. Whether the out-state delegates agreed with those from the Detroit area as to which were the most crucial deficiencies of the 1908 document, and how such deficiencies could best be remedied, is a more complex matter.

Table 1

REPRESENTATION IN THE CONSTITUTIONAL CONVENTION OF THOSE COUNTIES FAVORING CONSTITUTIONAL REVISION

1 County	2 % of Michigan population, 1960	3 No. of delegates to Con-Con	4 % of total	5 "Value of Vote" index*	6 Partisan division of delegation	
					Dem.	Rep.
Wayne (Detroit)	34.08	45	31.25	91.7	37	8
Oakland (Pontiac and Detroit suburbs)	8.82	7	4.86	58.5	1	6
Macomb (Detroit suburbs)	5.19	4	3.47	66.9	3	1
Washtenaw** (Ann Arbor and Ypsilanti)	2.20	3	2.15	97.7	0	3
Totals	50.29	59	41.73	82.97	41	18

* This is the familiar David-Eisenberg index developed in their *Devaluation of the Urban and Suburban Vote* (Charlottesville: Bureau of Public Administration, University of Virginia, 1961). It is obtained by dividing column 2 by column 4 and measures the degree of under- or overrepresentation. Perfect population apportionment is 100. A district with half the population which should be required for a representative has an index of 200.

** Washtenaw County, which adjoins Wayne County, is not part of the Detroit metropolitan statistical area, nor is it considered to be politically aligned with the interests of Detroit residents, since Washtenaw votes Republican. But, it is the home of the University of Michigan, and a partial explanation of the approval by the county of the Constitutional Convention may be the interest of the university community in constitutional revision.

The "gateway amendment" specified that one delegate should be elected for each senator and each representative but left the other details of their election to the legislature. That body determined that delegates should be nominated in party primaries, elected on a partisan ballot, and receive a salary of $1,000 per month (but no more than a total of $7,500) for the term of the convention. The salary, which was double the amount the Michigan legislator receives on a monthly basis, was intended to make it possible for distinguished citizens to serve without financial sacrifice; and the political parties seemed to take very seriously their responsibility for recruiting capable persons to rewrite Michigan's basic law. The prospect of party support, coupled with their conception of the importance of the tasks faced by the convention, enticed many leading citizens into candidacy. Many of these persons would not have been interested in other elective offices.[1]

The importance of the issues at stake also led important actors on the Michigan political scene to seek election as delegates who would normally exert influence on the political process from vantage points outside the formal governmental institutions. This list would include at least William Marshall, vice president of the Michigan AFL-CIO; Tom Downs, AFL-CIO attorney; Stanley Powell, legislative agent of the Michigan Farm Bureau Federation; D. Hale Brake, former state treasurer and educational director of the Michigan Association of Supervisors (made up of township and county officials); and Mrs. Katherine M. Cushman, of the League of Women Voters. The result was that many of Michigan's active pressure groups were represented in

[1] A non-exhaustive list of such personages would include Charles Anspach, president emeritus of Central Michigan University; John Hannah, president of Michigan State University; William Marshall, executive vice president of the Michigan AFL-CIO; and Dan Karn, president of Consumer's Power Company.

161

the convention by members of their own leadership elite who had been elected as delegates.[2]

Fifty-two of the 144 delegates listed their primary occupation as "attorney," which is certainly no surprise in American politics, although several of these delegates were of a distinction (and income) in the legal profession that would not usually be found in the state legislature. Several ladies were elected to the convention who would not normally have sought a legislative career. Several others, including Stephen Nisbet, president of the convention, had retired from their lifetime occupations. Election to the Constitutional Convention represented for them the culmination of a long interest in public affairs.

In sum, the delegates to the Constitutional Convention were a group generally conceded to be more capable and distinguished than those representatives normally elected to the Michigan legislature. Many of them had had less direct political experience than legislators, however, and the convention as an institution did not have established and traditional methods of procedure, such as a seniority system, which legislatures tend to develop.

Because of the lack of precedent in determining the procedures of a constitutional convention, the decisions of the majority party in this regard would be of crucial importance. And Democrats who opposed calling the convention feared that the Republicans would control the substantive decisions of the convention.

The principal objection of the Democrats to the calling of a constitutional convention in 1958, when the question automatically appeared on the ballot as stipulated by the 1908 constitution, was that a convention elected on the basis of three delegates from each senatorial district would simply duplicate the

---

[2] At the instigation of Delegate Walter deVries, political science teacher at Calvin College, who had written a doctoral dissertation on lobbying in the Michigan legislature, the convention provided rules for the regulation of lobbying which were rather more stringent than those in force in the legislature. Studies of lobbying techniques at the Constitutional Convention were frustrated, however, because many interest groups counted on the influence of elected delegates rather than traditional lobbying methods.

unrepresentative nature of the Michigan senate. Michigan elected a Democratic governor every two years from 1948 to 1960, but the Democratic party never captured either house of the legislature. In 1958, 12 Democratic and 22 Republican senators were elected. The 12 Democrats together received nearly 46,000 votes more than the total vote cast for the 22 Republicans. This was due not only to the overrepresentation in the senate of areas outside the Detroit metropolitan area but also to the heavy concentration of the Democratic vote in that area.[3] If the party division had remained the same in the election of 102 Con-Con delegates, as provided in the 1908 constitution, 36 Democratic delegates would have faced a majority of 66 Republican delegates. Citing similar statistics, an AFL-CIO pamphlet in 1958 commented:

> The foregoing facts in relation to a Constitutional Convention are never mentioned in our daily newspapers in their enthusiastic drive for a Constitutional Convention. However, they are well aware that less than 50% of the people would elect more than 2/3 of the delegates and that as a result of the fashion in which these districts are divided, the Republican Party would dominate any constitutional convention held in the next decade.[4]

The Democratic legislators were willing to support a constitutional convention if three delegates were elected from each district of the house of representatives.[5] It remained for citizens' groups to put forward the obvious compromise, however. If previous party voting patterns were repeated in the Con-Con election, the Republicans would have a majority of about ten delegates. The compromise plan did not arouse universal enthusiasm in Republican hearts, in spite of the enthusiastic support for Con-Con by Paul Bagwell, the Republican nominee for governor in 1958 and 1960. Many conservative Republicans

---

[3] Several Detroit districts regularly cast a Democratic vote of the magnitude of 80 or 85 percent. "Safe" Republican districts out-state have smaller populations and also a smaller Republican majority in percentage terms.

[4] *The Case for Representative Government* (Detroit: Michigan State AFL-CIO, not dated), p. 13.

[5] *The Detroit News,* January 26 and 28, 1958.

were satisfied with the 1908 document, particularly the 1952 amendment providing frozen senatorial districts. With neither party unified on the issue, citizens' organizations carried out the petition campaign for the calling of a constitutional convention. The Junior Chamber of Commerce, the League of Women Voters, and the Michigan Education Association were among the leading groups. The final impetus carrying the petition drive to its goal was provided by Citizens for Michigan, a small but well-financed organization headed by George Romney, president of American Motors.[6]

The special election of September 12, 1961, did not result in a constitutional convention mirroring the party division of the legislature. Ninety-nine Republican and 45 Democratic delegates were elected. Five Democratic legislative districts in Michigan's upper peninsula returned Republican delegates; this was readily explained by the insistent "one man, one vote" campaign slogan of Democratic candidates in the Detroit area. The upper peninsula, chronically depressed since the closing of many of its mines around 1910 (and Democratic in seven or eight of its ten legislative districts since the New Deal) was one of the principal beneficiaries of the existing apportionment system. It had been hostile to the proposal for a constitutional convention. But Republicans also won in the traditional Democratic strongholds of southeastern Michigan. Wayne County, which usually sends no Republicans to the senate and only one to the house (from the swank residential area of Grosse Pointe), elected eight Republican delegates. In Oakland County, the city of Pontiac, which elected a Democratic representative by 62 percent in 1958 and by 58 percent in 1960, elected a Republican Con-Con delegate by a 2 percent margin. The third district of Macomb County, which elected a Democratic legislator in the two previous

---

[6] In urging an affirmative vote for Con-Con, Romney stated that "the near-equilibrium representation offers the voters of Michigan their best chance . . . to undertake a constitutional convention on terms that assure balanced representation of all Michigan interests without urban or one-party domination." *Lansing State Journal*, November 4, 1960.

elections by a slender margin, gave a Republican candidate nearly 60 percent of its vote.

The most obvious explanation for the Democratic defeat was the light turnout. Approximately 17 percent of the state's registered voters participated in the election.[7] In district after district, there was a dramatic decrease in participation. In the city of Pontiac, for example, the total vote cast in the presidential year of 1960 had been 30,222; in the non-presidential year of 1958, it had been 22,041; but the Con-Con election brought only 4,955 voters to the polls. The low turnout could be explained partly on the basis of timing: a campaign during the hot summer months; an election at an unusual time, with no national or even state-wide office to capture attention; voters perhaps more interested in getting the children ready for school than in paying attention to politics.

That a light turnout should favor the Republicans is due to the fact that the voters with the most pronounced Democratic affiliation are those of lower socio-economic and educational status who would be most likely to be uninformed concerning the nature of the Constitutional Convention, the attitude of party leaders on the question, and the impact of constitutional revision on their own interests.[8]

Because the special election attracted so little public notice, the Democratic party organization faced a formidable task in getting its voters to the polls. Several commentators noted an additional source of Democratic trouble. The Con-Con salary

---

[7] 839,219 went to the polls, but only 720,000 voted for Con-Con delegates. The remainder were attracted only by local issues, which some cities chose to place on the ballot at the same election. The elections director said that the turnout was the lowest since the April election of 1945, a wartime year. *The Detroit News*, October 28, 1961.

[8] Many recent studies of voting behavior establish the conclusion that the incidence of nonvoting is highest among groups with a Democratic party identification. Perhaps the most authoritative are the studies of the University of Michigan Survey Research Center. See Angus Campbell, Philip E. Converse, Warren E. Miller, and Donald E. Stokes, *The American Voter* (New York: Wiley, 1960), pp. 110-15.

of $1,000 per month was intended to provide adequate compensation for capable delegates. Faithful ward workers in Detroit who had built up the party organization during the Williams era may have seen the delegate position as a just reward. When the party leaders sought candidates elsewhere, the enthusiasm of the ward workers for the campaign would be considerably lessened. Primary elections in metropolitan districts were characterized by a great number of candidates, and the divisive effect of a primary free-for-all is certain to lower party efficiency in the general election.

The winners of an election, however, do not seek the meaning of their victory in the preferences of non-voters or in the organizational troubles of the opposition party. A mandate is sought in the preferences of those making the trip to the polls. The assumption is that votes cast by individuals are based at least in part on campaigns waged by the candidates. Victorious Republicans read the election results as a negative reaction to the position of the Democrats. It was harder to discern a consistent Republican theme which might have aroused a positive reaction.

The Republican party was confident of controlling the convention; but none of its factions was confident of controlling the party. Furthermore, the majority of the Republican delegates were certain to be elected from areas which had opposed the calling of a constitutional convention. Paul Bagwell's insistence on a platform plank favoring constitutional revision had succeeded in achieving a party endorsement in 1958 and 1960. When it seemed clear that the call to a convention would actually be issued, however, conservative opposition was redoubled. The Republican Convention preceding the April election took a neutral position on the matter. When the call of the convention was approved, there were no further party conventions before the campaigns began and no chance to develop a party statement on the issues Con-Con would face.

Democrats were beset by no such woes. Democratic Governors Williams and Swainson had been assailing the misrepresentative nature of the legislature for 13 years; metropolitan Democratic leaders had battled for population representation in the 1952 initiative campaign; and the AFL-CIO had published concise data concerning the present and projected population of the established districts.[9] There was no surprise, therefore, when the Democratic State Central Committee adopted a platform on behalf of Democratic delegate candidates which pinpointed apportionment as the key issue in constitutional revision.[10]

The much amended constitution of 1908 had serious flaws. The governor's powers were far short of his political responsibilities, for members of his Administrative Board (or cabinet) were elected independently; the administrative branch of state government had grown into an awkward monster of more than 120 departments, agencies, and commissions; the amount of money the state could borrow without a vote of the people was limited to $250,000; tax monies were earmarked for local governments, school districts, and roads, so that the legislature really could not determine the fiscal policies of the state; and the nature of township and county government was specified in the constitution, hampering the development of local government responsive to the needs of urban areas. Ignoring all these, Democrats in southeastern Michigan campaigned for "one man, one vote" apportionment.

Republican reaction was varied. In out-state districts, Republican candidates painted the usual campaign portrait of the Democratic city candidates as the willing creatures of UAW President Walter Reuther and August Scholle, president of the Michigan AFL-CIO. The Democratic purpose, they claimed, was to reapportion the state so that the urban counties of southeastern Michigan would "control" the legislature. In Wayne County, Republican candidates were frustrated by the refusal

---

[9] *The Case for Representative Government, op. cit.*

[10] One political commentator wrote that Democratic "candidates have been pledged to push apportionment of the legislature as the over-riding purpose of the Con-Con, even to the point of holding out against any other changes in the basic law until they get what they want on a reshuffle of legislative seats." William Kulsea, *The Ann Arbor News*, July 29, 1961.

of their Democratic opponents to debate issues other than apportionment. Weldon Yeager, a young member of the Republican State Central Committee who was running in a traditionally Democratic senatorial district, first attempted to ignore the issue in his campaign. Unable to debate other problems with his opponent, Yeager felt it necessary to formulate a position on apportionment. He proposed a formula by which the apportionment of the senate would be based "sixty per cent on population and forty per cent on area." Yeager won the election by a margin of 777 votes of 55,807 votes cast. The total vote of the district had been 155,655 in 1958 and 229,664 in the presidential contest of 1960.

Most conservative Republican candidates conceded that the lower house should be apportioned periodically on the basis of population, in order to "balance" an upper house based in part on other considerations. No Republican candidate, even in the underrepresented suburban areas, was reported as supporting strict population apportionment in both houses of the legislature. The source of disagreement between Republicans was the matter of how nearly the upper chamber should approach a population standard. Positions on this matter were rather vaguely defined, save for those who wished no change in the existing frozen-district senate.

The question of legislative apportionment was the single issue upon which party positions were most clearly defined and on which the electorate was most likely to be informed, due to its perennial appearance as an issue in Michigan campaigns. The day after the election, George Romney, the newly elected delegate from the Oakland County senatorial district, defined the meaning of the election. The people of Michigan, he stated, do not wish both houses of the legislature to be apportioned strictly on the basis of population.[11]

---

[11] George Romney, quoted on television newscast, September 13, 1961; George Romney, speech at Central Michigan University, Mt. Pleasant, December 2, 1961.

If this was indeed the mandate of the election, the Republican party had a comfortable majority to carry it out. There were other aspects of the Constitutional Convention, however, which affected its performance as a representative institution. To begin with the most obvious, the convention was a temporary body. Its proposal would be judged by the state-wide electorate, but the individual delegates would not be required to submit voting records to their districts at another election. This aspect of the convention drew some editorial comment, based on the notion that delegates for whom re-election was impossible would be more likely to act the role of a statesman than that of a politician. In its most extreme form, this argument was the basis for a prediction of the reduced influence of the party affiliation of the delegates:

> Constitutional delegates differ from legislators in that they have power to establish basic organic law which embodies fixed principles and expresses the fundamental philosophy of govern-ment . . . while we do not imply any dereliction of duty on the part of the legislator, the mere fact that the delegate does not seek re-election could make him less sensitive to party pressures.[12]

The nature of the convention as a temporary body did have an effect on the performance of some delegates, but a lessening of party ties was not the result. For some delegates, their elec-tion to the convention was the beginning of a political career, and the Michigan legislature was well aware of the fact that the convention nurtured a pack of eager political rivals. For others, the delegates' experience was the capstone of their careers, and they had no future political ambitions. They were free to adopt a theory of representation based even more ex-clusively on personal judgment than that of Edmund Burke. This seemed to be the approach of several of the convention delegates, including some of the surprise Republican winners in Wayne County. Because the multi-member district system in that county has effectively excluded Republicans from the leg-

---

[12] *Challenge,* publication of the Michigan State Chamber of Commerce, quoted in *The Detroit News,* September 27, 1961.

islature for many years, the Republican organization simply does not expect victory in a legislative contest and did not expect victory in the Con-Con election. The candidates in such districts tended to be those willing to represent a pronounced conservative point of view, even though it was an unpopular one. The most striking example of this phenomenon was J. Harold Stevens, a retired school teacher and practicing attorney elected from Wayne County's Twelfth District, which includes the western area of the city of Detroit and has nearly 200,000 inhabitants (it is a two-member district). Mr. Stevens earned a reputation as one of the most conservative delegates at the convention.

Arthur T. Iverson, long active in state Republican affairs, was elected from the neighboring Tenth District of the city of Detroit, also a solidly Democratic area, and his views were conservative enough for him to become the chairman of the Republican caucus. The other delegate elected in the two-member Tenth District was Miss Adelaide Hart, former vice chairman of the Democratic State Central Committee, and a leader in the formation of the liberal-labor coalition under G. Mennen Williams. Miss Hart served as leader of the Democratic caucus at Con-Con.

There is no mystical method by which a representative informs his constituents of the issues placed before him, determines their attitudes, and then votes according to the majority preference of his district.[13] He may attempt to interpret the mandate of his own election. Even if he correctly interprets the will of the majority voting for him, he still runs the risk of performing

---

[13] Professor V. O. Key, perhaps the most noted American student of political parties, has written that "few of his constituents have even the slightest awareness of most of the questions on which the legislator must stand up and be counted. On those few issues about which awareness is widespread among his constituents . . . [he] may hear from a few people on a few issues. He must always, as he votes, assume the risk of antagonizing some constituents, but he is rarely faced by the difficult choice of rejecting or accepting the mandate of his constituency, for he does not know what it is. And, indeed, there may be none." *Public Opinion and American Democracy* (New York: Knopf, 1961), pp. 482-83.

some action which will so enrage the non-voters that they will flock to the polls at the next election and turn him out of office. The delegates to the Constitutional Convention faced no further election.

But the Constitutional Convention was designed to be a representative institution. It was not an appointed commission ready to make recommendations to the legislature or to the people; nor was it a group elected from the state at large, in order to represent "the interests of the whole state" in preference to the regional or parochial concern. The delegates were elected from legislative districts; and, if the delegates voting for the proposed document should support its adoption in those same districts, one of the most important explanations they would be forced to make would be the rationale for any change in the representation of that district in the legislature.[14] It was a serious problem for the delegation from Kent County, which was generally one of the most progressive and capable groups of Republican delegates. Kent County (the Grand Rapids area) had been represented by two senators for over 60 years, but its population increase had not kept pace with other areas of the state, and the apportionment of the senate more nearly on the basis of population could cause the loss of the second senator.

The inescapable factor determining the nature of the convention, however, was the election of its delegates on a partisan ballot. The political party is the most important single reference group which guides the voter in determining political choices. With a two to one Republican majority in the convention, the document was bound to wear a Republican label.

---

[14] Delegates heard a great deal on other issues from their districts as the convention progressed. The delegates from areas with race tracks were very busy indeed when it seemed that the proposed constitution might prohibit pari-mutuel betting. The 1908 constitution prohibited lotteries, but a Supreme Court decision held this did not include horse racing. On this, as on the question of constitutionally earmarked tax funds, the delegates recognized the power of established interests and decided to continue the provisions of the old document.

THE DEMOCRATIC DILEMMA

THE DEMOCRATIC PARTY in Michigan had been made into a formidable power during the decade of G. Mennen Williams' tenure of the executive office. The Michigan Democrats developed a program which was aggressively liberal in content, particularly after the Teamsters Union was defeated by the AFL-CIO in a contest for party influence. Matching liberal programs with a genius for party organization, the Democratic liberal-labor alliance in that brief period changed Michigan from a Republican state to one with a normal Democratic majority. That the state clung to its Republican habits so long after the advent of the New Deal seems to be explained by the fact that Democratic Governor Frank Murphy developed a strong personal following based on support for his liberal views but neglected to tend to the organizational spadework which could permit the transfer of allegiance to a chosen successor. Governor Murray Van Wagoner, on the other hand, won office on the basis of the patronage he dispensed as highway commissioner, but he could not form a coalition of interest groups based on adherence to party programs. The permanence of the Democratic majority established by the combination of Williams' leadership, liberal programs, and union support seemed proven by the election of Lt. Governor John B. Swainson as Williams' successor in 1960.

The Democratic delegates elected to the Constitutional Convention, therefore, were partisans accustomed to being members of a victorious coalition, and they often acted as though convinced that the Republican delegates represented minority opinions which had won a delegate majority through deception or fraud.[1] The Democrats were faced with a dilemma in planning party strategy. In its most simple terms, the choice was between serving as an active force in the convention (seeking alliances with a group or groups in the majority party) in order to exert an influence on its product, or holding themselves aloof from the real negotiations in order to avoid being tainted with the

---

[1] Because of Republican victories in underrepresented Detroit area districts, the apportionment of the unicameral convention did not discriminate against the Democratic party in a substantial manner. Twenty-five of the 34 senatorial districts elected Republicans, so that Republicans held 73.5 percent of those seats. The population of those districts was 69.8 percent of the state total, so that the apportionment of senate districts gave the Republicans one extra delegate. Seventy-four of the 110 house districts elected Republicans, so that Republicans held 67.3 percent of the house seats. Republican districts contained 66.8 percent of the state's population, so that the Republicans gained half a delegate because of the apportionment of house seats. This was a total Republican advantage of one and one-half delegates over the outcome of strict population apportionment. During the course of the convention, however, two Republican delegates resigned, and Governor Swainson appointed Democrats to fill the vacancies.

odor of a document which could fall considerably short of their desires. If the final outcome should be not to their liking, enthusiastic participation in the writing of the document might hamper effective opposition to its adoption.

Complicating this decision was the appearance on the political horizon of George Romney. Although Romney had announced no political aims beyond the convention, Democrats were aware that his potential as a candidate posed a real threat to the continued domination of the Democratic party in the state. They were not eager to add brilliance to his political luster by cooperating in the writing of a document with which Romney would be closely identified.

The solidarity of the Democratic delegation varied according to the issue concerned. But the position of the metropolitan area Democrats on the question of legislative apportionment was publicly staked out. Expressed in the stark principle of "one man, one vote," the Democratic position left little room for maneuver or compromise.

THE REPUBLICAN RESPONSIBILITY

GIVEN THE POLITICAL SITUATION which has developed in Michigan over the last 14 years, the task of the Michigan Republican party is analagous to the duty of the Democratic party on the national scene. Just as the Democratic party must somehow contain in a single organization both the southern rurally oriented conservatives and the northern urban-based liberals, the Michigan Republican party, if it wishes to become an effective vehicle for popular government, must build a bridge of understanding between the Michigan of the Farm Bureau Federation and the Michigan of the United Automobile Workers.

The national Democratic party has lived with its problem longer, and with greater success.

Within three elections, Williams' party organization converted his narrow personal victory into a Democratic party majority. Republicans could win hardly any state-wide office. But conservative Republican senators were safely in control of their chamber and secure in their individual districts. The stage was set for a classic struggle between executive and legislature. That their performance would form the image of the Republican party in the minds of Michigan voters did not distress the senators. Each seemed to feel that the interests of his own district and the demands of his conservative ideology should take precedence over the state-wide interests of the party.

The leaders of the state Republican organization clearly perceived that the Republican party could win state-wide office only by appealing to the urban centers, which house a majority of Michigan's citizens. In recent years, the state chairmen have been elected by party conventions which provide adequate representation for urban areas. But the state Republican organization (represented by the staff of the central committee) can exert little influence over the actions of county organizations and none over the voting patterns of party members in the legislature. There was open hostility between the leadership group in the senate and state chairmen John Feikens and Lawrence Lindemer. Paul Bagwell, Republican candidate in 1958 and 1960, campaigned vigorously in southeastern Michigan but made few dents in Democratic solidity there. Conservative Republicans claimed that the liberal wing was alienating true Republicans in the out-state area without winning any strength in Detroit.

The division in the Republican ranks was not one between farm Republicans and city residents. Some of the most conservative Republican legislators have represented cities outside the Detroit area, such as Grand Rapids, and large corporations, including the automobile companies, have influenced Republican policies.[1] It was rather a contest between those who would accept the presence and problems of the Detroit area and attempt to rebuild the party on a state-wide basis, on the one hand, and those on the other hand, who would abandon Detroit and the labor vote to the Democrats, retreat into barricaded safe districts, and oppose the political demands of the Detroit area with every weapon at hand.

At the time of the Con-Con election, the Republican party had suffered a string of defeats in state-wide elections. It was made up of a collection of mutually hostile groups, held together only by the party label, and no individual could legitimately claim leadership over all party factions.

Thus the Republican party faced the responsibility of a commanding majority in the Constitutional Convention with no agreement on procedures to be followed, no platform which could be the basis of one faction's appeal to public opinion over the power of another, and with each candidate owing his election only to the constellation of political forces in his own district. It seemed likely that the proposed constitution would be submitted for voter approval in the election of November 1962. If approved, the constitution could carry into office the Republican nominee for governor and give the Republicans a chance to begin rebuilding a state-wide party. If the document were rejected, however, Republican fortunes might be eclipsed for another decade.

These were the considerations that faced party members as the elected Republican delegates jockeyed for power in the organization of the convention. Two-thirds of the elected Republican delegates attended an annual party rally at a resort hotel in St. Joseph, Michigan, ten days after the election. An initial alignment of forces became clear, but the only decision made

[1] The history of Michigan's party system from 1900 to 1956 is outlined in Stephen B. and Vera H. Sarasohn, *Political Party Patterns in Michigan* (Detroit: Wayne State University Press, 1957).

was that there be a caucus meeting in Lansing the week end before the convention was scheduled to open on October third.

One identifiable party group was composed of party professionals with a conservative outlook and strong support in rural areas. Included in the group was Stanley Powell, registered lobbyist for the Michigan Farm Bureau Federation, who had led the Farm Bureau fight against the calling of a constitutional convention in 1958, in coalition with the Michigan AFL-CIO. The combination of the Farm Bureau and the CIO is as rare in Michigan politics as it is unbeatable.

The best known member of the conservative bloc was D. Hale Brake, former state treasurer, now education director of the Association of Supervisors. Brake had been the out-state candidate for the gubernatorial nomination in 1954 but had not won the ballot designation. Brake enjoyed the title of "Mr. Republican" in rural Michigan and had opposed the campaign policies of the Bagwell group in the two preceding elections. It became clear at the St. Joseph meeting that the conservative group had chosen, as its candidate for president of the convention, Edward Hutchinson, of Fennville, a veteran state senator and unsuccessful aspirant for the 1960 nomination for lieutenant governor. The rural base of this faction is perhaps indicated by the fact that both Brake and Hutchinson had been defeated in state-wide primary elections. *The Detroit News* stated that "Hutchinson is able and an expert on constitutional questions. In a political vacuum he would be a first-class con-con president. But con-con will not operate in such a vacuum . . . Hutchinson would be no better a president than the obstructionist company he keeps." [2]

Hutchinson's leading opponent was George Romney, president of the American Motors Corporation. Romney was a newcomer to partisan politics, which alone disqualified him in the eyes of some aging professionals. Others saw in him a potential candidate for governor, who, if elected, might rebuild the Michigan

---

[2] September 27, 1961.

Republican party in a manner not to their liking. Publicity as Con-Con president plus his own charismatic personality would give Romney a better chance at election than Paul Bagwell had ever enjoyed. Oakland County Republicans had long urged Romney to become a candidate for state-wide office, and he had refused to support a movement to enter his name in the Republican primary election for United States senator the previous year. Romney claimed as his primary objective the achievement of recommendations for constitutional revision formulated by his organization, Citizens for Michigan. He described himself as an "Oakland County Republican" when seeking the position of delegate. He had made no announcement of further interest in public office, but his supporters clearly wished to make him president of Con-Con in order to strengthen his candidacy for governor. Both his friends and enemies seemed convinced that he would decide to seek the gubernatorial nomination, and his name had already been mentioned in speculation concerning Republican presidential candidates for 1964.

Romney's base of support was in Oakland County, and he could expect aid from other delegates concerned with attempting to win state-wide victory. But neither of the leading contenders could count on the support of a majority of the delegation, partly because of the large number of delegates who were relative newcomers and were not clearly identified with either party faction. The prospect of a deadlock in the caucus between the Romney and Hutchinson forces led to the mention of possible compromise candidates. Two of these were nominated in the caucus at the same time as were Hutchinson and Romney. They were President John A. Hannah of Michigan State University and Professor James K. Pollock of the University of Michigan Political Science Department.

During the campaign, Michigan newspapers had launched a crusade of their own for an "open convention," claiming that the news media should not be denied access to any of the deliberations of the convention. Commitments were obtained from most delegate candidates that they would oppose executive sessions of the Con-Con committees as well as of the full convention. In the opening minutes of the Republican caucus, the first blow to Hutchinson's candidacy was struck when the first vote opened the caucus to the public. The conservatives were defeated on other questions of convention procedure as the liberals determined that there should be no party floor leaders or whips; that the convention rules should be determined in consultation with the minority party; that Democratic delegates should be elected to some of the offices of the convention; and that staff recruitment should be based on civil service examinations, rather than political patronage. All of these decisions were aimed at keeping the door open for bipartisan compromise in the writing of the new constitution.

But the liberals did not wish to compromise the responsibility of the Republican party. If the Republican caucus was hopelessly divided against itself, a Republican faction might combine with the Democratic minority to elect the convention officers. To preclude such a possibility, the caucus agreed that its designee for president should receive 73 votes, a majority of all delegates elected to the convention. Balloting went on all day Friday, with neither Romney nor Hutchinson able to secure the required majority, or even a majority of those present. Both Hannah and Pollock kept a handful of votes.

Hopelessly deadlocked, the caucus recessed over the week end. On Monday morning, three ballots proved that there had been no substantial change in the alignment of support, in spite of frantic politicking by both the Hutchinson and Romney supporters. Romney attempted to shift his support to Hannah, but his followers were not agreed on Hannah as their second choice. The floor was then opened for further nominations. The delegation from his home district presented the name of Stephen Nisbet, retired Gerber Foods Company executive and former member of the State Board of Education. Nisbet had opposed calling the convention, preferring revision by amendment, but he had cancelled a long-planned vacation in Florida when the Republicans insisted that he become their candidate. Motivated by a strong sense of public duty, he was a respected senior figure in the party who had not been a participant in its most intense factional struggles. Neither the Romney nor the Hutchinson forces had strong objections to his candidacy, and the caucus flocked to his standard with obvious relief. In Nisbet the Republicans had chosen a presiding officer who would be scrupulously fair in his rulings and who would try to smooth the wounded feelings of individuals and groups within the convention. But he was a person without strong commitments as to the language the new constitution should contain, and he would not use his official leadership position to influence the outcome of the convention process. In choosing Nisbet, the Republicans postponed the inevitable confrontation of rival party factions.

The postponement of conflict was confirmed by the selection of both Hutchinson and Romney as vice presidents of the convention, with a third vice president to be designated by the Democrats. The "troika plan" of organization was extended to Con-Con committees, with the chairman and first vice chairman designated by the Republicans and the second vice chairman designated by the Democrats.[3]

Democratic leaders seemed prepared to oppose the election of either Romney or Hutchinson. Hutchinson's record and associations were too conservative, and Romney's potential can-

---

[3] The latter designation was intended as a public gesture of bipartisan cooperation, rather than as a grant of power. This was made clear when the convention adopted a rule empowering the president to appoint a new chairman if both the chairman and first vice chairman were absent from committee meetings for a "prolonged" time, so that no Democrat would actually preside over a committee. A democratic delegate moved to abolish the office of second vice chairman, "which would have cost Democrats no real power, and made them underdogs on paper as well as in fact." *The Ann Arbor News*, October 11, 1961. See also Michigan, State of, *Journal of the Constitutional Convention*, October 10, 1961. (Cited hereafter as *Journal*.)

didacy for governor threatened to end the 13-year Democratic monopoly of that office. The only chance for Democratic participation in the election of the convention president lay in combining their voting power with a group of disgruntled Republicans. But Stephen Nisbet had no further political ambitions. Democratic leaders who had worked with him in public affairs testified to their respect for him as a "real gentleman." The Democratic minority prepared to give their blessing to the Republican choice for convention president.

The Constitutional Convention opened the next day. Nisbet's nomination was seconded by a Democratic leader and he was elected by acclamation. The convention was organized in an atmosphere of bipartisan harmony that belied the tensions beneath the surface. Republicans agreed that Democrats should receive one-third of the membership on all committees, reflecting their numerical position in the convention, and no serious conflict developed over the adoption of the procedural rules of the convention.

The convention delegates were organized into three procedural and nine substantive committees, the latter being assigned specific sections of the old constitution. The potentially explosive matter of the appointment of committee chairmen and the selection of committee membership was made the task of the president, in consultation with the three vice presidents. Because of the unified leadership within the Democratic delegation, the Democratic caucus was able to agree on committee assignments, and President Nisbet accepted the recommendations of the Democratic caucus as transmitted by Tom Downs, AFL-CIO attorney elected as the third vice president of the convention. But the Republicans could boast no such unified purpose, and the committee assignments were made by Nisbet, on the advice of Romney and Hutchinson. Each delegate submitted his preference for committee assignment to Nisbet, and this preference was honored in so far as possible, but the president announced that his selections were guided by the desire "to balance the committee memberships geographically, philosophically, and by qualifications." [4]

Following these principles, Nisbet's appointment of committee chairmen gave positions of influence to prominent Republicans—men of knowledge and experience—of every point on the liberal-conservative spectrum represented by the elected Republican delegates. Of the nine substantive committees, no more than five were headed by men clearly identified with the liberal faction. The potentially most difficult assignment was chairman of the Committee on Legislative Organization, which would handle the issue of legislative apportionment. This assignment went to John A. Hannah, president of Michigan State University, who had presided over the development of that institution from a first-rate agricultural college into a major university, earning a reputation for political adroitness.

The assignment of these influential positions represented a recognition of the most experienced and powerful members of the Republican contingent. The result was a diffusion of party leadership and a further postponement of the inevitable factional collision. That the collision had again been satisfactorily postponed was evidenced by the general satisfaction expressed by both Republicans and Democrats with their committee assignments. The only real source of complaint was not related to political ideology. None of the Republican women had been assigned to the first vice chairmanship of any committee, and no Republican lady was assigned to more than one committee. This oversight was rectified within the Republican caucus.

---

[4] *The Detroit News,* October 11, 1961.

THE COMMITTEE ON LEGISLATIVE
ORGANIZATION

THE KEY COMMITTEE on Legislative Organization consisted of 21 members. Reflecting the two-thirds Republican majority, 14 of its members were Republicans and seven were Democrats. President Nisbet's goals of geographical and ideological variety were achieved. As Table 2 demonstrates, the members of the committee represented districts which were well distributed over the state, including one of the four Democrats elected from the upper peninsula. Factional distribution within the Republican group was quite uneven, however. Only two or three could be solidly identified with the more liberal group.

Arthur Elliott, who was to become George Romney's campaign manager, could not devote full energies to the question of legislative apportionment, because of his problems as chairman of the Committee on Local Government. The balance of the Republican delegation in varying degree was aligned with the conservative bloc.

It is interesting to notice, as Table 2 demonstrates, that nine of the committee members (five Republicans and four Democrats) came from districts which had fewer members in the legislature than would be allocated on the basis of strict population. Twelve members of the committee (nine Republicans and three Democrats) came from overrepresented districts. Districts of the lower house were due for reapportionment after the 1960 census, which would reflect population changes since 1950, but the moiety provision (assigning a seat to any area with one-half of 1 percent of the state's population) would favor rural districts. Republicans Dehnke, Kirk, Plank, and Rood, together with Democrat Sablich, came from such "moiety districts." But the frozen senate seats could never reflect population changes. Republicans Yeager and Hannah, and Democrats Liberato and Marshall, came from underrepresented senatorial districts, while Oakland County, home of George Romney and Arthur Elliott, was the most populous senatorial district in the state.

If the primary concern of the delegates was to protect the interests of their own districts, the committee would have a majority of two for a plan providing minimal change in the status quo. Assuming that motivation, members from the overrepresented districts would be the most vehement defenders of the existing system. Lee Boothby, the youngest Republican delegate and a protege of D. Hale Brake, fulfilled this prediction admirably. He introduced several schemes for establishing various systems of frozen senate districts, and he later led an abortive attempt, on the floor of the convention, to retain the existing districts. But the theory of district interest as the primary motivation of delegates ignores the fact of party affiliation. William Hanna, who became identified as the author of the original committee proposal which required little alteration in the existing senate apportionment, came from an under-represented district, while Melvin Nord, the author of the Democratic minority report, came from an area of declining population in Detroit which enjoyed substantial overrepresentation.

The Republicans were agreed that the upper house should be based on population "and other factors." The most likely source of disagreement between the Republicans was over how closely the senate apportionment should approach a population standard. The Democratic party, however, called for a strict population standard in both houses and expressed their belief that a convention controlled by the Republicans could never produce a satisfactory apportionment formula. The Democrats on the committee were in a position to make this a self-fulfilling prophecy. By combining with the liberal Republicans, they could, at least in theory, have forced the committee to adopt a proposal more closely reflecting population distribution than any which would have been acceptable to the conservative Republicans. Or they could remain aloof from the procedings, attempt to maximize the Democratic advantage in a new apportionment formula, and drive the liberal Republicans toward a conservative position.

After the committee was organized, several meetings were devoted to familiarizing its members with the facts of legislative apportionment. Presentations were made by members of the committee staff and by visiting academicians on a variety of matters. These included the history of legislative apportionment in Michigan, the effectiveness of legislative representation in Michigan compared to other states, and the techniques of predicting population growth and establishing population projections. Chairman Hannah established the fact that overrepresented districts were not confined to rustic areas. Districts of

(*Text continued on page 191.*)

Table 2

ANALYSIS OF REPRESENTATION ON THE COMMITTEE ON LEGISLATIVE ORGANIZATION

1	2	3	4	5	6	7
Name	Occupation	Name of district	Location of district	% of state's population, 1960 census	% of representation in house or senate	"Value of Vote" index[*]
		REPUBLICAN MEMBERS				
John A. Hannah, chairman	president, Michigan State U.	14th senatorial	Ingham and Livingston Cos.	3.17	2.94	93
Robert H. Blandford	lumber dealer	Kent County—1st rep. dist. (3 member dist.)	northern 1/2 of county, excluding Grand Rapids	2.25	2.73	121
Lee Boothby	attorney	7th senatorial	Berrien & Cass Cos., southwestern corner of Michigan	2.37	2.94	124
Garry E. Brown	attorney	6th senatorial	Kalamazoo & St. Joseph Cos., southwestern Michigan	2.78	2.94	116
Herman Dehnke, 1st vice chairman	retired circuit judge	Alpena rep. district	three counties, eastern shore of upper lower peninsula	.66	.91	138

187

Table 2—(Cont.)

ANALYSIS OF REPRESENTATION ON THE COMMITTEE ON LEGISLATIVE ORGANIZATION

1	2	3	4	5	6	7
Name	Occupation	Name of district	Location of district	% of state's population, 1960 census	% of representation in house or senate	"Value of Vote" index*
REPUBLICAN MEMBERS—(Cont.)						
Donald D. Doty	farmer and township supervisor	Monroe rep. district	Monroe County southeastern Michigan on Ohio border	1.29	.91	71
Arthur G. Elliott	real estate & Oakland Co. chairman	Oakland Co. 5th rep. dist.	Detroit suburbs	1.38	.91	66
William F. Hanna	attorney	Muskegon Co. 2nd rep. dist.	west central Michigan	1.07	.91	85
Shuford Kirk	farmer	Tuscola County rep. district	thumb area of lower peninsula	.55	.91	165
Blaque Knirk	farmer	9th senatorial	Calhoun & Branch Cos., south central Michigan	2.22	2.94	132

Name	Occupation	District	Description			
**Kent T. Lundgren	pharmacist	30th senatorial	Eastern 1/2 of upper peninsula	1.64	2.94	179
Raymond A. Plank	radio station owner	Mason rep. district	three counties, northern lower peninsula	.52	.91	175
James R. Rood	attorney	Midland County rep. district	industrial area, central Michigan	.66	.99	138
Weldon O. Yeager	personnel agency operator	18th senatorial (in Wayne Co.)	Ward 22 of Detroit & suburban cities	6.55	2.94	45
DEMOCRATIC MEMBERS						
Theodore S. Brown	attorney	Wayne County 20th rep. dist.	Garden City & 2 urban twps.	1.92	.91	84
William O. Greene	deputy sheriff Wayne County	3rd senatorial (in Wayne Co.)	6 Detroit wards & Highland Park	3.14	2.94	94
Robert G. Hodges	attorney	Wayne County 1st rep. dist.	Detroit, ward 21 (2 member dist.)	1.43	1.82	127
Ralph A. Liberato	automotive design checker	11th senatorial	Macomb County	5.18	2.94	57
William C. Marshall	executive vice pres., Michigan AFL-CIO	21st senatorial (Wayne County)	6 suburban cities & 12 townships	8.28	2.94	36

Table 2—(Cont.)

ANALYSIS OF REPRESENTATION ON THE COMMITTEE ON LEGISLATIVE ORGANIZATION

1	2	3	4	5	6	7
				% of state's popula-tion, 1960 census	% of rep-resentation in house or senate	"Value of Vote" index*
Name	Occupation	Name of district	Location of district			
		DEMOCRATIC MEMBERS—(Cont.)				
Melvin Nord, 2nd vice chairman	patent attorney	Wayne County 6th rep. dist.	Detroit ward 16 (3 member dist.)	1.96	2.73	139
Joseph F. Sablich	attorney	Iron representa-tive district	four counties, western upper peninsula	.54	.91	169

* This index is explained in the note to Table 1, page 160. It is obtained by dividing column 6 by column 5.

** Kent Lundgren did not participate in floor debate of the proposed apportionment formula. He resigned from the Constitutional Convention after winning a special election held to fill a vacancy in the legislature.

declining population in the city of Detroit were substantially overrepresented, as Democrats Hodges and Nord could testify.[1]

One of the early discussions centered on the feasibility of following county lines in the construction of legislative districts. It was demonstrated that the house of representatives could not be apportioned within a 15 percent deviation of population apportionment following county lines, because of substantial differences in the population of neighboring counties. On November 15, the committee heard from Robert Montgomery, the state director of elections, and Bernard Apol, an employee of the Bureau of Elections. These gentlemen agreed that it was "administratively feasible" to divide along other lines and that districts could even be divided along precinct boundaries, although this would add to the burden of county clerks in the administration of elections.

But Apol and Montgomery did not mention the convenience to the political parties of county boundaries. The single issue concerning legislative apportionment upon which bipartisan agreement developed was that districts should follow county lines. The reason was obvious: the parties are organized on a county basis, and a legislative district cutting across a county boundary requires the establishment of a separate party organization.

Having completed their basic education, the committee next listened to the proposals of interest group representatives. August Scholle, president of the AFL-CIO, made a detailed case for "one man, one vote" apportionment. He presented a series of quotations on equality at the ballot box ranging from the *Federalist Papers* to President Kennedy, demonstrating that this principle was not "a plot by the CIO to capture control of state government." He also supplied a list of key votes through which

---

[1] These and other meetings of the committee were open to the public. This discussion of the hearings of the committee is based on the mimeographed minutes of the committee meetings prepared by the committee clerk and the printed testimony presented to the committee by various witnesses.

measures were defeated by the senate majority elected by a minority of the state's population and a list of nominations made by Democratic governors which had been rejected by the Republican senators.

The opposite viewpoint was presented by former state Senator Creighton Coleman, author of the 1952 "balanced legislature" amendment. He argued that, if the validity of the existing state senate were challenged, the basis of the United States Senate would also be brought into question. The lobbyist for the Michigan Manufacturers' Association stated that his group favored retention of the "balanced legislature" and was pledged to join with the Michigan Farm Bureau Federation in preserving it. Delegate Stanley Powell, of the Farm Bureau, stated that the meaning of the Con-Con election was that the people of Michigan wanted no tampering with their legislature.

Such attitudes were predictable, as the economic interest groups reiterated their estalished positions. But the citizens' organizations also rejected the one man, one vote formula. Mrs. Howard Lichterman, representing the League of Women Voters, a prime force in the movement to call the convention into being, stated the League's position. The house should be based on population, she said, while the senate should be based on population and area together, with a provision for periodic reapportionment of both houses. A delegation from the Michigan Municipal League stated the policy of that organization, that the lower house should be based on population, while the senate should be "apportioned in some other manner than a population basis to recognize area and economic factors." [2] A Detroit city councilman (the late Eugene Van Antwerp) supported this view.

---

[2] Questioning by committee members emphasized the fact that this recommendation was formulated by a vote of the Municipal League membership, with each city or village casting one vote. The size of member units ranges from the city of Detroit to the village of Lake Ann, with a population of 97. *Minutes of Committee on Legislative Organization*, November 14, 1961, p. 2.

These hearings provided the official contact between committee members and spokesmen for "public opinion." Other than labor union members, few voices were raised in support of "one man, one vote." If any further reinforcement of Republican attitudes was needed, it came on December 13, 1961, from the titular leader of the party, former President Eisenhower, who addressed the convention at the invitation of George Romney. He confined himself to the topic of relations between the states and the Federal Government and the need for a clearer definition of the responsibilities of the states. During the question period, he was asked to comment on the implications of *Baker* v. *Carr*, the Tennessee apportionment case then pending before the United States Supreme Court. Mr. Eisenhower replied:

> Each man in the legislative body is to represent the views of a region. If these people are difficult to reach, it is obviously more difficult for him to represent them accurately if he does it completely by the population ratio. I would think therefore that there must be a good common sense compromise, although I think always the correct way would be according to number. But certainly, if you have a big city, you can much more easily reach these people than by large districts where populations are sparse. As I say, I believe the basic thing must be population, the rest of it some modification because of special conditions.[3]

The Republican members of the Committee on Legislative Organization perceived that their task was to determine how far either house should depart from the population standard. Even before the committee finished its public hearings, delegate proposals relating to reapportionment were received by the committee, and, by December 22, 38 such proposals had been received. A great range of ideas was represented, from a unicameral legislature based on population, to a bicameral body with frozen districts in each house. Certain of these proposals deserve more specific description, as much for the chronology of their introduction as for their content.

---

[3] *Journal*, December 13, 1961, p. 228. In response to a further question, Mr. Eisenhower rejected the federal analogy, stating that "a county or a subdivision of a state is not sovereign."

On October 26, Weldon Yeager submitted the first proposal on the subject of legislative apportionment to be sponsored by a member of the committee. Having been forced to concern himself with apportionment by the demands of a Wayne County campaign, Yeager worked out a detailed plan which presumably implemented his campaign promise of a senate based 60 percent on area and 40 percent on population. The scheme provided for the specification of senatorial districts to be described in the constitution. Each district was to be guaranteed one senator. The remaining seven seats of a 34-member senate were to be allocated to the districts according to population by the mathematical process of equal proportions used to allocate congressional seats among the states. The districts were to be as nearly square in shape as possible, and the State Board of Canvassers was appointed as the apportioning agency, with their decisions subject to judicial review.[4] The use of the equal-proportions formula would find its way into the committee proposal, but the ratio of population to area in determining representation would be expressed more directly.

A plan with some features which the committee members found attractive was presented by Professor Pollock on November 29. Concerned that the convention might become bogged down in the political task of drawing actual district lines, Pollock proposed the immediate addition of five senators (two for Oakland, one each for Wayne, Macomb, and Genessee Counties) to remedy the most glaring underrepresentation of suburban areas. After the 1970 census, he proposed the application of a strict formula which would permit the population of senatorial districts to deviate only 15 percent above or below the ratio of representation obtained by dividing the total population by the number of seats.

---

[4] This discussion, and that of other delegate proposals, is based on the mimeographed *Summary of Proposals Received as of December 22, 1961*, produced by the Committee on Legislative Organization and the issues of the *Journal* for the days on which the proposals were originally introduced.

Implementing his declaration that the mandate of the Con-Con election was that both houses should not be apportioned on the basis of population, George Romney on November 27 introduced a proposal calling for districts in the lower house to be equal in population, while senate seats would be apportioned on the principle of "sparsity." Senate districts would be established on the basis of county lines, with an initial assignment of seats on the basis of population but with additional seats assigned to districts with sparse population, on the theory that the vast area of the large district presents the representative with special problems of maintaining contact with his constituents. Mr. Romney advanced the proposal, which resulted from careful study, as a compromise between "one man, one vote" and the defenders of the existing system, but Democratic critics claimed that it would result in only a minimal change from the existing system.

The prospects of bipartisan compromise on the issue, if they ever existed, had been dealt a death blow even before Mr. Romney's proposal was introduced.

On November 14, a series of five proposals was introduced on the convention floor by Democratic delegates. The groups of sponsors for the various measures differed, but all of the lists included Tom Downs, Democratic vice president of the convention. Each of the measures proposed a constitutional standard which would insure strict population of both legislative chambers. Two of the measures specified a population percentage for each district; two specified the numbers of citizens to reside in each district (for example, no senatorial district would contain less than 140,000 persons or more than 144,000 persons). The fifth measure simply provided that representative districts should be of equal population.

These measures were the means to implement the Democratic campaign promise of "one man, one vote" apportionment, and they should not have surprised any delegate. But Melvin Nord, second vice chairman of the Committee on Legislative Organization, also introduced a proposal on that day which contained many of the features that would later be found in the Democratic minority report of the committee.

Nord had been trained as an engineer before preparing for the legal profession, and he was at home with mathematical formulas and their relevance for apportionment. He quickly became the Democratic party's expert on the matter, as William Marshall was deeply involved with the work of the Democratic members of the Committee on the Executive Branch. Nord's proposal of November 14 reflected his knowledge that no system of single-member districts based on population could guarantee a Democratic majority in the legislature, due to the heavy concentration of Democratic strength in Wayne and Macomb Counties. If the voting habits of the state continued, the Democrats would continue to obtain a state-wide majority and elect the governor by a slender but adequate margin. But this was possible only because of the heavy Democratic vote, particularly in Detroit. All of the Democratic votes in a district voting 85 or 90 percent Democratic counted toward the election of a governor, but in a single-member district, the votes for the legislator above the 50 percent plus one needed to elect him were wasted since they had no effect in determining the party division in the legislature.

Nord proposed a unicameral legislature, consisting of a senate only. Senatorial districts would be of roughly equal population, but this fact was of lesser significance than the real innovation of the plan. It provided that each district should elect two senators, one from each major party. A third senator would be elected by a minor party achieving 20 percent of the total vote. Using electronic equipment, each senator in voting on proposed legislation, would cast the number of votes which he had received in the election, and the membership of each party on committees of the legislature would be proportionate to the percentage of the state-wide vote received by each party.

This "tote vote" scheme represented a considerable departure from the usual practices of American legislatures, and Republican delegates attacked it as a blatant attempt on the part of the Democrats to construct a system of representation which would insure maximum advantage for the Democratic party. Such attacks did not point out that the traditional system of single-member districts protected Republican interests very comfortably.

On November 29, two weeks after the Nord proposal had been introduced and referred to the Committee on Legislative Organization, a group of Republican delegates supplied their answer. They proposed that each of the 83 counties, regardless of population, would have one senator. The proposal was sponsored by 39 Republican delegates, including five members of the Committee on Legislative Organization (Boothby, Kirk, Knirk, Plank, and Rood). A senate elected on such a basis would have perhaps 15 Democratic members opposing 68 Republicans. Wayne County would have approximately 1,300 times the population of the smallest senatorial district.

One of the sponsors of the measure claimed it was necessary because of pending action by the U.S. Supreme Court on the Tennessee and Michigan apportionment cases; he claimed that there could be no constitutional objection to an upper house modeled on the U.S. Senate and representing area without regard to population.[5] Lee Boothby, conservative member of the Committee on Legislative Organization, regarded the measure as a warning to the Democrats. He stated that the Democrats had been introducing measures which were just as one-sided in favor of their own party, implying that the minority needed to be taught the fact of their own impotence.[6]

---

[5] Retired Circuit Judge Karl K. Liebrand, of Bay City, quoted in *The Detroit News*, November 30, 1961. Liebrand later cited this reason for voting against the proposed constitution.

[6] *Ibid.*

The proposal caused little comment at the time, and no great effort was expended on its behalf. Its nature was quite in keeping with the flavor of the convention, which by that time had divided sharply along party lines on several issues. But the proposal may be cited as a kind of official notice of the fact that bipartisan compromise would never be achieved on the issue of legislative apportionment. It was a concrete expression of the hostility that made such compromise impossible.

Committee discussions continued, and the deadline for the introduction of committee proposals drew near. Chairman Hannah, apparently hoping to leave open the possibility of bipartisan compromise, postponed the formulation of substantive decisions as long as possible. The committee did not vote on any substantive issues during the months of November and December. None of the suggestions made to the committee stimulated enthusiastic response, and committee members of each party began to reach separate decisions as to the nature of apportionment formulas they would be willing to support. On December 17, Delegate William Hanna presented a proposal which was destined to become the basis for the Republican position. The committee had heard many suggestions as to the nature of principles of representation that might be applicable to the senate. Historic communities, political subdivisions, and economic interests were all suggested as possible determinants of a representative system. Hanna's proposal dispensed with all these and settled upon land area as the "other factor" which should modify the population standard for senate apportionment. He proposed that population should receive a weighted value of 80 percent and area a weighted value of 20 percent in determining senate districts.

On January 19, the committee began a series of ten decisive meetings. Exploratory discussions were held at the first of these, and "advisory votes" were taken. On January 20, Dr. Nord, the Democratic spokesman, outlined the plans which he was prepared to present to the Democratic caucus as being worthy of their support on the floor of the full convention. Each of the three plans provided a population basis for senate apportionment. The "tote plan" which Nord had introduced so many months before was included but modified to apply to the upper house of a bicameral legislature. After reconsidering his plans, Nord at the next meeting suggested that the "tote plan" might include districts drawn on the basis of representation for area, as long as the voting power of senators was equal to the vote received by each party member in the election. As an alternative, he announced that the Democrats were prepared to support Professor Pollock's plan, provided that the population apportionment take place immediately, instead of being postponed until after the 1970 census.

After recessing for a caucus, the Republican members of the committee reported that they wished to base discussion of senate apportionment on the proposal made by William Hanna. Chairman John Hannah announced to reporters that the failure of Democratic committee members to compromise on the issue made it necessary for the Republicans to write their own proposal.[7]

On January 23, the committee began to reach its decisions. The first of these was that the legislature would be bicameral in nature. Next it was decided that legislative districts should elect only one member and that districts would be "compact, contiguous, and as nearly square as possible." Over the objection of Republican Yeager, the committee next determined that districts in both houses should follow county lines. Delegate William Brown pointed out that Democratic members were abstaining on all these questions and that the record should make note of this fact.

William Hanna's plan was discussed next and adopted. It provided for apportioning the senate by adding four seats to the metropolitan areas immediately and redistricting according

---

[7] *The Detroit News,* January 23, 1962.

to an "80 percent population—20 percent area" formula after 1970.[8]

Democratic members again abstained, and they were joined by Republicans Boothby and Garry Brown, who felt that the proposal was too liberal. Because four members were absent, the key senate apportionment formula was approved by only 11 out of 21 committee members.

Distressed by the nature of the Republican senate plan, Democratic members on January 24 offered to support two proposals that had previously been presented to the committee by Republican convention leaders. The Democrats proposed combining the two plans as the official committee proposal and offered to support the new constitution if it were adopted. The two plans were those of John Hannah for the reorganization of house districts and that of Professor Pollock for apportioning the senate. Hannah's proposal called for a lower house based on population by removing the "moiety clause" of the 1908 constitution. The Pollock senate proposal called for the addition of five seats to the southeastern counties at once and a cooling-off period until the 1970 census. At that time the senate would be apportioned on the basis of population, with a 15 percent deviation permitted above or below the required ratio of representation. As a final effort at compromise, the Democrats agreed to accept even the waiting period. Republican members of the committee scorned this belated offer of compromise.

The committee next reached a decision on the potentially crucial matter of defining the nature and duties of the apportionment agency, having agreed that the legislature could not be expected to perform that task. The Republican committee members proposed to establish an eight-member commission

---

[8] Hanna's proposal of January 17 had called for an immediate application of the 80-20 formula, but committee members had become enamoured of the "cooling-off period" featured in the Pollock proposal, although they would not accept his proposal for population apportionment after the period had expired.

on legislative apportionment. These members were to be selected "by each of the state organizations of each of the two political parties casting the highest vote for governor at the last preceding election" from four specified regions. The regions described were roughly equal in area. Southeastern Michigan, with well over half the state's population, would supply only two members of the commission; four members would come from an area with 8 percent of the total population. Decisions of the commission would be subject to the "same provisions of referendum as apply to acts of the legislature." [9] This brief provision opened up great possibilities to the opponents of legislative reapportionment—the same forces that had succeeded in freezing the senate districts in 1952.

The committee next considered districts in the lower house. The Democrats felt released from their promise of support for Chairman Hannah's proposal and voted against apportionment of 110 seats on the basis of population, insisting on a house of 115 seats. The 110-seat formula would have reduced the representation of the democratically-inclined upper peninsula, but a house with 115 seats would have permitted the retention of those seats for another decade.

Republican committee members thereupon chose the proposal of Delegate Blaque Knirk which granted a first seat in a 110-member house to areas containing seven-tenths of 1 percent of the state's population and assigned additional seats on the basis of population according to the method of equal proportions. The seven Democratic members of the committee voted against this proposal for house apportionment, and they were joined by Republican Boothby, who claimed that the formula was too liberal.

---

[9] Quotations are from the version of the committee proposal (committee proposal number 79 of the convention) reported to the convention and referred to the Committee of the Whole on February 2, 1962. *Journal,* February 2, 1962, p. 455.

The committee proposals were reported to the convention on February 2 and placed on the calendar of debate by the Committee of the Whole. Because the convention leadership felt that other matters should be decided before dealing with the explosive issue of reapportionment, more than a month would elapse before debate by the entire convention. But the outline of the committee proposals became known, and that knowledge affected the delegates' actions in the intervening weeks. Events transpiring outside the convention in that month further affected delegate attitudes toward the committee proposals. For these reasons, it is best to analyze the impact of the committee proposals in order to understand their meaning for the convention process and the significance of the changes later made in them.

The provision for apportionment of the lower house included two important changes. The first was the modification of the moiety provision from one-half of 1 percent to seven-tenths of 1 percent. The second was the stipulation that all districts would elect a single member, which would permit the election of some Republican legislators in Wayne County.

The Democratic members of the committee, in filing their minority report, discussed the proposal in straightforward partisan terms. The bias in favor of non-metropolitan areas would be reduced from a margin of ten seats to one of five, they reported, by the modification of the moiety clause. Yet, Republicans would still control the lower house because the single-member seat provision would result in the Republicans winning "some seats in . . . Democratic strongholds . . . while the Republicans will continue to win 100 per cent of the seats in their strongholds." [10] The minority report accepted single-member

---

[10] *Journal*, February 7, 1962, p. 546. The effects of the apportionment systems of both the old and the new constitutions are analyzed by John P. White on pages 233-361 in this volume, "An Analysis of the Apportionment System Proposed by the Michigan Constitutional Convention of 1961-1962." The purpose here is to study the perceptions of the delegates at the time, concerning the effect of apportionment proposals, rather than to measure their actual impact according to the indices devised by political scientists.

districts, providing for a 115-member house with districts "as nearly equal in population as may be."

The committee provisions for the lower house were destined to survive virtually intact. But the nature of the lower house was a secondary question. The source of governmental stalemate in Michigan has been the contest between the Democratic governor and the Republican state senate.

The committee proposal for senate apportionment provided for the election of "not less than 36 nor more than 40 members" from single-member districts "for four-year terms concurrent with the term of office of the governor." The districts frozen into the constitution by the 1952 amendment were to be continued, but an additional senator was granted to Wayne, Oakland, Macomb, and Genessee Counties, thus increasing the present 34-member senate to 38. Following the 1970 census, however, senate districts would be rearranged by the Apportionment Commission on the basis of a mathematical formula. The proposed constitutional language defined the formula very carefully:

> . . . each county shall be assigned an apportionment factor according to the following formula: the percentage of the state's population as shown by the last regular federal decennial census computed to the nearest 1/100 of 1% shall be multiplied by 4 and there shall be added thereto the percentage of the state's area computed to the nearest 1/100 of 1%.[11]

The formula was, and is, simply a method of giving a value to area one-quarter as great as that assigned to population. The result of the operation is to give to each area (counties or groups of counties) a number of apportionment factors, which will be used to determine the number of representatives assigned to that area.

The crucial point, therefore, is the method of applying this number to make that allocation. The original committee proposal

---

[11] *Journal*, February 2, 1961, p. 457. Other citations of the committee proposal are from the same place.

provided various and conflicting standards for this determination, constituting a grant of authority to the Apportionment Commission to make minimal change in the existing districts. Dividing the total of 500 factors available at any time for assignment (400 for population, 100 for area) by the number of seats in a 38-member senate gives a quotient of 13. An area with 13 factors therefore deserves one representative. The proposal provided that

> . . . counties with 13 or more apportionment factors shall be entitled to one senatorial district for each 13 apportionment factors . . . [and] the remaining counties of the state shall be arranged into senatorial districts that are compact, contiguous by land and as rectangular in shape as possible, having as nearly as possible 13 apportionment factors. . . .

So much of the provision seemed completely equitable. But the phrase continued:

> . . . as nearly as possible 13 apportionment factors, but in no event less than 10 or more than 16. Insofar as possible existing senatorial districts at the time of each reapportionment shall not be changed unless there shall be a failure to comply with the above standards.

This provision made it possible for one district to exceed another district of equal area by six factors. The value of six "population factors," computed on the basis of the 1960 census, was 117,350 persons. If the 38 seats were apportioned equally by population, each district would contain 217,400 persons, so that the permissible variation of ten to 16 factors permitted a substantial population difference. But, it was also possible for a district to earn its representation on the basis of vast area alone, and the formula placed no limits upon the variation in population between districts. The district in the western upper peninsula, for example, would have over ten factors, and a senator, even if its population should vanish.

Calculations by the opponents of the plan, which probably paralleled those made by its supporters, revealed that nearly all of the existing non-metropolitan districts would, in fact, earn approximately ten apportionment factors in 1970. The Apportionment Commission, therefore, was encouraged to provide the non-metropolitan counties with systematic overrepresentation at the expense of the urban areas. Latitude for the accomplishment of such a purpose was further provided by allowing the commission to establish the total number of seats at any figure between 36 and 40.

Establishment of this provision created special problems for the sponsors of the proposal, however, for they wished to win the support of the Republican delegation from Kent County, which has been represented by two senators for 60 years. For Kent County to keep both senators, a special provision was inserted:

> Counties with 13 or more apportionment factors shall be entitled to one senatorial district for each 13 apportionment factors except that any county with 19.5 or more apportionment factors shall be entitled to not less than 2 senate districts.

Twenty-six apportionment factors were required to win two senators; Kent County would be allocated slightly under 20 factors.

This provision made certain that Genessee County (which had by 1960 attained a population greater than that of Kent County but had only one senator under the 1952 amendment) would retain the second senator allocated to it in 1963. But there would be a difference of 20 apportionment factors between two-senator counties and three-senator counties. If the area of the two districts were the same, the three-senator county would have over 400,000 more persons.

The committee proposal could only be explained as an attempt to devise a formula which would provide as little change as possible but would be derived by a seemingly reasonable method. The basic objection to the formula was the straight-forward equation of area and persons in determining representation. In attacking the original Hanna proposal, Professor Pollock had declared that based on the 1960 census one person would be equal to 19.05 acres of land.[12] The most glaring inequities (that Oakland and Macomb Counties, with substantially greater populations than Kent County, elected a single senator, while Kent elected two) would be modified upon the adoption of the constitution. After the 1970 census, the Apportionment Commission would have authority to apply the complicated formula in such a manner that little change would take place. The 1952 amendment, which had frozen into existence districts partly based on the population distribution of 1920, had no claim to a "reasonable standard" of legislative apportionment. The 80-20 formula, with a permitted variation between ten and 16 apportionment factors, could provide a "reasonable standard" for continuing the then existing senate districts in 1970.

The senate apportionment formula was a Republican invention. The Democratic committee members attacked its principle ("What better form could be found for the expression of contempt for people than to equate one person with a specific amount of dirt?")[13] and lamented the fact that the minority party did not participate in formulating the proposal.

> We submit that if this Convention is to achieve a bipartisan product, it can do so only by providing a bipartisan representation plan for the Senate. This is the only way to make sure that no group gets a special advantage.[14]

The minority report proposed a senate consisting of 19 districts, divided between four zones of equal area. Each zone was guaranteed a senator, and the remainder were to be allocated by population. Each district would elect the nominees of the two parties receiving the largest share of the vote plus the candidate of any third party receiving 25 percent of the vote. Each senator's voting strength in the legislature would then be equal to the number of votes he received in the election, save that each senator would have an equal vote in committees other than the Committee of the Whole.

---

[12] James K. Pollock, press release, January 25, 1962.
[13] *Journal*, February 7, 1962, p. 546.
[14] *Ibid.*, p. 548.

On the apportionment issue, therefore, the Democratic attitude was solidified: no compromise with the Republicans, stand fast for a system that would maximize Democratic party advantage. The Republicans, on the other hand, exhibited no desire even to recognize Democratic attitudes. The pattern of partisan stalemate was established in classic form.

As soon as the convention began the procedure of debate in Committee of the Whole, it became clear that the committee reports would have little status. In most legislatures, committee reports are accorded some privilege, because committee members are recognized as specialists in their fields. At Michigan's Constitutional Convention, however, such an attitude did not exist, partly because none of the delegates could claim prior experience. The final form of a committee report might be only a starting point for the whole convention to write different preferences into that section of the constitution. This implied that the proposal of the Committee on Legislative Organization might be modified substantially on the floor of the convention. But the senate formula and its application became pawns in the factional struggle within the Republican party. One of the prices of establishing harmony with the conservative Republican delegates was the promise to leave the senate proposal unaltered.

FACTIONAL DISCORD AND THE
ROMNEY LEADERSHIP

AS NOTED EARLIER, the election of Stephen Nisbet as president of the convention had signaled the postponement of factional conflict in the Republican ranks. Disagreement with the Democratic minority on several issues, together with bipartisan agreement on non-controversial changes, gave a surface appearance of Republican harmony for several months.

When the voting began on crucial committee proposals, however, temporary coalitions of liberal Republicans and conservative Democrats formed to defeat the desires of the conservative Republicans. An early instance was the constitutional 15-mill limitation on property taxation. This limit applied to counties, townships, and school districts and its retention was considered one of the primary goals of the Farm Bureau Federation. Although the limitation did not apply to charter cities, urban-oriented delegates saw it as an unnecessary restriction on the powers of local government. D. Hale Brake's Committee on Finance and Taxation recommended the retention of the constitutional limitation. Brake's proposal was defeated by the Committee of the Whole, in which an amendment was adopted permitting the legislature to limit the rates of *ad valorem* taxes but not specifying the amount of such limit. The recommendation of the Committee of the Whole was concurred in by the convention through a roll call vote of 65 to 53. Thirty-one Republican delegates joined 34 Democrats in voting against retention of the 15-mill limit.[1]

Two weeks later, the convention began debate on the proposed methods of selecting justices of the state supreme court. The 1908 constitution provided for the non-partisan election of justices. Statute provided for the nomination of candidates by party conventions and permitted an incumbency designation. With no party label to guide voter choice, incumbents have had a good chance for re-election. Since vacancies usually have occurred through death or resignation in mid-term, and the governor was empowered to fill such vacancies by appointment (without the consent of the senate) Michigan enjoyed a *de facto* appointive system, and the Democratic victories of G. Mennen Williams had brought a five to three Democratic majority to the court.

The Committee on the Judicial Article, made up of 20 attorneys and one pharmacist, was unable to agree on the proper method of selecting justices. A few Republicans were adamant in their support of the system of appointment from a Bar Association list. Democratic committee members favored the existing system, because of the power it gave to Democratic gov-

---

[1] *Journal*, February 9, 1962, p. 576.

ernors. Conservative Republican committee members supported a system of districts for the election of the high court judges, through which Democratic Wayne County would elect only three of the nine justices, and the other six would most likely be Republican. Eleven committee members finally signed this plan so there would be a committee proposal, but four of the 11 reserved the right to oppose it in debate.

The supporters of the district plan reintroduced it in one form or another for three weeks, but it was continually defeated by a coalition of liberal Republicans and Democrats. It was an undisguised attempt to prevent the normal state-wide Democratic majority from determining the make-up of the court. The nomination of candidates in the individual districts also would take that power from the party convention which the liberal Republicans have usually controlled, thereby upsetting the factional balance of the party. Some liberal Republicans also may have believed that judges do not perform a representative function analagous to that of legislators. The conservatives devoted considerable energy to the plan, which in one of its reincarnations was defeated by only two votes [2] and its defeat left them bitter and disappointed.[3] Conservative Republicans saw a chance to combine with the Democrats on one of the next issues for Committee of the Whole debate. It concerned the proposals of the Committee on the Executive Branch.

Many limitations were placed on the powers of Michigan's governor by the constitution of 1908. Not the least of these was the provision for the independent election of the members of

---

[2] *Journal*, March 12, 1962, p. 744.

[3] The final judicial article adopted by the convention reduced the court from eight to seven members. It stipulated the non-partisan election of justices and permitted their continued nomination by party conventions. Incumbent justices were permitted to renominate themselves, however, by filing a simple notice of intent. The governor's appointment power was eliminated through the provision that vacancies would be filled until a special election through the appointment by the court of retired justices to serve temporary duty. (Constitution of the State of Michigan, 1963, article VI, sections 2 and 23.)

the Administrative Board, or cabinet. The potential for frustration of such a system is most obvious when the governor is of one party and all members of the cabinet are of the opposition party, as happened during former Governor Williams' first term. Williams had in fact recommended to the Committee on the Executive Branch that the governor be given the authority to appoint the Administrative Board. But the system constitutes no less a danger to the unified authority of the governor if all members of the Board are members of his own party. Nominations for the Administrative Board positions are made by the party conventions following the primary elections for the offices of governor and lieutenant governor. Although the gubernatorial nominee exercises great influence at the convention, partisan logic dictates that the ticket give recognition to competing party factions and cement the party for its campaign task.[4] Conservative Republicans, most notably former Treasurer D. Hale Brake, had won party prominence through election to Administrative Board positions, and they felt this limitation on the governor's power should be retained.

Although the Democratic party has been considered the party favoring increased executive authority since at least the time of Franklin D. Roosevelt, short-range party advantage dictated an opposite attitude among the Democratic delegates at the Constitutional Convention.

During the opening months of the Constitutional Convention, George Romney had not played a leading role. His position as president of American Motors placed demands on his attention, although his participation in the convention was as diligent as that of most delegates. During these same months, however,

---

[4] This feature of the system had been demonstrated as recently as 1960. Lieutenant Governor John B. Swainson, with massive support from organized labor, was the surprise winner of the Democratic primary, defeating the popular secretary of state, James M. Hare. Hare was thereupon renominated to the secretary of state position. Interestingly enough, Hare's vote total led the Democratic ticket in 1960 and again in 1962, when Hare and all other Democratic nominees for Administrative Board positions survived Romney's gubernatorial victory.

Romney became a focus of attention for the national news media. Pictured as the brightest new star in the Republican firmament, he was portrayed as the most likely compromise candidate for the Republican presidential nomination in 1964. His business achievements, athletic practices, religious convictions, and political opinions were featured by nearly every national news-magazine and television network. This publicity redoubled the pressures forcing him either to declare his intention of pursuing a further political career, or promise a return to his responsibilities with the automotive concern.

At the regular board meeting of American Motors in mid-February, Romney submitted his resignation as president of the company and announced his intention of seeking the Republican gubernatorial nomination. He announced to the convention that his first resposibility was to the convention, and that he would engage in no campaigning until after the Constitutional Convention was completed. But the campaign began in the convention hall. Democrats discovered in the proposed article on the executive branch a means to frustrate Romney's conception of the powers necessary to the governor by combining with the conservative Republicans.

The chairman of the Committee on the Executive Branch was John Martin of Grand Rapids, Republican National Committeeman, who was solidly identified with the party faction eager to win state-wide victory. Liberal Republican members of the committee proposed making all positions on the Administrative Board appointive. Conservative Republicans wavered, and there was some indication that a number of Democratic members might vote with the liberal Republicans. This hope was dashed as early as November when a meeting of the Democratic State Central Committee passed a resolution favoring the election of all members. Democratic opposition solidified Republican attitudes, and the Republican members presented a proposal for the appointment of all state executive officers except the governor and lieutenant governor. The Democratic minority report called for the election of all officers elected under the terms of the 1908 constitution, as well as the highway commissioner, who had been made an elective official by statute.

The Democratic delegates referred to the principles of Andrew Jackson, but their main argument was that the malapportioned senate established by the Republican formula could never be expected to confirm the appointments of a Democratic governor.[5] This claim was based on bitter experience with the existing senate. The failure to reach a bipartisan agreement on apportionment had made the Democrats lose interest in compromise with the liberal Republicans on other aspects of the constitution. Their attitude was that the system of representation was so fundamental that other improvements would be of little significance.

Republicans asserted that the Democratic position resulted from fear that Mr. Romney would be elected governor, thus jeopardizing political empires held by Democrats in the persons of Secretary of State James Hare and Highway Commissioner John Mackie. It had taken several years for the popularity of Governor Williams to establish a Democratic Administrative Board, and the Democrats assumed—correctly—that Democratic Administrative Board members might weather the storm of a Romney gubernatorial victory.

Leaders of the conservative Republican faction did not agree with the action of their colleagues on the Committee on the Executive Branch. They felt that the power of the governor should be restricted by providing for the independent election of other officers (although they wanted Mr. Mackie, the highway commissioner, removed from office by one means or another). Conservative Republicans, therefore, threatened to vote with the Democrats to retain the elective Administrative Board. Also, there were indications that conservative bitterness over

---

[5] See *Journal,* February 2, 1962, pp. 450-51, for the majority report. The minority report is found in *Journal,* February 8, 1962, pp. 562-63.

the formation of coalitions between liberal Republicans and Democrats might inspire retaliation in the form of combinations by conservative Republicans and Democrats to protect the status quo. The smouldering factional conflict within the Republican party had at last burst into flame.

Liberal Republicans were in danger of becoming the minority element of the convention. Democrats were willing to work against a constitution with a Republican label, whether or not it provided improvements over the old document. Some conservative Republicans, of course, had been hostile to constitutional revision in the first place and would not be overly distressed at the defeat of the proposed document. Either the defeat of the new constitution or the unabated hostility between the two wings of the party could ruin Republican chances (and Romney's) for winning state-wide victory.

Faced with these unpleasant alternatives, George Romney made perhaps the most fateful decision of the convention. After consultation between Romney and the leaders of the conservative faction, a series of Republican caucuses hammered out agreement on the major controversial issues. Although details of the agreement were never published, its main features seemed to include provisions dealing with the Administrative Board, taxation, and legislative apportionment. The conservative Republicans, with decades of legislative experience, drove a hard bargain.

The provision for the Administrative Board included the election of four members, the appointment of two members by independent commissions, the appointment of the state treasurer by the governor, and the selection of an auditor by the legislature.[6]

---

[6] Specifically, the governor, lieutenant governor, secretary of state, and attorney general were to be elected. A bipartisan, appointed, four-member Highway Commission would choose a director of highways. The Superintendent of Public Instruction would be appointed by an elected eight-member Board of Education.

In the field of taxation, the agreement included reinstatement of the constitutional 15-mill tax limitation, which had been defeated on first reading. It was also decided that the practice of earmarking tax funds constitutionally for certain purposes should be continued. In the field of apportionment, the agreement apparently stipulated that the senate districting formula proposed by the Committee on Legislative Organization should not be altered in any way by the full convention.

Democrats greeted the news of the Republican "package deal" compromise with cries of derision. In a stormy session, the Democratic delegates threatened to walk out of the convention, since there seemed no longer any useful purpose to be served by an opposition party. One by one, Democratic delegates asked permission to be excused from that session (a permission usually granted *pro forma*). Republican delegates systematically objected to the granting of such permission.[7] On the convention floor, Romney stated that the agreement was necessary to prevent the conservative Republicans from combining with the Democrats to frustrate the goals of constitutional revision. The official organ of the Democratic State Central Committee proclaimed in black headlines, "ROMNEY SELLS OUT."[8]

Partisan tempers cooled following a convention recess, and the Democratic members rejoined the convention to participate in its deliberations. The result of the explosion was to solidify control by the Republican caucus of controversial decisions. Such matters were decided through compromise between the Republican factions rather than through the combination of one Republican faction with the minority party. The "package deal" agreements on the executive branch and on taxation survived all attacks and were adopted as part of the proposed constitution. An outside influence intervened, however, to modify the proposal for the apportionment of the state senate.

---

[7] *Journal,* March 16, 1962, pp. 775-77.
[8] *The Michigan Democrat,* March 1962.

ECHOES OF A DECISION IN
WASHINGTON

TEN DAYS AFTER THE SUPREMACY of the Republican caucus had
been established, the United States Supreme Court rendered its
decision in the Tennessee reapportionment case, *Baker* v. *Carr.*[1]
The Tennessee legislature had ignored the command of the Tennessee Constitution for periodic reapportionment for half a
century, and the Court ruled that the people of Tennessee
(where there are no provisions for initiative or referendum)
could seek a judicial remedy. Overruling the precedent of *Cole-*

---

[1] 369 U.S. 186 (1962). The legal issue of legislative apportionment is
analyzed in this volume by Professor William Pierce on pages 1-114.

grove v. *Green*,[2] the Court held that the guarantees of the fourteenth amendment applied to the organization of state legislatures.

The Supreme Court decision had an electric effect on the Michigan Constitutional Convention. John Hannah, chairman of the Committee on Legislative Organization, was also head of the President's Commission on Civil Rights, and was able to have 150 copies of the decision air mailed to Lansing. The decision caused a marked change in the attitudes of certain individuals. Most notable of these was William Hanna, author of the committee formula for apportioning the senate.

Committee of the Whole consideration of the proposals of the Committee on Legislative Organization began on Friday, March 30, nearly a month after the committee had completed its work. The proposed apportionment commission was considered first. Delegate Nord proposed that the votes cast by members of the Apportionment Commission be "equal to the vote obtained by the gubernatorial candidate of his political party in the previous general election," but this amendment was rejected by a voice vote.[3] On behalf of his committee, Chairman Hannah proposed an amendment striking out the provision which made the determination of the commission subject to voter referendum. Hannah's proposal was accepted by a voice vote, and the prospects for orderly reapportionment were considerably improved. But the standards which would guide the commission in its work were yet to be determined.

On Tuesday, April 3, the convention debated and defeated, on a party-line vote, the committee minority proposal for the election of two senators from each district who would cast the number of votes they had received in the election. On Wednesday morning, Professor Pollock introduced a series of amendments which were the fruit of an analysis of the committee proposal begun prior to the Baker decision. There seemed no

---

[2] 328 U.S. 549 (1946).
[3] *Journal*, March 30, 1962, p. 848.

hope that the Republican caucus would abandon its commitment to the 80-20 formula as a method of assigning a value to area. Professor Pollock's purpose, therefore, was to amend the proposal so that the formula could not be applied in a manner that would further discriminate against the metropolitan counties. Three of these "perfecting amendments" were adopted by voice vote. The first inserted the word "land" into the definition of the formula, so that the area of lakes would be excluded. The second amendment affected a substantial change and aroused the ire of the conservative supporters of the committee proposal.

The "Kent County provision" had modified the application of the apportionment formula so that Kent County, with only 20 factors, could retain its second seat, by providing a second senator for any county with 19.5 factors. The purpose of the provision was pointed out by Democratic Delegate Robert Hodges, who introduced, and then withdrew, an amendment stating "Kent County shall always have two Senators." Professor Pollock proposed that every county entitled to more than one senator would receive a senator for each 13 apportionment factors and an additional senator for each remainder of six and one-half factors. The provision would have kept the two senators for Kent and Genesee but would have added one seat to Wayne and one to Oakland Counties, thus removing the disparity between a two-senator county and a three-senator county created by the committee proposal.

The third amendment inserted the word "thereafter" into the description of the application of the formula, so that seats would be assigned first to the urban counties, and, only after their fair share had been received, to the rural areas. This reversed the standard procedure of the Michigan legislature, which assigned first seats to the rural areas and the remainder to the cities.

The convention thereupon recessed for lunch, and the Republicans held a caucus. After lunch, Professor Pollock proposed an amendment specifying "the closest possible approach to thirteen apportionment factors per district" as the standard to be followed by the Apportionment Commission. A roll call vote was demanded, and only eight Republicans joined with the Democrats to support the proposal, which was defeated by 77 to 50. The Republican caucus had invoked the package compromise, insisting that the decisions of the convention not be reached through collusion with the Democrats.

But the problem of Kent County remained. The Baker decision made it clear that any formula would be reviewed by the courts; and there seemed to be no reasonable principle of classification which would grant a second senator to Kent but deny further senators to other metropolitan counties. Caucus members apparently insisted that the Pollock amendment granting additional senators for a remainder of six and one-half apportionment factors was objectionable.

Following the caucus, Delegate William Hanna introduced an amendment granting additional senators to each county for 13 apportionment factors or major fraction thereof, which would have had an effect similar to that of the Pollock amendment. Chairman John Hannah moved that further consideration be postponed until other pending amendments to the committee proposal could be considered. Hannah was faced with a revolt by the conservative Republicans and needed time for further discussion in the caucus. The convention then proceeded to reject amendments proposed by Democrats, which were more liberal than the committee proposal, and by conservative Republicans, which departed radically from the intent of the committee proposal. Delegate Boothby's proposal to re-enact the language of the 1952 amendment, which froze established districts into the constitution, won only 20 votes, and the proposal to elect one senator per county, which had won 39 sponsors when originally introduced was defeated by 107 nays to 14 yeas, with Lee Boothby the only member of the Committee on Legislative Organization supporting it. The Baker decision had considerably dampened Republican enthusiasm for apportionment on the basis of area alone.

Professor Pollock next proposed to amend the provision for districting the lower house so that one representative would be assigned to an area with seventy-five hundredths of the state's population, rather than seven-tenths. The Legislative Organization Committee staff had determined that this was as close to a strict population standard as the use of county lines for district boundaries would permit. The proposal was defeated, 81 to 37.[4]

The following day, after all pending amendments to the proposal had been dealt with, William Hanna withdrew his "major fractions" proposal and Chairman John Hannah proposed to amend the committee proposal by eliminating completely the "Kent County provision." The first reading of the committee proposal finished, therefore, by adding four senators, one to each of Wayne, Oakland, Macomb, and Genessee Counties, and adopting a provision which would, after 1970, probably take the new second senator away from Genessee County and reduce Republican Kent County to representation by a single senator. Substantial discrimination against urban areas would be the result. Professor Pollock's amendments attempted to remedy the situation, but the Republican caucus found them objectionable. Chairman Hannah promised a new remedy when the apportionment formula should receive a second reading.

On April 25, as the convention proceeded with the order of second reading of proposals, a Democratic delegate moved that the convention postpone consideration of legislative apportionment until the state supreme court should render a decision in the case of *Scholle* v. *Hare*. This case, in which AFL-CIO President August Scholle had challenged the constitutionality of the 1952 amendment providing senate apportionment, had been declared non-justiciable by the Michigan court in 1960.[5] Appealed

---

[4] The fate of the Pollock amendments is reported by the *Journal*, April 4, 1962, pp. 864-70. The Boothby amendment is found on p. 867. The McAllister proposal for one senator per county is reported by the *Journal*, April 5, 1962, p. 879.

[5] 360 *Michigan*, 1-125.

to the United States Supreme Court, the case had been remanded to the Michigan court following the decision in *Baker* v. *Carr*. The motion to postpone was defeated by 94 nays to 38 yeas (all Democratic). The Scholle case tested the constitutionality of the existing senate, which all but 20 of the delegates were prepared to change. Adoption of a new constitution would make Scholle's claim a moot issue. Furthermore, the Republicans felt they did not require whatever standards of equitable apportionment might be defined by the Democratic majority of the Michigan Supreme Court.

On behalf of the Legislative Organization Committee, Chairman Hannah presented a substitute proposal which completely redefined the application of the 80-20 apportionment formula. Again identified as substantially the creation of William Hanna, the new proposal can be explained only in terms of the impact of the decision in *Baker* v. *Carr*. The apportionment factors were determined as before, but their application was specified in three clear steps:

1. Counties with 13 or more apportionment factors would be separated as a class from all other counties. These metropolitan counties (Wayne, Oakland, Macomb, Genessee, and Kent) would be assigned a number of senators proportional to their share of the total number of apportionment factors of all counties. After an initial allotment of one senator, additional seats would be assigned within each metropolitan county according to the mathematical method of equal proportions applied to the apportionment factors.

2. Counties with fewer than 13 factors would be combined with adjoining counties to form senatorial districts, which would have as nearly as possible 13 factors, but no more than 16 and no less then ten factors.

3. Counties entitled to more than one senator would be subdivided by the apportionment commission into single-member districts "as nearly equal" in population "as possible but shall

221

not have less than 75 per cent nor more than 125 per cent" of the ratio of representation obtained by the dividing of the county's population by its number of senators.

These provisions strictly limited the operations of the apportionment commission. Out-state districts could vary considerably in population and existing districts could be preserved—but not at the expense of the metropolitan counties, because the districts were separated into two separate classes. The method of constituting the apportionment commission became a matter of minor importance, as the application of the formula strictly limited their discretion.

The Pollock amendments aroused the anger of the conservative Republicans when they realized that two more senate seats would be granted to urban areas; and that anger was reinforced by the realization that the Pollock amendments were being adopted by a coalition of liberal Republicans and Democrats. Yet the final provision, worked out by Republicans and supported by the Republican caucus, gave even more certain protection to urban areas than that envisioned by the Pollock amendments. On the complicated issue of apportionment, delegates such as William Hanna had developed recognized expertise. The Republican caucus would listen to its own experts, but it rejected any proposition having Democratic support as intrinsically suspect.

This account of partisan conflict on certain key issues should not obscure the fact that many provisions of the new document —ranging from elimination of the fee system in lower courts to the reorganization of the administrative branch—caused relatively little controversy. There was, in fact, bipartisan agreement on many matters.[6]

---

[6] An analysis of convention roll call voting showed that there was substantial partisan agreement (90 percent of the Republicans voting with 90 percent of the Democrats) on about 70 percent of such votes. James K. Pollock, *Making Michigan's New Constitution, 1961-62* (Ann Arbor: George Wahr Publishing Co., 1962), p. 48.

Agreement by the Republican caucus on controversial issues, however, left the Democrats determined to vote against the proposed constitution in the convention and to oppose its adoption by the people of Michigan.

Convention action was completed by May 11. The convention then adjourned until August 1, in order to seek a further legislative appropriation to finance the conclusion of the convention's work [7] and to await a judicial determination of when the proposed document should be placed on the ballot. [8]

While the convention was recessed, the Michigan Supreme Court rendered a decision in the case of *Scholle* v. *Hare*. The justices were divided four to three along party lines, with one justice disqualifying himself. In the light of the U. S. Supreme Court's ruling in the Baker case, the Michigan court found that the 1952 "balanced legislature" amendment was unconstitutional according to the fourteenth amendment of the federal document. The legislature was ordered to reapportion the state senate before August 20, according to the provisions of the original document, which required the use of a population standard in each house. The legislature was given 33 days to accomplish this task, which

---

[7] Hostility had been the hallmark of relations between the legislature and the convention from the beginning. Because of a failure to agree with the governor on the method, the legislature did not establish a preparatory commission. Preparatory work was finally financed by the Kellogg Foundation of Battle Creek. The work of the convention was limited to seven and one-half months because of the exhaustion of the legislative appropriation for delegate salaries. The additional appropriation was needed to finance the preparation of the verbatim record of convention debate and the distribution of copies of the proposed constitution. $75,000 was finally supplied for these purposes.

[8] Opinions were divided as to whether the wording of the 1908 constitution as amended would permit the submission of the new document to the people in the November 1962 election. Republicans hoped that discussion of the new document as an issue in that campaign would aid both the constitution and George Romney in winning voter approval. Democrats feared that the Republican perception was correct. Court action initiated by the convention to win a judicial determination of the question was delayed until it became impossible to place the document on the November ballot.

included reducing the number of senate seats, since two had been added by the 1952 amendment. If the legislature should fail to comply with the court order, then elections to the senate would be at large, and the secretary of state was restrained from issuing writs of election for the party primaries in the existing legislative districts.

On July 27, Justice Potter Stewart of the U. S. Supreme Court issued a stay of execution of the Michigan court's order. Justice Stewart noted the judgment of the Michigan court that both houses of the legislature should be apportioned on the basis of population. This represented an extension of the *Baker* v. *Carr* decision into an area which had not been specifically presented to the United States Court for determination.

One Justice cited a decision of the Michigan court, rendered at the turn of the century, which held that the population principle required that no district contain more than twice the number of citizens in the least populous district. This was an intimation that the proposal of the Constitutional Convention would be regarded as unconstitutional, since the 80-20 formula placed no limit upon the difference between the most populous and the least populous district. Applied to the 1960 population distribution, the formula provided one district over four times as populous as the least populated district. The details of the senate apportionment proposal had been formulated before the Scholle decision, and the Republican delegates were in no mood to modify it. After consultation with members of his committee, however, Chairman John Hannah did propose exclusion of that part of the Schedule and Temporary Provisions of the proposed document which delayed implementation of the formula until after the 1970 census.

At the final session of the convention, Hannah's proposal was passed by a vote of 94 to 47, with two Democrats joining the Republicans in Hannah's support, while six conservative Republicans joined the Democrats in opposing it.[9] Assuming adoption

---

[9] *Journal,* August 1, 1962, p. 1345.

of the constitution, this action precluded a judicial determination of the constitutionality of the districts established by the 1952 amendment. Those districts, modified only by the addition of four senators, would otherwise have been retained until 1970. Ironically, the application of the formula to the 1960 census figures resulted in Republican Kent County losing its second senator. All of the energy expended in behalf of representing Grand Rapids, Michigan's second largest city, was futile. In terms of population, Kent County would be the most under-represented area in the state. The four counties of southeastern Michigan, with 53 percent of the 1960 population, would have 17 of the 38 senatorial districts.[10]

The convention then voted 98 to 43 in favor of adopting the proposed constitution. Although Democratic Governor Swainson had personally intervened with wavering Democratic delegates, five Democrats voted with the Republicans in favor of the new document. Only two Republicans joined the Democrats in opposing it, on the grounds that the constitution would be too liberal.[11]

In spite of repeated Democratic requests that controversial sections of the new document be placed on the ballot separately, the convention determined that it should be voted on as a whole, with the citizen indicating either "yes" or "no" in regards to the entire document. Thus the apportionment formula became only one of many changes proposed by the convention.

---

[10] More exactly, these four counties, with 52.87 percent of the 1960 population, would have 44.73 percent of the senatorial representation. The value of an individual vote in these counties would be 84.6 percent according to the David-Eisenberg index.

[11] *Journal*, May 11, 1962, p. 1322.

CONCLUSIONS

CONFLICT BETWEEN A Democratic governor and a controlling Republican "veto bloc" in the state senate brought to Michigan more than a decade of governmental stalemate and bitter partisan strife. The Democratic party diagnosed the source of the conflict as being the unrepresentative nature of Michigan's upper house, which had not been reapportioned to reflect the growth of urban areas in southeastern Michigan. Republican legislators seemed to accept the diagnosis, feeling they had substantial power stakes in the existing system, and organized interest groups developed rigid positions on the question. The political parties could not agree on calling a constitutional convention because they were not able to agree on a method of apportioning delegates.[1]

The compromise on the method of selecting delegates combined the representative features of both houses of the legislature. The four counties voting in favor of constitutional revision contained just over half of the state's 1960 population; and these counties had 41 percent of the delegates elected to the Constitutional Convention.

Although many of the delegates had opposed calling of the convention, and represented areas voting "no" on the question, the convention early determined to undertake a thorough revision of the 1908 document.

Delegates were elected in legislative districts, and the convention was intended to be a representative institution. The representation of narrow geographic interest was overshadowed, however, by the influence of powerful organizations directly represented by elected delegates: the AFL-CIO, the Michigan Farm Bureau Federation, the Michigan Association of Supervisors, and the League of Women Voters.

The convention method of constitutional revision may not produce that document which would win the praises of political scientists; just because so many diverse political forces gain representation in the convention, however, there is a better chance of establishing a consensus that will lead to the acceptance by the voters of the proposed document. At Michigan's

---

[1] The drawing of district boundaries is only one of the influences on the outcome of the legislative process. A group of young "moderate" Republican senators was formed after the 1960 election. With the retirement or electoral defeat of key members of the "veto bloc," the moderate senators were able to capture control of the senate Republican caucus after the 1962 election. Senator Stanley Thayer of Ann Arbor was elected caucus chairman (with power to determine committee assignments) and newspapers hailed the end of the era of senatorial obstruction. An improved outlook for the passage of legislation responsive to urban needs was therefore effected without a change in the method of senate apportionment.

Con-Con, a consensus of sorts was developed among themselves by the Republican caucus. On the crucial questions, a bipartisan consensus became impossible.

Citizens' organizations carried the burden of bringing the Constitutional Convention into being, but the convention was manned by the political parties. Citizens' organizations are not by nature prepared to exercise the responsibilities of public office. The election of delegates on a partisan ballot injected party responsibility into a potentially chaotic campaign, and permitted the recruitment of outstanding candidates, but the convention could not change the nature of partisanship in Michigan. Michigan's parties were ideologically oriented before the convention and were perhaps more bitter in their partisanship after its conclusion.

The special election of delegates held in September 1961, resulted in a convention with a two-to-one Republican majority. The most encompassing explanation of the Republican victory was the low turnout of voters. Both Republicans and Democrats behaved as if the Con-Con election had been something of a freak. In particular, the Democrats assumed that their normal state-wide majority would continue, but that Republican strength would be distributed over the state in such a manner that no system of single-member districts could assure the election of a Democratic majority in the legislature. The conservative Republicans seemed determined to retain every advantage enjoyed by the out-state areas resulting from the existing constitution, such as the 15-mill tax limitation, and some of the conservative Republicans insisted that little or no change be made in the existing legislative apportionment. A second Republican faction, however, was interested in building a state-wide Republican majority by making both their party and Michigan's governmental institutions responsive to the needs of the Detroit metropolitan area.

Any two of these three factions could control the convention. When coalitions were formed between liberal Republicans and

Democratic delegates, the conservative Republicans reacted with violence. Liberal Republicans felt that the fortunes of the party (and those of George Romney) could not survive a permanent split between the two Republican factions. The decisions on most controversial issues, therefore, were made in the Republican caucus through agreement between the Republican factions.

The work of the Committee on Legislative Organization presented in miniature the political aspects of the convention at large. Democratic delegates had taken a firm campaign stand in favor of population apportionment in both houses. Even the most liberal Republicans interpreted the mandate of their own election as a rejection of the Democratic position by the voters, although the voting turnout was so slight—and so highly selective in favor of the Republicans—that it hardly constituted a sampling of majority opinion on any issue. The Republican preference for the use of "other factors" in apportioning the senate was reinforced by the testimony of the citizens' groups which had been most active in supporting the call of the convention. Some of the members of the committee wished as little change as possible in the existing system. The liberal Republicans were unable to combine with the Democratic committee members and there is little evidence that such a combination was even attempted. A last-ditch offer by the Democrats to compromise on the issue was rejected by the majority party, and the committee reported a proposal which would have permitted substantial and systematic discrimination against urban areas.

The proposal of the committee became one of the articles of the agreement within the Republican caucus, and conservative Republicans were able to convince the caucus that any amendments to the proposal given substantial support by the Democrats should be defeated. But the thinking of Republican leaders on the issue was profoundly altered by the decision of the U. S. Supreme Court in *Baker* v. *Carr*. Amendments introduced and passed by the Republicans markedly increased the representation of the urban counties of southeastern Michigan. Thus, the United States Supreme Court exerted a substantial influence in molding the Michigan apportionment formula, although it did not decide the substantive issues of a single Michigan case.

Any hopes that the convention would produce a model document proved futile. The production of model constitutions is best left to academic committees meeting in cloistered chambers, rather than elected delegates meeting in the full glare of publicity generated by the modern media of communication. The Michigan Constitutional Convention was a political institution, and its delegates were concerned with both personal and party political fortunes. The oft-amended 1908 Michigan Constitution had created vested interests with overpowering voices that limited the discretion of the 1962 convention in such matters as tax earmarking, sanctions for pari-mutuel betting, and the constitutional framework for local government. The Democratic party had taken certain positions with such finality that any compromise would seriously damage the party's image of aggressive liberalism; and the Democrats were also afraid that George Romney might be credited with advances made by the convention. The Republican party was an uneasy combination of hostile factions, which were finally brought together by George Romney through substantial concessions to the conservative point of view.

In November of 1962, Romney was elected governor by a majority of 80,000 votes, after intensive campaigning in southeastern Michigan and with a substantial vote in the Detroit suburbs. All other state-wide offices were won by Democratic incumbents. The proposed constitution was not a key issue in the election, since the submission of the document for voter approval had been delayed until the April election.

Because voters tend to judge candidates, rather than issues, the danger to the Democratic party was that the new unity of the Republican party, reinforced by the acceptance of the new "Republican" constitution, would provide the foundation for establishing a renewed normal Republican majority in the state. Republican unity was marked in the acceptance by conservative

Republicans of the apportionment formula, which lessened considerably the legislative influence of rural areas. But the formulation of a new basic law did not bring harmony to the state. The party contest over adoption of the document was as bitter and violent as any other political campaign in Michigan. Adoption of the new constitution might alter the outcome of political conflict, but it could not change the nature of the contestants.

AN ANALYSIS OF THE MICHIGAN PLAN OF LEGISLATIVE APPORTIONMENT

By John P. White

INTRODUCTION

ON AUGUST 1, 1962, the Michigan Constitutional Convention voted 99-44 to adopt a proposed constitution, and adjourned *sine die*. The final decision on whether to accept the proposed document or to retain the constitution of 1908 was referred to the voters in the regular spring election on April 1, 1963. The voters accepted the new constitution by a narrow margin.

The most divisive issue in the convention was that of legislative apportionment. In its "address to the people," the convention majority maintained that the apportionment provisions adopted "will bring Michigan to the forefront of the states in the fairness and equity of its system for allotting legislative representation among its population."[1] All but five of the delegates voting to submit the constitution to the people were Republicans, and the remaining Democratic delegates took quite a different view. Immediately after the preliminary vote to adopt the constitution, 33 Democratic delegates inserted into the journal of the convention a statement of their reasons for voting against adoption. Their first reason had to do with apportionment, which the Democrats said was "the major reason for the calling of the Convention." The statement continued:

> The proposed document perpetuates legislation without fair representation, because the apportionment problem has not been solved. . . . A minority of the voters will continue to elect a clear majority in both houses of the legislature.[2]

The subsequent campaign preceding the ratification referendum reflected the Democratic-Republican convention split. Republican county and state conventions enthusiastically supported the proposed document, while Democratic conventions bitterly condemned it.

But while the constitutional revision campaign in Michigan would make an interesting study in state politics, the apportionment provisions of the new constitution have an intrinsic importance far beyond the boundaries of the state, and beyond the transient interests of Republican and Democratic political leaders in Michigan. The apportionment system in the new constitution represents a direct response by the highest constitutional authorities in a state to the warning implicit in *Baker* v. *Carr* that state legislative apportionments will henceforth be subject to federal judicial scrutiny, and that any apportionments found to be invidiously discriminatory will be invalidated. Moreover, the plan adopted for apportioning the senate is unique among American

---

[1] Michigan Constitutional Convention, *What the Proposed New State Constitution Means to You* (Lansing: Constitutional Convention Office, 1962), pp. 5-6.

[2] Michigan, State of, *Journal of the Constitutional Convention*, May 8, 1962, p. 1331. (Cited hereafter as *Journal.*)

state constitutions. It grants specific, mathematical consideration to land area in the computation of entitlement to senate seats. Having been approved by the people of Michigan, it will—if it survives the inevitable judicial examination—almost certainly be considered by other states that wish to adopt a legally defensible method of granting special consideration to sparsely populated areas.

Two outstanding academic experts on apportionment, Professors Paul T. David and Ralph Eisenberg, in a recent monograph summarizing major current trends and actions in the apportionment battle, discuss the Michigan plan in one paragraph of a section dealing with actions by "defenders of the status quo."[3] They assert that the Michigan convention was "almost unable to function on the issue of representation in the light of *Baker* v. *Carr* because of its own built-in unrepresentative character."[4] Whether the Michigan convention was unable to function "in the light of *Baker* v. *Carr*" depends on one's estimate of the light shed by that decision. If one takes *Baker* v. *Carr* to require a standard of strict population equality in both houses of a bicameral legislature, it is true that the Michigan convention was unable or unwilling to act. But, as demonstrated by Professor Lamb in his study of the evolution of the Michigan apportionment provisions, the Baker decision had the most profound effect on the delegates to the convention, and was unquestionably responsible for the adoption of very important amendments to the original "80-20" senate plan.[5] The delegates apparently did not perceive the light of *Baker* v. *Carr* in the same way as David and Eisenberg. In any event, the convention product will doubtless be scrutinized by federal judges and the deviations from population equality

---

[3] Paul T. David and Ralph Eisenberg, *State Legislative Redistricting: Major Issues in the Wake of Judicial Decision* (Chicago: Public Administration Service, 1963), p. 22.

[4] *Ibid.*, p. 24.

[5] Karl A. Lamb, "The Political Evolution of the Michigan Apportionment Formula," on pp. 153-231 of this volume.

held up to whatever light is then emanating from the supreme bench. Students of the apportionment problem might find it interesting to examine an application to the proposed Michigan apportionment system of the "Index Values of the Right to Vote" devised by David and Eisenberg.[6] The present study makes extensive use of an index of representation identical to that employed by David and Eisenberg.[7]

In judging whether an apportionment system is good or bad, constitutional or unconstitutional, an individual or a judge must have a set of standards against which to measure the system. So far, standards based on personal political philosophy and real or perceived political party and group interests have not been lacking. As of this writing judicial standards have not been formulated by the United States Supreme Court. The most fundamental question which must be asked by those viewing the Michigan apportionment plan is whether both houses of a state legislature must be based as closely on population as is reasonably and administratively possible so that legislative districts in each house vary only within a narrow range from the state-wide average population per district.

It must be said at once that if the United States Supreme Court should subsequently hold that such a standard is imposed by the fourteenth amendment, or if one's personal political philosophy, or his calculation of the interests of groups with which he identifies requires such a standard, the Michigan plan must be condemned. It is based on a different conception of the fourteenth amendment, a different political philosophy, and a different calculation of group interests. It represents a gamble that ultimately the United States Supreme Court will fulfill the prediction made by the Solicitor General of the United States, Mr. Archibald

---

[6] Paul T. David and Ralph Eisenberg, *Devaluation of the Urban and Suburban Vote* (Charlottesville: Bureau of Public Administration, University of Virginia, Vol. I, 1961; Vol. II, 1962).

[7] Needless to say, Professors David and Eisenberg bear no responsibility whatever for the utilization made in this study of their measuring device.

Cox in a speech to the Tennessee Bar Association. Mr. Cox said that:

> I do not mean to suggest how the question should be decided, but it would not surprise me greatly if the Supreme Court were ultimately to hold that if seats in one branch of the legislature are apportioned in direct ratio to population, the allocation of seats in the upper branch may recognize historical, political, and geographical subdivisions provided that the departure from equal representation in proportion to the population is not too extreme.[8]

It is only if we accept the possible validity of the Solicitor General's prediction that extended analysis of the Michigan plan is of much practical value. The study that follows is therefore based on the supposition (possibly incorrect) that apportionment of one house of a state legislature on a basis other than populations is not inevitably prohibited by the United States Constitution. It does not follow from such an assumption that one house of a state legislature may be based on any principles found pleasing to a convention or even to a vote of the people. Both Mr. Cox's statement and the Michigan Constitutional Convention clearly accepted the doctrine that even in the less popular house, there should be a reasonable relationship between population and the apportionment of seats. Before we can decide whether the relationship is reasonable, we must know what it is, and only a detailed analysis of an apportionment plan will enable us to understand clearly the full effects of a constitutional formula for legislative apportionment.

We hope to establish how the Michigan plan compares to other existing systems of state legislative apportionment and to an apportionment based on population alone. We can analyze its immediate and future effects. We can also evaluate it for what it purports to be: a system that bases one house on population and the other on a combination of area and population. Whether

---

[8] Quoted in Supplemental Opinion of O. Bowie Duckett, Maryland Committee for Fair Representation v. Tawes, Circuit Court for Anne Arundel County, No. 13920, Equity, p. 3.

the plan is desirable is a question the voters of Michigan decided; whether such a system is in harmony with the United States Constitution is a question for the federal judiciary, and whether it is a good or a bad system is a question that each interested individual must refer to his personal philosophy of representative government.

The evolution of the apportionment provisions of the new Michigan Constitution has been fully analyzed by Professor Lamb in another monograph, and need not be discussed at length here. As Professor Lamb points out, the historic decision of the United States Supreme Court in *Baker* v. *Carr*, and the subsequent remand action by that court in *Scholle* v. *Hare* had a profound effect on both the Republican majority and the Democratic minority at the convention. The Republicans became convinced of the necessity of moving much closer to a population-based legislature than anyone could have foreseen. The minority became convinced that a legislature based strictly on population was a distinct possibility—not through convention action, but through judicial action. The Democrats reasoned that if the apportionment of the senate under the 1952 "balanced legislature" amendment could be nullified by the courts, the state would revert to the original apportionment provisions of the 1908 constitution, which required apportionment of both houses by population. Furthermore, it would no longer be possible for the legislature to avoid its constitutional responsibility to reapportion the legislature, since the courts would intervene just as they had against the recalcitrant Tennessee legislators in the Baker case.

This general prognosis was partially and temporarily borne out by the decision of the Michigan Supreme Court on remand of *Scholle* v. *Hare*. But for the stay of execution granted in the Scholle case it would have produced at-large senate elections in November 1962. The stay of execution, however, did not in any way nullify the legal prognosis that had been accepted by the opponents of the new constitution. Much of the opposition to the constitution was based on a firmly held belief that its apportionment provisions represented a last-ditch attempt to prevent "one-man, one-vote" apportionment of both houses of the Michigan legislature.

The opposition was all the stronger because of the difficulty in predicting the ultimate judicial disposition of the proposed apportionment. Most Democratic leaders in and out of the convention were almost certain that the old senate apportionment, so reminiscent of the Tennessee apportionment castigated by Mr. Justice Clark in his opinion in the Baker case, would be overthrown by the courts. There could be no such certainty, however, about the proposed apportionment provisions.

At the very least, the adoption of the new constitution rendered the Scholle case absolutely or practically moot, and the whole tedious legal struggle has to begin all over again, with no certainty of final success. For whatever the final judgment of the people of the state as well as of the courts of law, the apportionment provisions of the new constitution were and are sharply different from those of the old constitution. The method of apportioning the senate is not only different from the old constitution, but different from the apportionment system used in any other state in the union.

GENERAL FEATURES OF THE NEW APPORTIONMENT
SYSTEM[1]

BEFORE BEGINNING A DETAILED analysis of these proposals, we can sum up their general intent and effect as follows:

1. The house of representatives is to be based closely on population, modified slightly by the requirements that districts follow county lines, that multi-member districts be outlawed, and that any county or group of counties having no less than .7 percent of the state's population may be granted a seat (whereas the full quota per seat would be .91 percent). After representative dis-

---

[1] The full text of the apportionment provisions of the 1963 constitution may be found in Appendix A, p. 343.

tricts have been created and allocated one seat each, all remaining seats are allocated among the districts by the method of equal proportion.[2]

2. The senate is to be based essentially on a strict representation of weighted population—the weighting to be supplied by the "80-20" formula, with actual population counting for 80 and land area for 20 in computing entitlement to senate representation.

3. Decennial reapportionment of both houses is guaranteed, with the legislature being relieved of all responsibility for reapportionment, and the task handed over to a bipartisan apportionment commission, whose discretion is very limited due to the highly mathematical character of the apportionment formulas. Provision is made for judicial review of reapportionment actions by the commission, and for intervention by the state supreme court in case of a deadlock in the commission.

There was no substantial opposition to the concept of an independent apportionment commission. The futility of expecting a legislature to reapportion itself without fear or favor had long since been demonstrated in Michigan and other states. There has been opposition to the requirement that two of the members of the commission (one Democrat and one Republican) must be residents of each of four geographic zones, roughly equal in area, but most unequal in population. In an extended commentary on the proposed constitution, Delegate Melvin Nord, probably the leading Democratic expert on apportionment, comments that:

> Basically, the "apportionment commission" here proposed would be bi-partisan, and its members would come from the "four corners of the state" in *equal numbers* regardless of population. In other words, it is based on 0% population plus 100% area.

---

[2] This is the method used by Congress to allocate seats in the House of Representatives among the states. A full explanation of the technique may be found in Lawrence F. Schmeckebier, *Congressional Apportionment* (Washington: The Brookings Institution, 1941).

> The latter feature is very objectionable, since it gerrymanders the apportionment commission from the outset, by allowing about 6% of the people to have as much voice in the Commission as the remaining 94%! [3]

In early (and pre-Baker) versions of the apportionment plan, the commission would have had wide latitude in the construction of senate districts, and would have included four legislative members. There was consequently considerable reason for apprehension regarding the effects of the area system of appointment. It would have been at the discretion of the commission to determine how many seats metropolitan counties would have, and this might have been a function of the number of rural seats the commission could carve out. The final plan was far different. It removed from the commission any discretion to determine the allocation of seats to metropolitan counties. This became a pure ministerial function, consisting of the application of the apportionment formula.

The major discretion remaining with the commission consists in their power to draw district boundaries in multi-seat counties. Even here, elaborate guidelines are provided. Still, the lines might be drawn in such a way as to favor one party or the other. But the issue here would be between the parties, not between metropolitan and out-state areas, since the commission will have no discretion in deciding the number of seats a given metropolitan county will have. Since the commission is bipartisan, and since its members will be chosen by the state central committees of the two major parties,[4] there is a safeguard against a partisan gerrymander. The other significant area of discretion remaining to the commission is in combining out-state counties into legisla-

---

[3] Melvin Nord, *Why You Should Reject the Con Con Proposition* (Campaign Brochure, Lawyers to Reject the Con-Con Proposition, 1963), p. 6 (emphasis in original document).

[4] If any third party should receive as much as 25 percent of the gubernatorial vote in the last election preceding a reapportionment, it would be entitled to appoint four members to the commission, which would then be enlarged to 12 members. Article IV, section 6.

tive districts. Again, any possible discrimination that might arise would be against a political party rather than against urban areas and in favor of rural areas. Criticism of the apportionment commission was a minor part of the opposition to the apportionment system of the new constitution. If one believes the system itself is bad, it is little consolation that the system will be scrupulously applied. If the commission were to be appointed on a strict population basis, it would still have to carry out a plan which the opponents find obnoxious, and it seems most unlikely that the resulting apportionments would differ significantly from those adopted by an area-based commission.

That the make-up of the apportionment system is a minor issue and that, in the eyes of the opponents of the constitution, the real villain is the system itself, is clearly indicated by Dr. Nord:

> The most remarkable thing about this section is the great lengths its drafters have gone to, in order to provide "fair" and "effective" apportionment *machinery,* to administer a grossly unfair and ineffective apportionment *formula!* It is a political Alice in Wonderland.[5]

---

[5] Nord, *loc. cit.* (emphasis as in original).

APPORTIONMENT OF THE
HOUSE OF REPRESENTATIVES

CONVENTION DEBATE REGARDING house apportionment was rather desultory on the whole, since there was never very much controversy about the major outlines of house apportionment. An overwhelming majority of the convention and of both parties was agreed that representation in the house should be based closely on population, and that the existing house was very close to straight population. Nevertheless, significant changes were made in the old apportionment provision for the house.

Two of these changes should properly be considered together, because they involve two provisions of the existing apportionment system. One provision gave a special advantage to the Republican party in the out-state area, while the other gave the Democrats a corresponding advantage in Wayne County. These were, respectively, the moiety clause and the multi-member district system.

The moiety clause originated in the constitution of 1850, and in its original form it was not designed to reduce the representation of urban areas (since the total number of seats was not fixed). In the 20th century, however, it came to have that effect. Strictly speaking, there has been no moiety clause in the Michigan Constitution since 1952.

The 1952 amendment, however, still permitted the creation of undersized districts by retaining the language of the old moiety clause (granting a seat for one-half of 1 percent of the state population), which was based on a 100-member house, while increasing the size of the house to 110. The full ratio for a seat therefore became .9091 percent of the population, so that one-half of 1 percent was no longer a moiety or half a ratio, but 55 percent of a ratio. Nevertheless, the term "moiety clause" continued to be used to describe this arrangement for districts with less than a full ratio of population. Most of these districts have been normally Republican.

Counterbalancing this was the requirement in the 1952 amendment that cities and townships entitled to more than five representatives should elect them in multi-member districts of not more than three members. Since, in the city of Detroit, the representative districts (drawn by the county board of supervisors) had traditionally followed ward lines, and since ward lines ran from the center of the city to the periphery, the net effect was to fragment suburban Republican communities and the Democrats regularly won all but one of the 38 Wayne County seats.

The new constitution retains what has been called a moiety clause, although the minimum requirement for a seat is again moved closer to a full population quota. To constitute a "representative area," a county or group of counties must contain .7 percent of the state population. Since the number of seats remains at 110, the full quota continues to be .9091 percent, and the minimum requirement becomes, therefore, 77 percent of a quota.

The multi-member district, however, is outlawed completely. Democratic convention delegates argued that if the Democratic advantage arising from multi-member districts were to be outlawed, fairness would require the total abolition of the last vestiges of the moiety clause. In other words, no district should be formed which would be at all undersized.

However, it is impossible to require that all districts have a full quota of population so long as county lines must be followed. Even if there were no such requirement, some administrative tolerance must be allowed, and is always included even in the strictest straight population proposals. But where it is necessary both to follow county lines and to create single-member districts, a requirement for a full or nearly full quota for the creation of a district becomes either meaningless or futile. For example, if we have a county containing eight-tenths of a full ratio, and we initially deny it a seat and therefore find it necessary to attach it to an adjacent district with 1.2 of a ratio, we have then created a district which is fully entitled to two seats. If two single-member districts must be created, following county lines, the county, which has only 80 percent of a full population quota, will receive a seat after all.

This sort of problem is inherent in the system of single-member districts following county lines. Inevitably there will be undersized districts "piggy-backing" on adjacent counties of larger size. Little is gained by establishing strict initial qualifications for the creation of districts if in the final allocation of seats the standards must be relaxed.

The major dilution of the population principle in the proposed Michigan House of Representatives, then, is not the feeble remnant of the old moiety clause, but the insistence on county lines and single-member districts. Actually, even the .7 rule cannot always be met due to the problems just discussed. This is the reason for the provision in the new constitution which states that "any county which is isolated under the initial allocation as provided in this section shall be joined with the contiguous representative area having the smallest percentage of the state's population."[1]

The necessity of such an escape hatch provision is illustrated by the problem of Van Buren County under the 1960 population. This county has only .62 percent of the state population, and therefore does not qualify for separate representation under the .7 rule. It is therefore initially attached to Allegan County, the smallest adjacent district. But under the subsequent allocation of additional seats by the equal proportions formula, the Allegan-Van Buren "representative area" (to employ the term used by the constitution to refer to the initial allocation of seats) just barely becomes entitled to a second seat.[2] Since the two seats must be allocated to two single-member districts following county lines, Van Buren receives a seat by the grace of the piggy-back clause. This is a marginal case, and in subsequent apportionments it is entirely possible that the two counties will have to share a single representative. In other words, the "piggy-back clause" will in some cases, and perhaps more often than not, simply bring a somewhat undersized district nearer to a full population ratio by adding to it an adjacent county of small population. That situation can also be illustrated by reference to the probable first apportionment under the proposed constitution. Marquette County is the most populous county in Michigan's upper peninsula. While it does not have a full ratio (.9091 percent of the population), its 1960 population of 56,154 gives it .72 percent, and thus qualifies it for separate representation.

[1] Article IV, section 3.
[2] Under the possible apportionment illustrated in Figure 1, the Allegan-Van Buren area qualifies for the 108th of the 110 seats.

However, under the apportionment outlined in Figure 1, adjacent Alger county, with only 9,250 people, is initially isolated, and must be attached to Marquette. The resulting representative area has .84 percent of the population, and gets only one seat.

The use of the equal proportions formula for allocating the second and subsequent seats to the "representative areas" provides a well-tried statistical method of insuring the maximum equity in the distribution of these seats. It also reduces the discretion of the apportioning authority to the initial creation of areas entitled to at least one seat. The system has worked well in the apportionment of seats to the states in the federal House of Representatives. It should be stressed that the large disproportions existing in the size of congressional districts has nothing to do with the equal-proportions method. Once a state is allocated a certain number of seats, the subsequent creation of congressional districts is a responsibility of the states. The states use whatever standards of equity they think best, subject to possible congressional action to impose national standards, and perhaps in the future to judicial scrutiny.

The problems existing in congressional apportionment, despite the long-standing use of the equal-proportions methods, illustrate very well that it is not itself an apportionment system, but an intermediate process (though a highly important one) that may be associated with widely divergent systems. The equal-proportions method requires a prior creation of districts entitled to at least one seat. If single-member districts are required, it also demands a further independent method of sub-dividing the original districts.

The detailed and mathematical character of the apportionment systems proposed for both houses enables us to predict with considerable accuracy the composition of districts which will be set up by the first apportionment commission. A possible house apportionment is described in Table 1, and in the accompanying map (Figure 1). Table 1 gives the representation indices for each of the projected districts, and the distribution of these

(*Text continued on page 251.*)

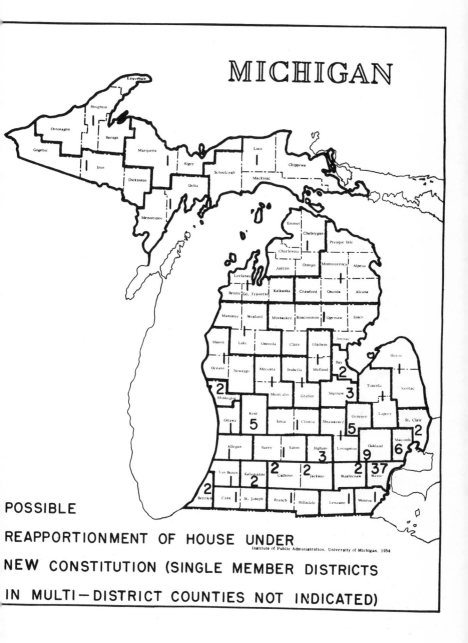

POSSIBLE
REAPPORTIONMENT OF HOUSE UNDER
NEW CONSTITUTION (SINGLE MEMBER DISTRICTS
IN MULTI—DISTRICT COUNTIES NOT INDICATED)

Figure 1

Table 1

Possible Allocation of House Seats[*]

House: 110 Single-Member Districts
Population, 1960: 7,823,998[***]
Average Population/Seat: 71,120

	Seats	Population 1960	Pop. per seat 1960	Index[*] 1960[**]
Allegan	1	57,729	57,729	123
Alpena Dist.	1	60,867	60,867	117
Bay	2	107,042	53,521	133
Berrien	2	149,865	74,933	95
Calhoun	2	138,858	69,429	102
Chippewa Dist.	1	60,288	60,288	118
Delta Dist.	1	58,983	58,983	121
Eaton Dist.	1	81,422	81,422	87
Emmet Dist.	1	61,799	61,799	115
Genesee	5	374,313	74,863	95
Gogebic Dist.	1	65,471	65,471	109
Gd. Traverse Dist.	1	55,027	55,027	129
Gratiot Dist.	1	72,360	72,360	98
Hillsdale Dist.	1	69,645	69,645	102
Houghton Dist.	1	55,806	55,806	127
Huron Dist.	1	66,320	66,320	107
Ingham	3	211,296	70,432	101
Ionia Dist.	1	81,101	81,101	88
Iosco Dist.	1	61,676	61,676	115
Jackson	2	131,994	65,997	108
Kalamazoo	2	169,712	84,856	84
Kent	5	363,187	72,637	98
Lenawee	1	77,789	77,789	91
Macomb	6	405,804	67,634	105
Manistee Dist.	1	56,441	56,441	126
Marquette Dist.	1	68,262	68,262	104
Midland Dist.	1	62,219	62,219	114
Monroe	1	101,120	101,120	70
Montcalm Dist.	1	56,846	56,846	125
Muskegon	2	149,943	74,971	95
Newaygo Dist.	1	62,636	62,636	114
Oakland	9	690,259	76,695	93
Ottawa	1	98,719	98,719	72
Saginaw	3	190,752	63,584	112
St. Clair	2	107,201	53,601	133
St. Joseph Dist.	1	79,264	79,264	90
Shiawassee Dist.	1	91,679	91,679	78

POSSIBLE ALLOCATION OF HOUSE SEATS* (con't)

House: 110 Single-Member Districts
Population, 1960: 7,823,998***
Average Population/Seat: 71,120

	Seats	Population 1960	Pop. per seat 1960	Index* 1960**
Tuscola Dist.	1	85,231	85,231	83
Van Buren	1	48,395	48,395	147
Washtenaw	2	172,440	86,220	82
Wayne	37	2,666,297	72,062	99
Mean deviation of indices:				8

* Where only the county name is given, the district is composed of one county, or one county has the number of seats indicated. No attempt has been made to subdivide multi-district counties. The apportionment commission is required to divide such counties into districts having population as nearly equal as possible but in no event smaller than 70 nor more than 125 percent of the county average.

** The index of representation used throughout this study is a measurement devised by Professors Paul T. David and Ralph Eisenberg. It is computed by dividing the state average district population (the population quota) by the population of a given district. Thus, if a district has a population of only half the state average, it would have an index of 200 (indicating that the population of this district has twice the average representation). Districts with indices below 100 are underrepresented, those with indices above 200 are overrepresented. See Paul T. David and Ralph Eisenberg, *Devaluation of the Urban and Suburban Vote* (Charlottesville: Bureau of Public Administration, University of Virginia, 1961 (vol. I) and 1962 (vol. II)).

*** Population total is as given in *Michigan Manual* varies slightly from final U.S. census total of 7,823,194.

indices gives us the means of analyzing the degree to which the apportionment is faithful to the ideal of straight popular representation. A brief summary of the distribution of the indices is found in Table 2.

In evaluating any apportionment system which claims to be based on population, it is reasonable to scrutinize closely the dis-

Table 2

DISTRIBUTION OF REPRESENTATION INDICES, POSSIBLE APPORTIONMENT OF MICHIGAN HOUSE OF REPRESENTATIVES

Range of indices	Number of districts	Population	Pct. of state pop.
1. Major underrepresentation: (Below 70)	0	—	—
2. Moderate underrepresentation: (70-84)	7	633,670	8.1
3. Optimum representation: (85-115)	90	6,464,899	82.6
4. Moderate overrepresentation: (116-130)	8	461,987	5.9
5. Major overrepresentation: (Over 130)	5	262,638	3.4
Total	110	7,823,194	100.0

tricts which deviate substantially from ideal population size. If there are many such districts, or if there seems to be no substantial and legitimate reason for their existence, we are justified in concluding that the apportionment is faulty.

As we have seen, under the possible apportionment outlined above, only five of the projected districts would have a representation index above 130, which we have taken as a somewhat arbitrary boundary of major overrepresentation. No district falls below an index of 70, which we have defined as the boundary line of major underrepresentation.[3]

Only two districts are below an index of 75. These are the districts in Monroe and Ottawa Counties, respectively. These counties have populations of awkward size, in that they would be considerably underrepresented with one seat each, and more considerably overrepresented with two seats. Monroe County

---

[3] It should perhaps be stressed again that the official apportionment cannot differ greatly from that projected in this study, due to the relative lack of discretion allowed to the apportionment commission.

has 1.29 percent of the state population, and thus on a straight mathematical basis would be entitled to 1.42 seats, while Ottawa's 1.26 percent of the population works out to an ideal of 1.39 seats. In the equal proportions allocations, both counties fail to qualify for a second seat, though Monroe would get the 112th seat, if there were one.

Given the limitations imposed by county lines and single-member districts, these two deviant districts certainly seem justifiable.

Moving to the overrepresented districts (i.e., those having 130 percent or more of their strict population entitlement), we see that the most overrepresented district would be Van Buren County, with a representation index of 147. We have already discussed the problem of this district as an example of the "piggyback" phenomenon. As previously noted, the problem is inseparable from the basic decision to adhere to county lines and single-member districts.

There are four districts (two in Bay County and two in St. Clair County) which have a representation index of 133, the next highest figure. These cases are the opposite side of the coin presented by Monroe and Ottawa Counties, discussed above. Like those counties, Bay and St. Clair Counties have populations which are large for one seat and small for two seats. Each of these counties has 1.37 percent of the state population, and would therefore be entitled to 1.51 seats. Like the underrepresented counties, Bay and St. Clair are marginal cases in the equal-proportions allocation, but having slightly larger populations, they barely qualify for second seats (being allocated the 106th and 107th seats, respectively). Again, our verdict has to be that no closer approach to straight population is possible, given the county line rule.

There are eight other districts which are significantly overrepresented. One of these is composed of Allegan County, and is a pure county line product. We are thus left with only seven districts which are significantly overrepresented, and these may be regarded as products of the residual moiety clause.

The actual and weighted populations of these districts are given in Table 3. As noted in that table, only 5.2 percent of the state population resides in these districts. The net effect of their overrepresentation on the representation of the remainder of the state population is negligible, reducing it from an actual 94.8 percent to a weighted 93.6 percent of the total. In terms of seats, the counties included in these districts are entitled on a mathematical basis to 5.68 seats. Assuming that in practice they would have to be accorded six seats as a minimum, even if there were no moiety clause, these counties will thus receive one extra seat as a result of the residual moiety clause. While this is a clear

Table 3

DISTRICTS OVERREPRESENTED AS A RESULT OF THE MOIETY CLAUSE

District	Actual population	Index	Weighted population*
Montcalm Dist.	58,846	125	71,120
Manistee Dist.	56,441	126	71,120
Gd. Traverse Dist.	55,027	129	71,120
Alpena Dist.	60,867	117	71,120
Houghton Dist.	55,806	127	71,120
Delta Dist.	58,983	121	71,120
Chippewa Dist.	60,288	118	71,120
Totals	404,258	123	497,840

	Moiety districts	Remainder of state
Actual pct. of state population	5.2	94.8
Weighted pct. of state population	6.4	93.6

* The "weighted population" is the average population of all districts in the house, i.e., the total state population divided by the total number of seats. Since each member of the house has 1/110 of the votes in the house, his constituents in effect have been weighted by the apportionment system at 1/110 of the total population. As explained earlier, the index is derived by dividing the average population per district by the actual population of a given district. Since indices are rounded to the nearest whole number, multiplying the actual population by the index will produce a weighted population varying slightly from the state average.

deviation from the ideal of straight population apportionment, it is hardly a major one.

Our earlier observation that the more important limitation on the equal population ideal is not the moiety clause but the necessity of following county lines is thus borne out by the fact that of the 20 districts whose populations fall outside the optimum range of representation indices (85-115), 13 appear to be county line problems, and only seven moiety problems. All 13 of the remaining deviant districts are located in relatively populous counties. Allegan, Bay, St. Clair, and Van Buren Counties are overrepresented, while Kalamazoo, Monroe, Ottawa, and Washtenaw Counties are underrepresented. In every case, the county population size is such that a substantial deviation from ideal population representation is unavoidable if county lines must be followed.

In evaluating both the major and minor deviations from ideal population size, the crucial question which should always be kept in view is the effect of "overrepresentation" on those "underrepresented." If one group of citizens is overrepresented, this can be done only at the expense of underrepresenting other citizens. Court actions challenging apportionments as violation of the fourteenth amendment take the form of asserting an injury to a citizen or group of citizens who are damaged by the dilution of their political power. It is therefore important that we examine the impact of all degrees of overrepresentation involved in the apportionment of the house.

It appears that some 74 districts will have a population larger than the average or norm, while the remaining 36 districts will have smaller than average populations.[4] It is possible to evaluate

---

[4] In this and in all other analyses of the apportionment provisions of the new constitution, no consideration is given to population variation of districts within counties entitled to more than one seat. Such districts are required to have populations as nearly equal as possible; city and township boundaries are to be followed "where applicable," but in no case can the population of such a district exceed 125 percent nor be less than 75

the effect of overrepresentation by computing the indices of representation for all overrepresented counties as compared to all underrepresented counties. The 36 overrepresented districts include 60 counties, while the 74 underrepresented districts include 23 counties. Comparative data on these two groups of counties and districts are contained in Table 4.

Table 4

ACTUAL AND WEIGHTED POPULATIONS OF OVER- AND UNDER-
REPRESENTED DISTRICTS, HOUSE APPORTIONMENT,
1960 POPULATION

	Overrepresented counties	Underrepresented counties	State totals
No. of counties	60	23	83
No. of districts	36	74	110
Total population	2,252,149	5,571,045	7,823,194
Ave. pop. per dist. ..	62,560	75,284	71,120
Representative index .	114	94	100

It will be observed that the overrepresented counties taken together have 114 percent of their theoretical entitlement on a straight population basis. On the other hand this 14 percent overrepresentation can be absorbed into 6 percent underrepresentation of the more populous underrepresented counties.

When it is kept in mind that many of the deviations from ideal population size are unavoidable within the context of a single-member district system following county lines, these overall disparities in representation between over- and underrepresented counties do not appear excessive.

---

percent of the average population per district within the county. It is clear that any systematic attempt to discriminate against one part of a county in favor of another would violate the intent of the constitution and would subject a proposed plan to judicial invalidation, even assuming bipartisan agreement within the apportionment commission could make such a discriminatory pattern possible.

Summary: Is the House Based on Population?

Although there was bipartisan agreement at the Michigan Constitutional Convention that the house of representatives should be closely based on the population principle, some of the opponents of the proposed constitution have claimed that the house apportionment formula finally approved is not so based. The Democratic minority of the Committee on Legislative Organization submitted a minority report which has subsequently been widely used as a basis for attacks on the house apportionment plan. The portion of the minority report dealing with the house is as follows:

D. *Reasons for a Change in the Apportionment of the House of Representatives.* We agree with the majority that the House in Michigan has always been based on population. The deviation from population at present is 10 area (rural) seats out of 110, or about 9% area, 91% population. This deviation may be small, but it has been enough to maintain Republican control of the House.

In the past 10 years, the popular vote for Representatives in the Michigan House favored the Democrats twice and the Republicans 2 times; yet in each case the Republicans maintained control of the House. Thus, the House has also been unresponsive to the public will, albeit only by a small margin. The point is, however, that this small margin was provided not by the votes of the people, but by the small degree of rural bias in the apportionment of the Legislature.

There is therefore ample ground for removing any such bias in favor of one group or another, and placing the House on a straight population basis in order to make it responsive to the public will, it certainly makes no sense to make half such a change. The majority Proposal reduces the "moiety" (or major fraction) effect from about 10 seats to about 5. (This can be seen if one compares a map based on the majority Proposal with one based on a 105-seat House based on population. The difference is substantially only in the addition of 5 more rural seats to the 105 based on population.) It should be emphasized that what is at stake here is not absolute perfection in equality of representation, but rather the more practical question of whether or not one desires to add extra seats in the rural region in order to keep control by a small margin despite the public will.

We have never insisted on perfection or near-perfection in equality of representation. Our position is simply that it should be as nearly equal as practical, but that in no event should a bias in favor of any group be thrown onto the scales of justice.

We note further that though the "bias" would not be reduced from 10 to perhaps 5 under the majority proposal, this will also in all likelihood be just enough for the Republicans to maintain control of the House. The reasons it can now be done with fewer "area" seats are: (1) the Wayne County Democratic stronghold has lost population percentagewise, and (2) the proposed provision for a single-member districts (with which we concur) will, in effect, approach proportional representation in the highly populated areas (thus winning some Republican seats in Democratic strongholds), while in the rural areas there will be no such change (hence the Republicans will continue to win 100% of the seats in their strongholds).

We therefore oppose any half-hearted effort to reduce the "area" effect in the House. We believe the House ought to be on a straight population basis. If this is not to be done, the House ought to be left alone altogether. Either make the change or don't. We regard the majority report as deceptive insofar as it leads one to believe that the apportionment proposed by the majority of the House "comes as close as possible to basing the House on population without breaking county lines. . . ."

The record on this point should be perfectly clear: The majority propose a House for 5% area, instead of the present 9% area. The minority on the other hand, propose a House with 0% area seats. There is no difficulty in doing this if you wish to do so. You simply specify a definite number of seats and provide that they shall be apportioned by population "as nearly equal as may be," together with a statistical test for the deviation from equality. In this way, while every district will not be exactly equal in population, there will be no seats added as an arbitrary bonus to any one group. That is, in fact, precisely what the minority proposal provides for the House.[5]

No purpose would be served by discussing in detail the comments of the minority report regarding the 1953 apportionment, but its criticism of the proposed house apportionment system appears to be based partly on faulty analysis and partly on a rejection of the basic principle of representation by geographical districts (despite the fact that the report specifically concurs in the requirement of single-member districts).

The calculation that the proposed apportionment will provide for five area seats is obviously incorrect. If the minority report's assertion means anything, it must mean that rural areas will have five more seats than they would be entitled to on a straight population basis. This conclusion is arrived at, according to the report, by comparing a map showing a 105-seat body based on straight population with a map showing a 110-seat body apportioned according to the majority proposal. It should be apparent that the proper procedure would be to compare a *110*-seat straight population map with the majority proposal map. Alternatively, one may examine the number of districts which appear to exceed whatever tolerance is appropriate, and decide how many of them are inevitable as a result of following county lines, and how many are accounted for by allowing rural counties representation on the basis of the moiety clause.

Apparently, the 15 percent tolerance used in the computations presented earlier in this study was acceptable to the authors of the minority report. One of them, Delegate Hodges, subsequently moved an amendment using the 15 percent plus or minus tolerance, and all six of the signatories of the minority report who were present and voting supported it.[6] At the end of the convention, all six signatories of the minority report voted for the

[5] *Journal*, February 5, 1962, pp. 545-46.
[6] *Ibid.*, March 26, 1962, p. 869. Delegates T. S. Brown, Greene, Hodges, Marshall, Nord, and Sablish voted affirmatively; Delegate Liberato did not vote.

Democratic substitute constitution, which employed the 15 percent limit.[7]

As we have seen, there will in all probability be seven true moiety districts among the 13 districts which are overrepresented by more than 15 percent. We have noted, however, this does not mean that the rural areas are given seven additional seats; it means that seven seats have been allocated to a population entitled to six, so that the overrepresentation of these rural counties is not seven or five, but only one—or to be mathematically precise, 1.32.

A more fundamental and thus more important aspect of the minority report is its insistence that a proper test of an apportionment is whether it reflects faithfully, in the distribution of seats between the political parties, the state-wide party division of the vote. It cannot be emphasized too strongly that no system of geographical districting, however close it may be to straight population, can guarantee such a result. Even if the districts are so constructed that they each include exactly the same population, a party which has a poor distribution of its party supporters will certainly elect a smaller percentage of legislators than the party's total percentage of the state vote.

It may certainly be argued that it would be more desirable to have a representative system geared to the reflection of a state-wide majority. The implication of such a position must be recognized, however. It involves the introduction of some variant of proportional representation or weighted voting. This fact was implicitly recognized by the minority report in its substitute for the majority senate apportionment proposal. The minority recommendation involved a system that came to be known familiarly as the "tote-board plan," because its adoption would require the use of some sort of computing machinery in counting legislative votes—machinery perhaps not unlike that employed by race tracks to calculate odds and payoffs. The tote-board plan

---

[7] *Ibid.*, May 8, 1962, pp. 1311 and 1321.

would eliminate at least one persistent problem of the American politician: no major party candidate could ever be defeated. The senatorial candidates of all parties receiving at least 25 percent of the vote would be declared elected, but in the senate, each member would cast the same number of votes he had received in the election.[8] At various times and by various Democratic delegates, versions of the tote-board plan were supported for one or both houses, or for a unicameral legislature.[9] In the end, however, the Democratic minority dropped the tote-board plan prior to the final vote on the revised constitution, and supported a more conventional system of geographical districting, using 15 percent population deviation limits, abandoning county lines, and permitting multi-member house districts in the larger counties.[10]

The final Democratic substitute would be slightly more advantageous to the Democratic party (because it would allow multi-member districts in Wayne County). Nevertheless, it would only have a relatively small effect in bringing the apportionment closer to straight population. This follows because only 20 of the 110 districts, under the proposal adopted by the convention, would fall outside the range suggested by the Democrats, and only five districts seriously exceed them. Moreover, the improvements proposed could only be accomplished by abandoning county lines, a step that even the Democratic minority was apparently rather reluctant to take, since earlier Democratic plans had adhered to county lines.

In summary, we can say that the plan finally adopted for house apportionment comes very close to straight population, as limited by county lines and single-member geographic districts. The Democratic minority report of the Committee on Legislative Organization is quite correct in saying that the plan does not come as close as possible to straight population following county

---

[8] *Ibid.*, February 5, 1962, pp. 543-44.
[9] Cf. Testimony of Delegate Melvin Nord, Democratic vice chairman, Committee on Legislative Organization, December 14, 1961 (mimeographed committee document), p. 29, and Appendix "Q."
[10] *Journal*, May 8, 1962, p. 1311.

lines. The remnant of the moiety clause appears to have inserted the equivalent of about one extra seat into northern Michigan. The effect of this extremely minor deviation on the representation of the rest of the state is, as we have seen, very small.

The effect on the five metropolitan counties is illustrated in Table 5. None of the five counties has an unrepresented full ratio of population, and only Oakland County has an unrepresented major fraction. Oakland would be entitled to 9.70 seats on a strict mathematical basis, and will actually receive nine. Wayne, Genesee, and Kent all have minor unrepresented factions, which would presumably not be represented even if the moiety clause were eliminated. Macomb County, on the other hand, will be slightly overrepresented, since it receives six seats, although mathematically entitled to 5.70 on the basis of its population.

The fundamental objections to the house plan then, probably do not rest on deviations from the population principle but are based on a theory of representation. This theory, often inchoate, assumes that a properly apportioned legislative body should reflect the party complexion and the public opinion of a state-wide majority. This is a doctrine which quite understandably suggests itself to a political party consistently frustrated by its inability to win legislative majorities although it normally commands a state-wide majority support for its candidates. It opposes itself to the

Table 5

REPRESENTATION OF FIVE METROPOLITAN COUNTIES, POPULATIONS
ENTITLEMENT COMPARED TO ALLOCATION UNDER
NEW CONSTITUTION

| | Number of seats | |
County	Straight population	Actual allocation
Wayne	37.49	37
Oakland	9.70	9
Macomb	5.70	6
Genesee	5.26	5
Kent	5.10	5

doctrine that legislators should represent community interests, and that a legislative majority should be a composite of community majorities.

A choice between these competing theories should perhaps be entrusted to the people themselves, or to constitutional authorities in a given state. Clearly, apportionment plans based on either philosophy can fulfill the obligations imposed on the states by the national constitution. There is much to be said on both sides of the philosophical argument, but this should not obscure the fact that the argument basically is not about apportionment as such, and certainly not about "one man, one vote," but about the nature of the political community. If this most interesting and important but (in the present context) irrelevant question can be separated from an evaluation of the house apportionment plan, there should be little difficulty in pronouncing it a successful application of the principle of representation by equal-population districts. We will have more to say about the house apportionment when we consider the combined effects of senate and house apportionments on the representation of the people of the state.[11] Our purpose in this section, however, was to make a judgment on the question of whether the house apportionment plan is or is not based closely on population. We conclude that it is.

---

[11] Analysis of such problems as the range in size between largest and smallest districts, minimum population needed to elect a majority, and comparisons of the proposed house apportionment with the apportionment of more "popular" houses in other states is presented at a later stage, since it is important to consider the net effect of both the house and senate apportionments together, and to compare the overall picture with that in other bicameral systems.

THE PROPOSED MICHIGAN SENATE

WHILE THE PROPOSED SYSTEM of apportionment in the house of representatives is a modern type of population apportionment, especially in its use of the equal-proportions device, it is in other respects a familiar system. But the plan proposed for the senate is totally unlike the apportionment system used in any other state legislative body. The senate plan represents an attempt to find a formula for granting weighted representation to sparsely populated areas in such a way as to avoid invidious discrimination. In his monograph, Professor Lamb has discussed the origin and development of the so-called "80-20" system.[1] As he points out, the opinion of the United States Supreme Court in the *Baker* v. *Carr* case unquestionably had a great influence on the evolution of the proposed senate apportionment system. The text of the senate apportionment provisions is contained in Appendix A, page 343. It is very far from being a simple plan. Perhaps the easiest way to grasp the procedures involved is to outline the steps which must be made in constructing an apportionment under the proposal. The process may be outlined as follows:

1. Each county's percentage of the total state population is computed to two decimal places.

2. Each county's percentage of the total state land area is computed to two decimal places.

3. The population percentage for each county is then multiplied by four, and is added to the county's total land area. Thus, population is weighted at four and area at one, i.e., population at 80 percent and area at 20 percent. This is the origin of the term "80-20" which has been used to describe the plan.

4. The figure obtained by adding the weighted population percentage to the area percentage is termed the total apportionment factors of the county. Under any state population, there will always be a total of 500 factors in the state, i.e., 400 population factors and 100 area factors.

5. At this point, the counties are divided into two groups: counties having 13 or more apportionment factors, and counties having less than 13 factors. The number 13 is selected because it is the nearest whole number to the average number of factors for all districts. Thus the first group of counties includes only those counties fully entitled to one or more senate seats. The apportionment factors for each class of counties is then totaled,

---

[1] Lamb, *op. cit.*

and it is ascertained what percentage of the total is possessed by each of the two groups of counties.

6. The percentage of the total apportionment factors possessed by each group is then multiplied by the number of seats, that is, by 38, in order to determine the entitlement of each group of counties to seats in the senate. The resulting product is reduced to the nearest whole number. Thus, if counties with more than 13 apportionment factors have a total of 250 apportionment factors, and the second class of counties (those with less than 13 apportionment factors) have the remaining 250 factors, each group would be entitled to 50 percent of the 38 seats, or 19 seats each.

7. Each of the large population counties (i.e., those with 13 or more factors) is initially allocated one seat, and the remaining seats to which this class of counties is entitled is distributed by the method of equal proportions, applied to the apportionment factors of the county.

8. Within each metropolitan county entitled to more than one senate seat, single-member districts are then constructed following incorporated city or township boundary lines where possible. The population of such districts within a single county must be as nearly equal as possible but may not be less than 75 percent nor more than 125 percent of the average district population of the county. The seats allocated to the class of counties with less than 13 factors are then apportioned into single-member districts so that no district shall have less than ten apportionment factors nor more than 16. Insofar as possible, districts are required to conform to an ideal of 13 factors, but it is further provided that existing senatorial districts shall not be altered unless there is a failure to comply with the standards set forth. These standards include, in addition to the minimum and maximum apportionment factors, a requirement of compactness, convenience, contiguity by land, and a final requirement that the districts be as rectangular in shape as possible.

An Analysis of the Effects of the New Senate Apportionment Plan

One of the major aspects of the new Michigan senate apportionment plan is that it provides a definitive method of settling apportionment disputes between metropolitan and non-metropolitan counties. The total number of seats is divided into two groups, metropolitan and non-metropolitan seats. Once the basic division of seats has been made, the creation of districts in non-metropolitan areas has no further effect upon the metropolitan counties. Since the initial allocation of seats to the two groups of counties is made by a rigid mathematical formula, the apportioning authority has no discretion to decide the number of seats which will be allocated to each of the two groups of counties. Given any set of population figures, it is possible to calculate exactly the division of seats as between the two groups. The responsibility of the apportionment commission in this regard will consist of making the necessary calculations.

The 1960 census revealed that 57.52 percent of the total population of Michigan was concentrated in five of the 83 counties. Four of these are contiguous counties in southeastern Michigan: Wayne, Oakland, and Macomb Counties are in the Detroit area, and Genessee County makes up the Flint metropolitan area. The fifth county is Kent, which includes the city of Grand Rapids. These five counties comprise the metropolitan group of counties under the 1960 census, and they are the only counties fully entitled to one or more seats each. The metropolitan county category is not a frozen one, however. If in the future other counties increase their percentage of the state's population so that they acquire 13 factors, they will enter the metropolitan group. However, there are few counties which have even an outside chance of joining the present five metropolitan counties in the foreseeable future. Only three other counties, Ingham, Saginaw, and Washtenaw, have over ten apportionment factors. Unless these counties increase their population at a rate considerably in excess of the state rate, they will not acquire the necessary additional factors. Table 6 indicates the allocation of seats to the five metropolitan counties.

Table 6

INITIAL ALLOCATION OF SENATE SEATS TO METROPOLITAN COUNTIES, 1960 POPULATION

County	Pct. of state pop.	Pop. factors	Area factors	Total factors
Wayne	34.08	136.32	1.06	137.38
Oakland	8.83	35.32	1.54	36.86
Macomb	5.19	20.76	.84	21.60
Genesee	4.78	19.12	1.13	20.25
Kent	4.64	18.56	1.51	20.07
Totals	57.52	230.08	6.08	236.16

Since the metropolitan counties are entitled as a class to the number of seats which will give them the closest possible percentage of seats to their actual percentage of apportionment factors, the computation for the number of seats may be expressed as follows:

$S = \dfrac{38\,F}{500}$. $S =$ the number of senate seats to which the metropolitan counties are entitled, where $F =$ the total number of factors in the metropolitan counties, 38 the number of seats, and 500 the total number of factors in the entire state. Applying the formula, we get:

$$S = \frac{38 \times 236.16}{500} = 17.95, \text{ or when rounded, 18.}$$

The application of the 80-20 formula reduces the weighted population of the five metropolitan counties from 57.52 percent of the total to 47.23 percent. This gives the metropolitan counties an entitlement of 17.95 seats or, when rounded to the nearest whole number, 18 seats. This automatically determines that the remaining counties of the state will receive the other 20 seats.

Once the metropolitan seats have been allocated, these seats are distributed among the counties in this class. As in the house of representatives, the equal-proportions device is utilized to allocate second and subsequent seats to districts. In the senate, however, the equal proportions table is applied not to population but to apportionment factors.

On making the necessary computations, we find that of the 18 metropolitan seats, Wayne County will be entitled to ten, Oakland to three, Macomb and Genesee to two each, and Kent to one. In order to evaluate the apportionment of the metropolitan counties, it is instructive to compare this allocation of seats both to the present senate apportionment and to an apportionment based entirely on population. A comparison of this kind is contained in Table 7.

Table 7

COMPARISON OF SENATE APPORTIONMENT IN THE FIVE LARGEST COUNTIES UNDER OLD CONSTITUTION, NEW CONSTITUTION, AND STRAIGHT POPULATION (1960)

	Number of seats			Representation index		
County	Old const.	New const.	Straight pop.	Old const.	New const.	Straight pop.
Wayne	7	10	13	60	77	100
Oakland ...	1	3	3	33	89	89
Macomb ...	1	2	2	57	101	101
Genesee ...	1	2	2	62	110	110
Kent	2	1	2	127	57	113
Totals ..	12(of 34)	18(of 38)	22(of 38)	61	82	101

An examination of this table indicates that the allotment of seats to the metropolitan areas under the new constitution will produce a decided improvement in the population representation of these counties, considered as a group. The individual counties will all move closer to their full population entitlement except for Kent County. Under the old constitution Kent was substantially over-represented, but by losing one of its two seats will be under-represented to an even more serious degree.

The problem of providing adequate representation for Kent County was one that the convention considered at length.[2]

---

[2] Cf. Lamb, *op. cit.*, pp. 205, 218 ff.

Several attempts were made to devise a modification of the plan finally adopted so that Kent County would receive its second seat. For example, an early version of the plan provided that a second senate seat would be allotted to every county having at least 19.5 factors. This proviso was so obviously intended to favor Kent County alone, that there was doubt that it would be upheld under judicial scrutiny. The convention, in approving an amendment proposed by Delegate James K. Pollock, deleted this proviso, in order to avoid any possibility that the senate apportionment plan might be held invidiously discriminatory.[3]

Since it appears at first glance that a more equitable allocation for Kent County would be two seats, the problem requires some further consideration. It must be stressed that Kent County is not deprived of its second seat because the equal proportions allocation is applied to apportionment factors rather than population. This can easily be ascertained by calculating the equal-proportions allocation of 18 seats to the five metropolitan counties, using population alone. Since the five counties have only a relatively small number of land area factors among them, the deletion of these factors and the subsequent recalculation of the equal-proportions computation does not change the allocation of the 18 seats and still results in Kent County barely missing its second seat. Thus, given the population distribution of the five metropolitan counties in 1960, and the fact that these counties are entitled to 18 seats, there is no ideal allocation which can be made. We must conclude, therefore, that the Kent County phenomenon is a chance product of the peculiar distribution of population in 1960, and that similar situations will not necessarily arise in future apportionments under the new constitution.

The basic problem of both Kent and Genesee Counties is one often encountered in any apportionment system following county lines. Situations often arise (as we have noted in dealing with the house apportionment), where a given county will be con-

---

[3] *Ibid.*

siderably underrepresented if it receives one seat, and considerably overrepresented if it receives two seats.

Is the Senate Apportionment Equitable to the Metropolitan Counties?

The answer to the question of equitability of the senate apportionment depends, of course, on the standards which are applied. Clearly, if the closest possible approximation to straight population is the sole criterion of equitability, the new Michigan apportionment formula is seriously defective. The five largest counties would be entitled to 22 seats if population were the only consideration. They will actually receive 18 seats. Thus the application of area weighting in the apportionment formula results in the loss of four metropolitan senate seats.

Two questions present themselves: First, will the under-representation of the metropolitan counties be excessive in the initial apportionment, and second, will continued population concentration weaken the representation of these counties in future apportionments? In order to answer these questions fully, we must remember that we are dealing with a bicameral system. In the lower house, these five counties with 57.52 percent of the total state population, will receive 62 of the 110 seats in the lower house or 56.36 percent of the total. In the senate the metropolitan counties will have a representation index of 82.1. In other words, they will have 82.1 percent of the representation to which they would be entitled on a straight population basis. How does this compare with the representation of similarly situated counties in other states? A proper evaluation should take into consideration the representation of such counties in both houses of the state legislature. A comparison of the representation of Michigan's metropolitan counties with that of similar counties in other states is made in Table 8.

After metropolitan seats have been allocated, the remaining seats are distributed to the other counties. Using the ground rules

(*Text continued on page 275.*)

Table 8

RANK ORDER OF INDICES OF REPRESENTATION, FIVE LARGEST COUNTIES IN EACH STATE, 1960 CENSUS*

I. House More Favorable to Five Largest Counties

Rank	State	Number of counties	Pct. of state pop.	Repres. index	Upper or lower house
1	New Jersey	21	53.6	106	L
2	Ohio	88	43.6	103	U
3	Rhode Island	5	66.2	103	L
4	California	58	60.0	102	L
5	Massachusetts	14	71.7	102	U or L
–New	Michigan Constitution	83	57.5	99	L
6	New York	62	52.8	97	U
7	New Hampshire	10	74.7	96	U or L
8	Arizona	14	83.9	94	L
9	Illinois	102	61.7	93	L
10	Maine	16	62.3	93	L
11	South Carolina	46	37.0	92	L
12	Pennsylvania	67	44.8	91	L
13	Washington	39	64.9	91	L
14	Wisconsin	71	42.6	90	U
15	Hawaii	4	79.1	89	L
16	Missouri	115	53.1	89	U
17	Oregon	36	57.0	89	L
18	Michigan (old const.)	83	57.5	88	L
19	Connecticut	8	79.0	88	U
20	West Virginia	55	32.0	85	L
21	Vermont	14	60.6	84	U
22	Montana	56	41.0	80	L
23	Arkansas	75	28.9	79	U
24	South Dakota	67	32.4	78	L
25	Colorado	63	57.3	75	L
26	Louisiana	64	33.6	75	U
27	Utah	29	78.7	75	L
28	Nevada	17	84.8	73	L
29	Indiana	92	39.6	73	U
30	Wyoming	23	53.4	73	L
31	Virginia	98	27.3	72	L
32	Alaska	24	67.8	70	L
33	Kentucky	120	33.6	69	U
34	Minnesota	87	48.7	68	U
35	Nebraska	93	42.6	68	U
36	Maryland	24	75.4	65	L

I. House More Favorable to Five Largest Counties* (con't)

Rank	State	Number of counties	Pct. of state pop.	Repres. index	Upper or lower house
37	Delaware	3	68.1	62	L
38	New Mexico	32	51.2	62	L
39	North Dakota	53	35.1	60	L
40	Idaho	44	43.3	59	L
41	North Carolina	100	22.5	59	L
42	Tennessee	95	45.7	56	U
43	Texas	259	39.0	56	L
44	Mississippi	82	23.5	48	U
45	Oklahoma	77	42.6	43	L
46	Alabama	67	41.2	41	L
47	Iowa	99	27.2	37	U
48	Kansas	105	40.0	34	L
49	Florida	67	50.4	29	L
50	Georgia	159	37.8	25	U

* In states with fewer than ten counties, data is for those counties containing a majority of the state population. In Rhode Island, Hawaii, and Delaware, data is for the largest county; in Connecticut, for the three largest counties.

RANK ORDER OF INDICES OF REPRESENTATION, FIVE LARGEST COUNTIES IN EACH STATE, 1960 CENSUS*

II. House Less Favorable to Five Largest Counties

Rank	State	Number of counties	Pct. of state pop.	Repres. index	Upper or lower house
1	Massachusetts	14	71.7	102	U or L
2	New Hampshire	10	74.7	96	U or L
3	New York	62	52.8	89	L
4	Washington	39	64.9	88	U
5	Wisconsin	71	42.6	87	L
–New	Michigan Constitution	83	57.5	82	U
6	Oregon	36	57.0	81	U
7	Maine	16	62.3	78	U
8	Pennsylvania	67	44.8	76	U
9	West Virginia	55	32.0	76	U
10	Illinois	102	61.7	75	U
11	Vermont	14	60.6	74	L

II. House Less Favorable to Five Largest Counties (con't)

Rank	State	Number of counties	Pct. of state pop.	Repres. index	Upper or lower house
12	Indiana	92	39.6	72	L
13	Rhode Island	5	66.2	72	U
14	Ohio	88	43.6	71	L
15	Colorado	63	57.3	70	U
16	Arkansas	75	28.9	69	L
17	Virginia	98	27.3	69	U
18	Louisiana	64	33.6	68	L
19	Nebraska	93	42.6	68	L
20	Minnesota	87	48.7	67	L
21	Kentucky	120	33.6	63	L
22	Connecticut	8	79.0	62	L
23	South Dakota	67	32.4	62	U
24	Michigan (old const.)	83	57.5	61	U
25	Utah	29	78.7	61	U
26	Delaware	3	68.1	60	U
27	Alaska	24	67.8	60	U
28	North Dakota	53	35.1	58	U
29	Wyoming	23	53.4	56	U
30	Missouri	115	53.1	54	L
31	Tennessee	95	45.7	52	L
32	Hawaii	4	79.1	51	U
33	North Carolina	100	22.5	51	U
34	Arizona	14	83.9	47	U
35	Maryland	24	75.4	46	U
36	New Jersey	21	53.6	44	U
37	Mississippi	82	23.5	38	L
38	Texas	259	39.0	38	U
39	Alabama	67	41.2	35	U
40	Nevada	17	84.8	35	U
41	Oklahoma	77	42.6	35	U
42	Iowa	99	27.2	34	L
43	Kansas	105	40.0	31	U
44	New Mexico	32	51.2	31	U
45	South Carolina	46	37.0	30	U
46	Florida	67	50.4	26	U
47	Idaho	44	43.3	26	U
48	Georgia	159	37.8	22	L
49	Montana	56	41.0	22	U
50	California	58	60.0	21	U

Note: For a similar rank ordering of the states according to the representation of the smallest number of counties including a majority of each state's population, see Appendix D, p. 356.

specified in the convention (a range of ten to 16 factors per district, retention of existing districts which meet constitutional qualifications, compactness, convenience and contiguity by land, adherence to county lines, and rectangularity of shape where possible), we have constructed an apportionment based on the 1960 census. As in the case of the house apportionment presented earlier, it is possible that some districts will be differently drawn by the apportionment commission, but because of the specificity of the apportionment formula, our sample apportionment will be close to the final product. In any event, the metropolitan counties cannot receive any other number of seats than we indicate, since there is no discretionary leeway in the allocation of seats to the metropolitan counties.

Table 9 gives the composition of senate districts, which are illustrated in Figure 2. We are now in a position to evaluate the entire senate apportionment in conjunction with the house apportionment.

Another method of evaluating the equitability of an apportionment system is to apply the so-called Dauer-Kelsay scale. In 1955, Professors Manning J. Dauer and Robert D. Kelsay computed for each state the total population of the smallest districts which could be combined to produce a legislative majority in each house of the state legislature.[4] Assuming that 50 percent is an ideal situation (i.e., it would require 50 percent of the population to elect a majority of each house) it is possible to add the percentage for each house of a bicameral legislature and to express the sum as a percentage of 100 and then to rank the states in the order of their approach to 100 percent. As of July 1, 1961, indices ranged from 95.9 in Oregon to 27.0 in Florida. Michigan ranked seventeenth with a total index of 74.4.

---

[4] Manning J. Dauer and Robert G. Kelsay, "Unrepresentative States," *National Municipal Review*, December 1955, pp. 571-75; revised in *ibid.*, April 1956, p. 198.

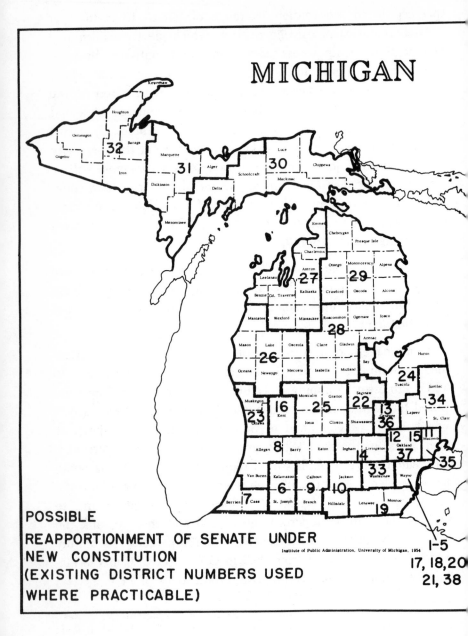

Figure 2

Table 9

POSSIBLE ALLOCATION OF SENATE SEATS
(NEW CONSTITUTION—1962)

State population, 1960: 7,823,998*
38 single-member districts

Districts	1960 population	Index
1-5, 17, 18, 20, 21, 38 (Wayne Co.)	266,630 (ave.)	77
6th	212,044	97
7th	186,797	110
8th	187,546	110
9th	173,761	118
10th	166,736	123
11th & 35th (Macomb Co.)	202,902 (ave.)	101
12th, 15th, 37th (Oakland Co.)	203,086 (ave.)	89
13th, 36th (Genessee Co.)	187,156 (ave.)	110
14th	249,529	83
16th	363,187	57
19th	178,909	115
22nd	244,198	84
23rd	248,662	83
24th	184,353	112
25th	153,908	134
26th	121,662	169
27th	119,975	172
28th	152,459	135
29th	82,962	248
30th	94,586	218
31st	114,006	181
32nd	97,360	211
33rd	172,440	119
34th	181,441	113
Mean deviation of indices		31.0

* Population total is as given in *Michigan Manual* varies slightly from final U.S. census total of 7,823,194.

The Dauer-Kelsay scale is not a measure of political power or influence. The legislative majorities measured by this scale are purely hypothetical majorities, and no known attempt has been made to ascertain whether the theoretical majorities assigned to each state bear any relationship to political realities.

However, this scale may be used as a rough measure of deviation from pure population apportionment, and it has been widely employed in the current apportionment controversy. Its application to the Michigan proposed apportionment reveals that the smallest possible percentage of the population which could elect a majority of the house of representatives would be 45.37. The 56 smallest seats would include the smallest districts in Wayne County. Although it is certain that Wayne County will receive 37 seats, the populations of these districts cannot be determined exactly at this time. The new constitution requires that the districts be as nearly equal in population as possible but that in no event shall any district have less than 75 nor more than 125 percent of the average population per district in the county. The index figure cited (45.37) is based on the assumption that the 20 smallest districts in Wayne County will have an average population of 90 percent of the average population size of Wayne County districts. It might be noted that the construction of a Dauer-Kelsay majority on the basis of the house apportionment plan clearly illustrates the difficulty in applying the Dauer-Kelsay scale to an analysis of the political effects of an apportionment. The majority thus constructed is one that appears impossible of attainment in the real world of Michigan politics. The 56 smallest districts will include such heavily Republican counties as Van Buren, Allegan, Midland, and Jackson. But they will also include the six districts in the Democratic stronghold of Macomb County, as well as Democratic districts in the upper peninsula, and the 20 districts in Democratic Wayne County. Barring a revolutionary party realignment, no such majority will ever become an active force in the Michigan legislature. It is also clear that neither party will be able to control the house without carrying districts including approximately 50 percent of the state population.

Turning to the senate, the construction of a Dauer-Kelsay scale here produces an index figure of 40.2. That is, the 20 smallest districts would include a population of 3,149,007 of Michigan's 7,823,194 people. The Dauer-Kelsay scale for the senate can be predicted with greater accuracy than for the house, since it is not necessary to estimate the size of districts within counties.

As in the case of the house, the theoretical majority used in computing the Dauer-Kelsay scale is one not likely to appear in reality. At least two of the three upper peninsula districts (all three of which are among the 20 smallest districts) seem very likely to be reliable Democratic districts, as does at least one of the two districts in Genesee County. Also included would be the two Macomb County districts, which seem to be reasonably safe for the Democrats. Thus, of the 20 smallest districts, at least five (and perhaps seven) may be expected to return Democrats. If we wish to ascertain the smallest Republican majority which it would be possible to achieve under the proposed senate apportionment, it would be necessary to delete at least the five probable Democratic districts and add to the list the next five smallest probable Republican districts. As it happens, these five districts all have populations greater than the state average. It appears that the smallest population that could elect a Republican majority in the senate would include 44.86 percent of the total state population.

However, using only the criterion of population size in each house and disregarding the politics of the districts, we find that under the new constitution Michigan's total Dauer-Kelsay index would be 85.7. As of July 1, 1961, only five states (Oregon, Massachusetts, New Hampshire, West Virginia, and Maine) had higher combined Dauer-Kelsay indices. A rank ordering of these indices is contained in Table 10.

Table 10

DAUER-KELSAY INDICES
PERCENTAGE OF POPULATION NECESSARY TO CONTROL
STATE LEGISLATIVE BODIES, AS OF
JULY 1, 1961, RANK ORDERED
(COMPARED WITH APPORTIONMENT ACCORDING TO
NEW MICHIGAN CONSTITUTION)

Rank	State	Total	Senate	House
1	Oregon	95.9	47.8	48.1
2	Massachusetts	89.9	44.6	45.3
3	New Hampshire	89.2	45.3	43.9
4	West Virginia	86.7	46.7	40.0
5	Maine	86.6	46.9	39.7
–New Michigan Constitution		85.7	40.3	45.4
6	Wisconsin	85.0	45.0	40.0
7	Alaska	84.0	35.0	49.0
8	Arkansas	77.1	43.8	33.3
9	South Dakota	76.8	38.3	38.5
10	Kentucky	76.1	42.0	34.1
11	Indiana	75.2	40.4	34.8
12	New York	75.1	36.9	38.2
13	Minnesota	74.6	40.1	34.5
14	Virginia	74.5	37.7	36.8
15	South Carolina	73.3	26.6	46.7
16	Michigan (old const.)	73.0	29.0	44.0
17	North Dakota	72.1	31.9	40.2
18	Ohio	71.3	41.0	30.3
19	Pennsylvania	70.8	33.1	37.7
20	Washington	69.2	33.9	35.3
21	Utah	68.9	21.3	33.3
22	Illinois	68.6	28.7	39.9
23	Missouri	68.0	47.7	20.3
24	Louisiana	67.1	33.0	34.1
25	New Jersey	65.5	19.0	46.5
26	Rhode Island	64.6	18.1	46.5
27	North Carolina	64.0	36.9	27.1
28	Mississippi	63.7	34.6	29.1
29	Wyoming	62.7	26.9	35.8
30	Colorado	61.9	29.8	32.1
31	Iowa	62.1	35.2	26.9
32	Vermont	58.6	47.0	11.6
33	Tennessee	55.6	26.9	28.7
34	California	55.4	10.7	44.7

Table 10—Continued

DAUER-KELSAY INDICES
PERCENTAGE OF POPULATION NECESSARY TO CONTROL STATE LEGISLATIVE BODIES, AS OF JULY 1, 1961, RANK ORDERED
(COMPARED WITH APPORTIONMENT ACCORDING TO NEW MICHIGAN CONSTITUTION)

Rank	State	Total	Senate	House
35	Utah	54.6	21.3	33.3
36	Oklahoma	54.0	24.5	29.5
37	Montana	52.7	16.1	36.6
38	Alabama	50.8	25.1	25.7
39	Idaho	47.3	16.6	32.7
40	Connecticut	45.4	33.4	12.0
41	Kansas	45.3	26.8	18.5
42	Nevada	42.0	8.0	35.0
43	New Mexico	41.0	14.0	27.0
44	Delaware	40.5	22.0	18.5
45	Florida	27.0	12.3	14.7
	Nebraska	—	36.6	(Unicameral)
	Arizona	N.A.	12.8	N.A.
	Georgia	N.A.	N.A.	N.A.
	Hawaii	N.A.	N.A.	N.A.
	Maryland	N.A.	N.A.	N.A.

N.A.—not available

Source: Derived from data in National Municipal League, *Compendium on Legislative Apportionment* as quoted in "Advisory Commission on Intergovernmental Relations," *Apportionment of State Legislatures* (Report A-15, Washington: 1962), pp. A-7, A-8.

POPULATION RANGE AS AN
EVALUATIVE MEASURE

ONE OF THE REASONS advanced by Democratic delegates for their vote against the proposed constitution was that the apportionment system would produce an excessive discrepancy between the populations of largest and smallest districts in each house. The Democratic statement inserted into the journal of the convention pointed out that:

> Senate districts . . . could vary in population by more than four to one . . . House districts could vary by approximately two to one.[1]

---

[1] *Journal*, May 8, 1962, p. 1331.

These estimates of deviations in population size are approximately correct. Under the probable apportionments illustrated in this study, the range between the largest and smallest senate districts would be 4.38, while the range in the house would be 2.09. Comparison with existing apportionments in other states, however, reveals that if smallness in range is a desideratum of good apportionment, the Michigan apportionment will rank very high among the states. In Table 11, we have rank ordered the states according to range; once for the house in each state which has the larger range, and once for the house with the smaller range.[2] It will be noted that the Michigan house would move from twentieth place to fourth place in the nation, while the senate moves from twentieth to third place. The house range would be the smallest of any house of representatives in the country, with only three state senates having smaller ranges.[3]

The relatively small ranges provided by the new constitution might well have been an argument for the defenders of the new constitution rather than for its opponents had it not been for the "two to one" rule set forth by Justice Kavanagh in the Michigan Supreme Court decision in *Scholle* v. *Hare.*

In that opinion, Justice Kavanagh stated that

> . . . when any apportionment plan provides some elective districts having more than double the population of others, that plan cannot be sustained. And so we hold in final summation that the Fourteenth Amendment and our own corresponding pledge of the protection of equal laws (Art. 2, Sec. 11) do require that the senatorial districts of Michigan be so arranged as to be consistent with the foregoing maximum 2 to 1 ratio.[4]

---

[2] This is a more meaningful classification than simply grouping all upper houses in one category and all lower houses in the other, since in some states the senate has a smaller range, while in other states the house range is smaller.

[3] As noted in Table 11, figures for other states are as of July 1961. Data on changes since then have not been calculated.

[4] Scholle v. Hare, 376 Mich. 176, 116 N.W. 2d 350.

(*Text continued on page 287.*)

Table 11

RANGE OF DISTRICT POPULATION SIZE, RANK ORDERING
OF STATES (AS OF JULY 1961)

I. House with Greater Population Range

Rank	State	Senate or House	
1	Oregon	S	2.3
2	Nebraska	—	2.7
–New Michigan Constitution		S	4.4
3	Wisconsin	H	4.5
4	South Dakota	H	4.7
5	Indiana	H	5.4
6	Maine	H	5.5
7	Hawaii	S	5.9
8	Kentucky	H	6.0
9	Arkansas	H	6.4
10	Virginia	H	7.1
11	Washington	S	7.3
12	Colorado	H	8.1
13	Texas	S	8.4
14	North Dakota	S	8.9
15	Ohio	H	9.4
16	Wyoming	S	9.8
17	New York	H	10.0
18	Illinois	S	10.6
19	Minnesota	H	11.9
20	Michigan (old const.)	S	12.3
21	Alaska	S	12.5
22	Missouri	H	13.4
23	Massachusetts	H	13.9
24	Mississippi	H	16.7
25	Iowa	H	16.8-median
26	Louisiana	H	17.4
27	North Carolina	H	18.2
28	New Jersey	S	19.0
29	Tennessee	H	23.0
30	South Carolina	S	25.1
31	Oklahoma	S	26.4
32	Utah	H	27.8
33	Pennsylvania	H	31.0
34	Kansas	H	33.2
35	Delaware	H	35.5
36	Alabama	S	41.1
37	West Virginia	H	57.6
	Average		68.8

Table 11—Continued

RANGE OF DISTRICT POPULATION SIZE, RANK ORDERING
OF STATES (AS OF JULY 1961)

Rank	State	Senate or House	
38	Arizona	S	85.8
39	Montana	S	88.4
40	Rhode Island	S	96.9
41	Georgia	H	98.8
42	Idaho	S	102.1
43	Florida	H	108.7
44	Maryland	S	132.2
45	New Mexico	S	140.0
46	Nevada	S	223.6
47	California	S	422.5
48	Connecticut	S	424.5
49	Vermont	S	872.5

23 senates, 25 houses, 1 unicameral

New Hampshire data not available
Nebraska (unicameral) is included in both sub-tables

II. House with Smaller Population Range

Rank	State	Senate or House	
1	Missouri	S	1.6
2	New York	S	1.8
3	Ohio	S	1.9
—New Michigan Constitution		H	2.1
4	Hawaii	H	2.1
5	Oregon	H	2.1
6	Alaska	H	2.2
7	Arkansas	S	2.3
8	Massachusetts	S	2.3
9	Nebraska	—	2.7
10	Maine	S	2.8
11	Wisconsin	S	2.8
12	Kentucky	S	2.9
13	New Jersey	H	3.0
14	Texas	H	3.1
15	North Dakota	H	3.2
16	South Carolina	H	3.4
17	West Virginia	S	3.4

Table 11—Continued

RANGE OF DISTRICT POPULATION SIZE, RANK ORDERING OF STATES (AS OF JULY 1961)

Rank	State	Senate or House	
18	Wyoming	H	3.4
19	Minnesota	S	3.8
20	Michigan (old const.)	H	4.0
21	California	H	4.2
22	South Dakota	S	4.3
23	Indiana	S	4.4
24	Washington	H	4.6
25	Illinois	H	4.7
26	Arizona	H	5.3
27	Virginia	S	5.5
28	North Carolina	S	6.0
29	Tennessee	S	6.0
30	Connecticut	S	6.7
31	Utah	S	6.9
32	Colorado	S	7.3
33	Louisiana	S	8.8
34	Mississippi	S	8.8
35	Iowa	S	9.0
36	Vermont	S	9.7
	Average		10.1
37	Pennsylvania	S	10.7
38	Maryland	H	12.5
39	Montana	H	14.0
40	Oklahoma	H	14.0
41	New Mexico	H	15.5
42	Alabama	H	15.6
43	Delaware	S	16.8
44	Idaho	H	17.8
45	Kansas	S	21.3
46	Nevada	H	22.0
47	Rhode Island	H	39.0
48	Georgia	S	42.6
49	Florida	S	98.0

27 senates, 21 houses, 1 unicameral

New Hampshire data not available
Nebraska (unicameral) is included in both sub-tables

The exact legal effect of these remarks is somewhat obscure. Justice Kavanagh did not derive the 2-1 rule from any previous judicial interpretations of the fourteenth amendment to the United States Constitution, but from two Michigan cases construing the state constitution of 1850.[5] That constitution required the senate to be apportioned according to population, and in the Giddings and Williams cases the Michigan court held this to mean that no district should be more than twice the population size of any other district.

Since Justice Kavanagh had found, earlier in his opinion, that the 1952 amendment to the constitution of 1908, which established the system of frozen senate districts, was invalid because the districts thus established "lack a rational, reasonable, uniform, or even ascertainable nondiscriminatory legislative purpose," he was construing the original version of the apportionment provisions in the 1908 constitution at the time he enunciated the 2-1 rule, and specifically article V, section 4 of that document, which requires that:

> At the session in 1913, and each tenth year thereafter, the legislature shall by law rearrange the senatorial districts and apportion anew the representatives among the counties and districts according to the number of inhabitants, using as the basis for such apportionment the last preceding United States census of this State. Each apportionment so made, and the division of any county into representative districts by its board of supervisors, made thereunder, shall not be altered until the tenth year thereafter.

Both the original state constitution of 1835, and the constitution of 1850 contained similar language.[6] The two to one rule has had scant acceptance in past Michigan apportionments. No house apportionment ever made in the State of Michigan produced a range of less than two to one, and of the 20 senate

---

[5] Giddings v. Secretary of State, 93 Mich. 1, and Williams v. Secretary of State, 145 Mich. 447.

[6] Constitution of 1835, article IV, section 3; Constitution of 1850, article IV, section 2.

apportionments made in Michigan from 1838 onwards, only five (1841, 1846, 1892, 1895, and 1901) produced a population range of less than two to one.

If it be held that the two to one rule was demanded by the federal constitution or by previous Michigan constitutions, and that the rule should have applied to both houses, it might be argued that Michigan has never had a constitutional legislature. Of course, judicial construction gives new meaning to constitutional provisions. But it is certain that the Williams and Giddings cases cited in *Scholle* v. *Hare* were not effective in establishing a two to one rule for either house of the Michigan legislature.

This, however, is not the important point. Under the new constitution, the two to one rule cannot be applied as a test of compliance with state constitutional provisions which appear to call for apportionment by population. The new constitution clearly demands apportionment by population *and* area, and if it is to be overthrown on the grounds of excessive population range, there will have to be a prior determination that the United States Constitution requires such a rule. In that event, the two to one rule may indicate what Justice Kavanagh, in *Scholle* v. *Hare,* called "the constitutional range of discretion."

The only federal authority for such an application cited by Judge Kavanagh is the dissenting opinion of Justices Douglas, Black, and Murphy in *MacDougall* v. *Green,* in which it was stated that:

> None would deny that a state law giving some citizens twice the vote of other citizens in either the primary or general election would lack that equality which the Fourteenth Amendment guarantees.[7]

Whether establishing one legislative district with twice the population of some other district is legally and constitutionally as objectionable as allowing a voter to cast two ballots in the same election may be regarded as a point that is not fully estab-

---

[7] 335 U.S. 281, 288.

lished, to say the least. Of course, Justice Kavanagh's basic finding rested on other grounds, as we have noted. For that very reason, his implication that the fourteenth amendment sanctions the application of the two to one rule may be regarded as dicta.

But the use of the range between the largest and smallest population districts as a criterion of constitutionality has not been confined to the State of Michigan. In the rash of apportionment cases following *Baker* v. *Carr*, it has become more or less standard procedure for the plaintiff attacking a state legislative apportionment to cite the existing range between largest and smallest districts, and to assert that this range is *prima facie* evidence of invidious discrimination. Some courts have come to accept a large population range as conclusive of the claims of the plaintiffs; others have apparently regarded it as a significant item of evidence, and in at least one case, a judge held that a range of 33 to 1 is not only not conclusive but was a "point of little merit."[8]

The fact that the initial apportionment under the new Michigan Constitution will establish population ranges which compare most favorably with those existing in other states prior to *Baker* v. *Carr* certainly does not dispose of the possibility that the new apportionment system will ultimately be voided by the courts. In the first place, it is conceivable that the United States Supreme Court will adopt the two to one rule or something close to it as a criterion of constitutionality, if it is finally determined that both houses of a state legislature must be based on population.

Since almost every other state would have larger ranges than Michigan, the effect of such a holding would be to invalidate all or practically all state legislative apportionments. That the United States Supreme Court would be willing to go so far in reconstructing the basic institutions of state government may be doubted, but the possibility cannot be ruled out. Secondly, it might be argued that however moderate the population ranges

---

[8] Opinion of Judge Duckett, Maryland Committee for Fair Representation v. Tawes, Circuit Court of Anne Arundel County, Maryland, upheld by Maryland Court of Appeals, 182-A, 2d 877 (1962).

might be under the initial Michigan apportionment, they will become progressively larger in the senate, due to the existence of a fixed area component in the apportionment factors of each county. This argument cannot be made about the house apportionment, where it is most unlikely that the population range will ever greatly exceed two to one, though it will usually not fully meet the two to one requirement. But a full assessment of the apportionment provisions must include an analysis of the future implications of the 80-20 plan to senate apportionment.

THE FUTURE OF SENATORIAL
APPORTIONMENT

CRITICS OF THE PROPOSED apportionment of the Michigan Senate seem to feel that the initial senate apportionment will probably be less objectionable than apportionments under future censuses. It is argued that the system contains a fixed area component which under no circumstances of population change will be affected in any way. It is further argued that as the trend toward urbanization and concentration of population continues, the underrepresentation of metropolitan cities will become progressively worse. This line of argument is understandable, but it arises from a fundamental misunderstanding of the system.

It is true that of the 500 apportionment factors, 100 are based on land area, and therefore not affected by population change. Every district and every county within a given district has a fixed area component. For example, Michigan's upper peninsula contains 29 percent of the total land area of the state, and therefore has 29 apportionment factors based on area. Since no senate district may contain more than 16 apportionment factors, the upper peninsula cannot be reduced to less than two senate seats, even if the entire population were to move away. In practice, the plan will virtually guarantee the upper peninsula at least three senate seats, since at any time that there are more than 32 apportionment factors in the upper peninsula, no two districts can be constructed so that both will be under the prescribed maximum of 16 factors. So long as the upper peninsula retains at least 0.75 percent of the state's total population, it will be entitled to retain its present three seats in the senate.

Similar examples could be given of the effect of the fixed area component on other northern districts. It is not surprising that critics of the new constitution have come to the conclusion referred to before: that the process of urbanization will cause a progressive deterioration in the relative position of urban populations under the proposed plan.

The fallacy of this line of argument lies in the unexamined assumption that a given degree of overrepresentation of a rural area automatically produces a corresponding and opposite effect of the same magnitude on the urban population. But this assumption is contrary to fact. While overrepresentation of any group or area can be accomplished only at the expense of some other group or area, the smaller the overrepresented group is in relation to the total population, the smaller will be the effect of the overrepresentation on the underrepresented majority. Let us make this point obvious. Suppose that by some chance the State of Michigan overrepresented lion tamers or sword swallowers by several hundred percent. The net effect on the political power of the other citizens of the state would clearly be negligible. Only an eccentric would feel himself so aggrieved as to bring suit in a federal court to redress the balance of political power.

While this example may be clear enough, many individuals and apparently some courts have overlooked the simple mathematical principles behind the example just cited. Whenever an apportionment system is declared unconstitutional solely on the basis of the range between the largest and smallest districts, the same fundamental error is made as if the court were to invalidate an apportionment on the ground excessive overrepresentation of lion tamers. The error consists in a failure to measure the effect of the overrepresentation on those underrepresented. Thus, if the population of the upper peninsula continues to decline, the range between the largest population and the smallest population of senate districts will continue to increase. It does not follow from this that the urban population will be correspondingly more and more underrepresented. In fact, it can be demonstrated that such can never be the case, and that the degree of underrepresentation of metropolitan areas will always be strictly limited, no matter what population changes may take place in the future. In most apportionment systems, it is impossible to predict with certainty the apportionment of seats to any given area, even assuming a certain population. The lack of rigid standards, or the lack of any effective means of insuring that a prescribed apportionment will actually take place, makes it difficult to predict the future status of legislative apportionment in most states.

However, the Michigan plan includes such definite standards, as well as a guaranteed method of securing reapportionment according to the provisions of the constitution. It is therefore possible to predict with certainty the number of senate seats which will be allocated to the metropolitan counties on the one hand and to the remaining counties on the other, given any projected population distribution.

The basic allocation of seats as between metropolitan and non-metropolitan counties can be understood much more readily if the whole system is presented in terms of a weighted population device. In order to make clear the future impact of the plan, it is convenient to reduce the apportionment formula to population percentages. Such a weighted population table is in Table 12. Using this table, it is possible to determine with certainty the exact number of seats which will be received by the two groups of counties, given the present or any projec'ted future population statistics. In other words, it is not necessary to have recourse to any further use of land area data, since the constant factor of land area is built into Table 12. Any future changes in the senate apportionment will result solely from shifts in the state population, since there will be no change in the area factors. We can thus determine that when the metropolitan counties attain 59.34 percent of the total state population, they will be entitled to a nineteenth senate seat, and that upon attaining 62.63 percent of the state's population, they will receive 20 seats. Another interesting aspect of this table is that it enables us to fix the smallest percentage of the state's population required by the non-metropolitan counties to retain a senate majority (20 seats). Since the metropolitan counties will gain a nineteenth seat when they achieve 59.34 percent of the state's population, the non-metropolitan counties must have no less than 40.67 percent of the population if they are to have a senate majority.

Table 12 indicates the exact limits of over- and underrepresentation of the metropolitan and the non-metropolitan counties. We observe that under no conceivable distribution of the population can the metropolitan counties receive less than 80 percent of the senate representation to which they would be entitled if the population were the sole criterion in apportionment. On the other hand, given the optimum situation (one in which the metropolitan counties just barely qualify for a given additional seat) the metropolitan counties will have an index of 83 to 86. In other words decennial reapportionment will reflect population changes in such a way that metropolitan representation will re-

Table 12

REDUCTION OF SENATE APPORTIONMENT FORMULA TO POPULATION: PERCENTAGE OF STATE POPULATION REQUIRED FOR FOURTEENTH TO THIRTY-FIRST SENATE SEATS, FIVE METROPOLITAN COUNTIES[*]

Metropolitan pct. of state pop.		Five metropolitan counties				Seventy-eight non-metropolitan counties		
				Index of population representation			Index of population representation	
Minimum	Maximum	Senate seats	Pct. of total seats	Min. pop.	Max. pop.	Senate seats	Min. pop.	Max. pop.
42.89	46.17	14	36.84	86	80	24	117	111
46.18	49.46	15	39.47	86	80	23	120	113
49.47	52.75	16	42.11	85	80	22	123	115
52.76	56.04	17	44.74	85	80	21	126	117
56.05	59.33	18	47.37	85	80	20	129	120
59.34	62.62	19	50.00	84	80	19	134	123
62.63	65.91	20	52.63	84	80	18	139	127
65.92	69.20	21	55.26	84	80	17	145	131
69.21	72.49	22	57.89	84	80	16	153	137
72.50	75.78	23	60.53	84	80	15	163	144
75.79	79.07	24	63.16	83	80	14	176	152
79.08	82.36	25	65.79	83	80	13	194	164
82.37	85.65	26	68.42	83	80	12	220	179
85.66	88.94	27	71.05	83	80	11	262	202
88.95	92.22	28	73.68	83	80	10	339	238
92.23	95.51	29	76.32	83	80	9	527	305
95.52	98.80	30	78.95	83	80	8	1,754	470
98.80	100.00	31	81.58	83	82	7	(No pop. required)	1,548

[*] Similar calculations for smaller numbers of metropolitan seats can be made, but are not presented since there seems little possibility that the metropolitan counties will decline to below 42.89 percent of the state's population. Their 1960 percentage was 57.52, and is increasing.

295

main within a rather narrow range of variation. No matter what population changes take place, the metropolitan counties will always have about the same degree of underrepresentation.

On the other hand, Table 12 shows that the indices of representation of the non-metropolitan counties will vary considerably. As the relative population of the non-metropolitan counties declines, so also does representation in the senate. However, the influence of the fixed area component means that the smaller the population of these counties, the greater will be the area component. Thus, the numerical overrepresentation of the non-metropolitan counties is allowed to increase as the concentration of population in the urban counties increases. The overrepresentation of these non-metropolitan counties is strictly limited by the maintenance of a more or less constant standard of population representation for the urban areas. A graphic representation of the comparison between straight population apportionment and the 80-20 system is presented in Figure 3.

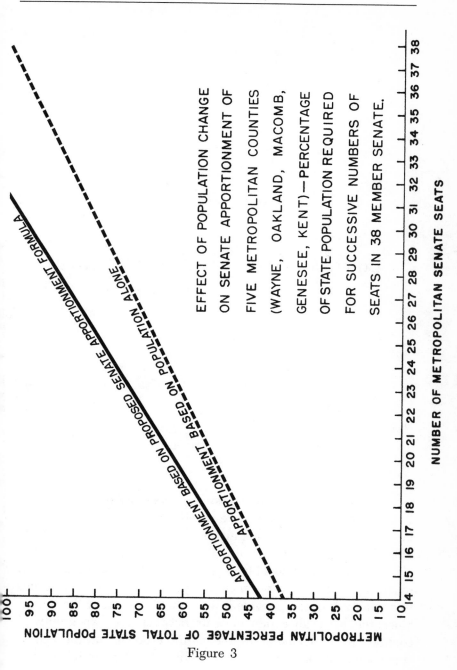

Figure 3

EFFECT OF POPULATION CHANGE ON SENATE APPORTIONMENT OF FIVE METROPOLITAN COUNTIES (WAYNE, OAKLAND, MACOMB, GENESEE, KENT)—PERCENTAGE OF STATE POPULATION REQUIRED FOR SUCCESSIVE NUMBERS OF SEATS IN 38 MEMBER SENATE.

NUMBER OF METROPOLITAN SENATE SEATS

METROPOLITAN PERCENTAGE OF TOTAL STATE POPULATION

APPORTIONMENT BASED ON PROPOSED SENATE APPORTIONMENT FORMULA

APPORTIONMENT BASED ON POPULATION ALONE

LONG-RANGE PROJECTIONS AND
SENATE APPORTIONMENT

WE HAVE NOTED THAT it is possible, given any projected population percentages to determine exactly the representation of the metropolitan counties. Population projections are notoriously difficult to make, and are not highly reliable. However, to get as clear a picture as is possible of the future effects of the proposed senate apportionment, we may apply existing population trends to an analysis of the possible future apportionment of the senate. Since the basic allocation of seats between the two groups of counties is fundamental to the entire rationale of the senate apportionment plan, we must consider the differential growth rate of the metropolitan and non-metropolitan areas in the state. During the decade between 1950 and 1960, the five largest counties increased their population by 25.9 percent. The remainder of the state increased by 18.8 percent, and the resultant of these differential rates of growth was a state-wide population increase of 22.8. In other words, while the metropolitan counties are growing at a significantly faster rate than the rest of the counties, the difference is not extremely large. Projecting these differential growth rates into the future, we find that the metropolitan counties will very slowly increase their total percentages of the state's population. The full computations are given in Table 13. There we see that the metropolitan percentage of the state's population would increase from 57.52 percent in 1960 to 58.93 percent in 1970, and ultimately to 63.07 percent in the year 2000. If senate seats were allocated purely on a population basis, the metropolitan counties would be entitled at present to 22 seats, and would still receive 22 seats after the 1970 census. This figure would go up to 23 after the 1980 census and would remain there until the year 2000 when it would increase to 24. Under the proposed apportionment, we have noted that the metropolitan counties would be entitled to 18 seats. Assuming the projected growth rate, the number of metropolitan seats would not change in 1970, but in 1980 would go to 19 and remain there until the year 2000 when it would increase to 20. In the same table, we have tabulated the indices of representation for each decennial year from the present until the year 2000. In none of the projections would the metropolitan counties fall below 80.4 percent of their full population entitlement. During the same period from the present to 2000, the indices of representation for the non-metropolitan counties will also fluctuate only slightly from a low of 123.9 in the initial apportionment to a high of 130.6 in the year 1990.

Table 13

EFFECTS OF PROJECTED POPULATION ON THE
APPORTIONMENT OF SENATE SEATS, 1960-2000*

Year	Population	State			Five metropolitan counties				Non-metropolitan counties			
		Senate seats	Ave. pop. per seat	Vote value index	Senate seats	Pct. of state pop.	Ave. pop. per seat	Vote value index	Senate seats	Pct. of state pop.	Ave. pop. per seat	Vote value index
1960	7,823,194	38	205,874	100.0	18	57.52	249,992	82.4	20	42.48	166,167	123.9
1970	9,613,445	38	252,985	100.0	18	58.93	314,740	80.4	20	41.07	197,406	128.2
1980	11,823,011	38	311,131	100.0	19	60.33	375,402	82.9	19	39.67	246,861	126.0
1990	14,552,155	38	382,951	100.0	19	61.71	472,631	81.0	19	38.29	293,271	130.6
2000	17,925,540	38	471,724	100.0	20	63.07	565,291	83.4	18	36.93	367,762	128.3

* This table is based on a straight line projection of 1950-60 population changes, and is not intended as an actual prediction of future state populations, but as an illustration of the effects of large-scale population changes on senate apportionment.

REPRESENTATION OF
OCCUPATIONAL GROUPS

ALTHOUGH THE DIRECT legislative representation of occupational groups is contrary to the American tradition of geographic districts, it is not unusual to hear allegations that an apportionment system favors or discriminates against certain occupational categories. An apportionment which greatly overrepresents rural areas at the expense of metropolitan cities obviously favors farmers and discriminates against industrial workers. Occupational categories are not evenly distributed throughout the area of a state. Farmers are as scarce in Detroit as automobile workers in rural Otsego County.

It is possible to arrive at a reasonably close measurement of the representation of occupation groups in a given apportionment by applying the same indices of representation we have used for other purposes. Tables 14 and 15 compare the weighted populations of ten major occupational groups in the senate and the house, respectively, for both the old and the new Michigan constitutions. In Table 14, we see that the old Michigan senate represented some groups rather closely in accordance with their actual numbers. The categories which tend to be rather evenly distributed throughout the state, will, as groups, tend to be evenly represented under almost any apportionment. This does not mean, of course, that all individuals in such groups are represented on a full population basis. Some are overrepresented and some are underrepresented. But the deviations tend to cancel each other out. However, other groups are most unevenly distributed, and no such cancelling out takes place. Farmers reside in rural areas, the rural areas were heavily overrepresented, and thus farmers as a group had roughly one and one-half times the weight in the old senate that would be warranted on the basis of population alone. The relatively small group of miners was even more heavily overrepresented, due to the concentration of this occupational category in the upper peninsula, where representation indices were extremely high. The most serious underrepresentation was at the expenses of industrial workers, who had about 90 percent of their population strength when their actual numbers were weighted by the senate apportionment. The proposed senate apportionment will not eliminate any of these major deviations, but it will sharply reduce all of them. As Table 15 indicates, discrepancies in the weighting of occupational groups was not nearly so serious in the old house, although again it was farmers and miners who were most seriously overrepresented, and industrial workers who were underrepresented. As in the senate, the new apportionment system will move all these categories closer to equality of representation. In the new house, no occupational category would be represented as less than 98 percent of its full strength, and the only significant overrepresen-

Table 14

REPRESENTATION OF OCCUPATIONAL CATEGORIES
1952 SENATE APPORTIONMENT AND APPORTIONMENT UNDER NEW CONSTITUTION

Occupation	1960 census	Weighted by 1952 apportionment	Index	Weighted by proposed apportionment	Index	Net change
1. Agriculture	93,662	145,489	155	115,250	123	−32
2. Mining	15,340	33,422	218	27,583	180	−38
3. Construction	125,562	134,129	107	129,910	104	− 3
4. Manufacturing	1,035,892	934,650	90	984,105	95	+ 5
5. Utilities	155,588	153,822	99	153,255	99	0
6. Trade	484,018	475,380	98	476,424	98	0
7. Finance	89,556	83,054	93	83,196	93	0
8. Business	195,226	190,279	98	190,879	98	0
9. Other services	347,601	356,329	103	341,199	98	− 5
10. Public admin.	94,837	92,546	98	93,946	99	+ 1

Table 15

REPRESENTATION OF OCCUPATIONAL CATEGORIES

1953 HOUSE APPORTIONMENT AND PROJECTED APPORTIONMENT UNDER NEW CONSTITUTION

Occupation	1960 census	Weighted by 1953 apportionment	Index	Weighted by proposed apportionment	Index	Net change
1. Agriculture	93,662	114,185	122	99,812	107	−15
2. Mining	15,340	23,980	156	16,939	110	−46
3. Construction	125,562	127,486	102	126,798	101	−1
4. Manufacturing	1,035,892	968,884	94	1,010,070	98	+4
5. Utilities	155,588	156,485	101	157,229	101	0
6. Trade	484,018	456,036	94	484,761	100	+6
7. Finance	89,556	86,566	98	87,739	98	0
8. Business	195,226	195,859	100	195,036	100	0
9. Other services	347,601	344,179	99	342,767	99	0
10. Public admin.	94,837	96,812	102	94,252	99	−3

tation, again of farmers and miners, would be relatively quite small.

Since manufacturing employees make up by far the largest single occupational category, and since there are many different kinds of manufacturing employees, not evenly distributed throughout the state, it is also useful to examine separately the representation of different kinds of manufacturing employees. In Tables 16 and 17, the data for the senate and house are presented. As might be expected, the concentration of heavy industry, and especially of the automotive industry, in the southeastern metropolitan region of the state, tended to produce a very serious underrepresentation of these groups in the old senate. The old apportionment had its most serious effects on the "Motor Vehicle and Motor Vehicle Equipment" workers—that is, on persons employed in the auto plants. Under the new senate apportionment system, these workers, as well as those in other underrepresented groups improve their situation considerably in the new senate apportionment, where no manufacturing category is below 90 percent of its full population strength. However, the automotive industry workers still have the lowest index number (90), and remain in last place, although they make the biggest percentage gain of any manufacturing category. Table 17 shows that in the new house no manufacturing category will be significantly overrepresented or underrepresented, with the lowest index being 98, and the highest 102. Again, this represents a sharp movement toward equality of representation compared to the last apportionment under the old constitution, where the indices of manufacturing categories ranged from 89 to 117.

The overall picture presented by this occupational analysis is basically very similar to that we have found in other types of analysis: the apportionments which will take place under the new constitution will move very definitely in the direction of population as the major criterion of representation, and in the house a very accurate reflection of population will be obtained. While the senate moves in the same direction, it will continue to give

Table 16

REPRESENTATION OF MANUFACTURING CATEGORIES

1953 SENATE APPORTIONMENT AND PROJECTED APPORTIONMENT UNDER NEW CONSTITUTION

	1960 census	Weighted by 1953 apportionment	Index	Weighted by proposed apportionment	Index	Net change
1. Furniture, lumber, and wood products	34,339	49,353	144	38,798	113	−31
2. Primary metal industries	71,670	68,099	95	65,667	92	− 3
3. Fabric'd metal industries	91,779	81,718	89	85,372	93	+ 4
4. Machinery, except electrical	147,059	132,113	90	137,921	94	+ 4
5. Electrical machinery, equipment, and supplies	31,695	35,051	111	31,754	100	−11
6. Motor vehicle and motor vehicle equip.	377,163	267,695	71	338,057	90	+19
7. Transportation equip., excluding motor vehicle	19,281	23,640	123	20,654	107	−16
8. Other durable goods	45,302	50,558	112	45,332	100	−12
9. Food and kindred products	62,382	66,614	107	61,115	98	− 9
10. Textile mill products	3,553	3,486	98	3,368	95	− 3
11. Apparel and other fabric'd textile prod.	8,582	10,850	126	9,478	110	−26
12. Printing, publishing, and allied products	45,742	40,910	89	42,750	94	+ 5
13. Chemical and allied prod.	40,909	41,593	102	42,304	103	+ 1
14. Other non-durable goods	56,346	62,929	112	58,263	103	− 9

Table 17

REPRESENTATION OF MANUFACTURING CATEGORIES

1953 HOUSE APPORTIONMENT AND APPORTIONMENT UNDER NEW CONSTITUTION

	1960 census	Weighted by 1953 apportionment	Index	Weighted by proposed apportionment	Index	Net change
1. Furniture, lumber, and wood products	34,339	40,012	117	33,801	98	−19
2. Primary metal industries	71,670	70,505	98	72,845	102	+ 4
3. Fabric'd metal industries	91,779	85,317	93	91,283	100	+ 7
4. Machinery, except electrical	147,059	138,301	94	145,187	99	+ 5
5. Electrical machinery, equipment, and supplies	31,695	31,132	98	30,961	98	0
6. Motor vehicle and motor vehicle equip.	377,163	336,300	89	369,563	98	+11
7. Transportation equip., excluding motor vehicle	19,281	20,134	104	19,808	103	− 1
8. Other durable goods	45,302	44,664	99	45,042	99	0
9. Food and kindred products	62,382	63,787	102	63,099	101	− 1
10. Textile mill products	3,553	3,372	95	3,597	100	+ 5
11. Apparel and other fabric'd textile prod.	8,582	9,660	113	8,911	104	− 9
12. Printing, publishing, and allied products	45,742	43,695	96	45,350	99	+ 3
13. Chemical and allied prod.	40,909	44,371	109	41,622	102	− 7
14. Other non-durable goods	56,346	56,242	100	55,228	98	− 2

greater weight to inhabitants of rural and sparsely populated areas than their numbers alone would warrant. It is also pertinent to note that the only occupational groups which are significantly overrepresented in either house (farmers and miners) are among the smallest groups. Even when weighted by the advantages given them by the senate apportionment, they make up only a small proportion of the electorate.

THE POLITICS OF REAPPORTIONMENT
IN MICHIGAN

THE FOREGOING ANALYSIS of the new apportionment provisions should make it clear that even using the "one man, one vote" in the representation criterion, the new Michigan apportionment undoubtedly compares favorably with the legislative apportionment system of any other state in the union. It is probable that urban groups in many other states who are seeking an improvement in their legislative apportionment systems would welcome as a considerable triumph the adoption in their respective states of an apportionment system as favorable from their point of view as would be the new Michigan system. Yet, it is a fact that the new constitution has encountered very heavy and very bitter opposition. The new apportionment system has been attacked in the most vigorous terms by representatives of the Democratic party, of organized labor, and of other urban-based groups and organizations.[1]

The proposed constitution therefore became deeply embroiled in partisan politics. In the gubernatorial campaign of 1962, the incumbent Democratic governor, John B. Swainson, opposed the proposed constitution, while the Republican challenger, George Romney, supported it. Subsequently, the respective spring conventions of the two political parties in 1963 took correspondingly opposite stands on the proposed document. A leading figure in the Democratic opposition to the proposed constitution was John C. Mackie, the Democratic highway commissioner. Mackie, as chairman of The Citizens' Committee to Defend Michigan's Constitution, alleged that the people have been "short-changed" by the apportionment provisions in the new constitution. Mackie's committee issued a campaign brochure containing the following description of the apportionment provisions:

> The historic American principle that each citizen is entitled to fair representation in the legislature is flouted in the proposed constitution. Residents who have the greatest need for services and pay more in taxes are denied an honest voice in their state government.
>
> Senate Districts would be formed in violation of an opinion by Michigan's Attorney General and a ruling by the majority of the Michigan State Supreme Court.
>
> (Both the ruling and the opinion were based upon the "equal protection" clause of the United States Constitution as interpreted by the United States Supreme Court.)

---

[1] It should also be noted, however, that some opposition to the proposed apportionment has come from rural groups, such as the Michigan Grange, as well as from the Michigan Township Association. These groups object to the proposed apportionment as being too generous to the urban areas.

Instead of throwing out bad apportionment, the proposed document tries to make legal that which no single state can make legal.

Michigan has been carved up to deliberately favor one political party over another in the face of a United States Supreme Court ruling that no state legislature can form districts discriminating against groups or individuals.[2]

This statement, enunciates the strong feeling of many Michigan Democrats that the new apportionment system is rigged against their party. The controversy over apportionment in Michigan cannot be separated from the whole fabric of Michigan politics in recent years.

There is probably no state in the union where state politics have been more polarized between an urban-liberal-labor coalition on the one hand and an out-state-rural-business coalition on the other. The division between the parties has been a very close one, which in itself would tend to exacerbate the bitterness of partisan controversy. In addition to the closeness of party competition, however, the partisan battle in Michigan is a highly sectional one. The political controversies in the state have tended in recent years to cast themselves into a struggle between the Detroit metropolitan area and the upper peninsula, on the one hand, and the rest of the state on the other.

Close party competition is a relatively recent phenomenon in the State of Michigan. For most of its history, Michigan has been a one-party state. In the early days of the state's history, the Democratic party was virtually unchallenged. The Whig party usually furnished only feeble opposition, winning only one of the ten gubernatorial elections they contested against the Democrats. (The only Whig victory occurred in 1839 when William Woodbridge won a narrow victory over his Democratic opponent.) The controversy over slavery, however, very nearly

---

[2] Citizens' Committee to Defend Michigan's Constitution, "Here's How the Proposed Michigan Constitution Hurts You!" (Campaign brochure, 1962).

killed the Democratic party in Michigan. In 1854, the Republican party was founded in Michigan, and overnight became the majority party there. Its first state ticket was nominated and elected in 1854, and from then until 1932 only three Democrats were able to win the governorship.[3]

The long years of Republican supremacy came to an end in 1932. In that year of great political upheaval throughout the United States, the Democratic candidate for governor of Michigan, William A. Comstock, was elected the first Democratic governor since Woodbridge Ferris left office at the close of 1916. Many of the Republicans who had crossed party lines to help elect Comstock in 1932 returned to the Republican fold in 1934, and it appeared for a time that Michigan would return to its traditional Republicanism. In the 1930's the Democrats were able to win the governorship only on the coat-tails of Franklin D. Roosevelt. The Republican gubernatorial candidates were successful in 1934 and in 1938, while in 1936 Democrat Frank Murphy, later Attorney General of the United States and Justice of the United States Supreme Court, was elected for a two-year term. Murphy was defeated for re-election in 1938, but in 1940, the Democrats were again successful with Murray Van Wagoner as their candidate. Van Wagoner was defeated for re-election in 1942 by Republican Harry Kelly, who was re-elected in 1944. In 1946 the nation-wide Republican landslide was reflected in Michigan by the one-sided victory of Kim Sigler. While these Republican electoral successes seemed on the surface to have reinstated the GOP as the majority party in the state, the electoral foundations of Michigan politics were shifting steadily in the direction of the Democratic party. The increasing concentration of the state's population in the southeast corner of the state, and particularly in the Detroit metropolitan area, was favorable to the Democrats. So also was the pattern of in-

---

[3] The successful Democrats were Josiah Begole, in 1882, who was the fusionist candidate of the Democratic and Greenback parties; Edwin B. Winans, in 1890; and Woodbridge N. Ferris, who was elected in 1912 and again in 1914 as a result of the Bull Moose split in the Republican party.

migration, in which Negro and white migrants from the southern states came into Michigan in large numbers during the 1930's and 1940's.

The basic ingredients for a Democratic resurgence were clearly present in Michigan by 1948. Prior to this time, however, the party had been greatly handicapped by a lack of effective leadership and by an almost non-existent state organization. In 1948 these defects were remedied in a dramatic fashion. In that year an effective political coalition was formed between liberal and labor elements in the state. The outstanding leaders of this coalition were G. Mennen Williams, later governor of the state, and subsequently Assistant Secretary of State of the United States, and Neil Staebler, who has served variously as a Democratic state chairman, Democratic national committeeman, and since the 1962 elections, as congressman-at-large. The Williams-Staebler leadership was able to mobilize the latent strength of the Democratic party in Michigan and lead it to an unprecedented series of political victories. No Michigan governor had ever been elected to more than three two-year terms, but Williams was elected to six consecutive terms, and finally retired undefeated in 1960. In the early years of his tenure as governor, Williams was far stronger than his own party, and in 1950 and again in 1952 was the only Democrat elected to state office. However, the effectiveness of the Democratic party organization was making itself felt, and by 1954 the Democrats were able to elect their entire state ticket. From that time until the present, no Republican has been elected to any major partisan office in the State of Michigan except George Romney in 1962. Even the very popular Mr. Romney had a difficult time in winning election, and the remainder of the state Republican ticket lost.

Democratic success was not complete, however. Not once during the six terms served by G. Mennan Williams and the single term of John B. Swainson did the Democrats control either house of the Michigan state legislature. The Republicans were able to hold a rather narrow margin in the house, except for the two years following the 1958 election when there was a 55-55 tie in house party membership, while in the senate the Republicans consistently maintained a heavy majority. The Democratic governor and the Republican legislature found themselves at loggerheads on most important issues of public policy. Their differences culminated in the bitter recriminations surrounding the fiscal crisis of 1959.

The inability of the Democrats to control the legislature was all the more bitter to them because the division of the total vote for the members of the legislature was close throughout this period. In several elections, the Democrats had a clear majority of all votes cast for senators and for members of the house of representatives.

Under these circumstances, it is not surprising that the doctrine has developed within the ranks of the Democratic party and its allies that the apportionment system in use in the legislature should be evaluated on the basis of whether or not it tends to produce a reasonably close correlation between the total statewide party percentage of the vote and the percentage of the number of seats won by the party. This doctrine was clearly enunciated on several occasions by Democratic delegates to the Constitutional Convention. For example, in the minority report of the Democratic members of the Committee on Legislative Organization (which was responsible for the apportionment provisions), the following statement appears:

> In the past ten years, ten legislative bodies have been elected in Michigan. On the basis of the popular vote for legislators, five of these bodies should have been Republican and five Democratic. In fact, all ten were Republican. Thus, (a) the legislature is not responsive to public opinion, and (b) it is biased against Democratic voters and in favor of Republican voters.[4]

It is certainly true that neither under the constitution of 1908 nor under the new constitution is the Democratic party likely to

---

[4] *Journal*, February 5, 1962, p. 545.

achieve a percentage of seats in the senate approximating its percentage of the total state-wide vote for senator. In recent years, the Democrats have been able to elect either 11 or 12 members of the 34-member senate, although their percentage of the total vote has always been close to 50 and has sometimes been substantially above a majority. Under the possible apportionment outlined in this study, it seems most unlikely that given a similar distribution of the vote, the Democratic party would be able to win more than 17 of the 38 seats. The question remains whether this discrepancy between the total percentage of the vote and the total number of seats won, is due primarily to the apportionment system as such, and whether the differences existing are evidence of any invidious discrimination against the Democratic party.

The basic political problem of the Democratic party in Michigan is graphically illustrated in Figure 4, in which the counties casting a Democratic majority for state senator in 1960 are shaded. Of the 83 counties in the state, only 14 returned Democratic majorities for state senator. An almost identical picture is seen in Figure 5, which shows the counties which voted Democratic for state representative in 1960. The only differences between the two maps are in three counties. Bay County, which was Democratic in the senate election, did not cast a majority for Democratic house candidates, but Mason and Lake Counties which were Republican for senator, were Democratic in the house elections. Thus, there were 15 counties which favored the Democratic candidates in the 1960 election of members of the house of representatives. The narrow distribution of Democratic party strength is quite evident when it is observed that only in the Detroit-Flint area, and in the western upper peninsula were the Democrats successful in commanding a majority for their candidates in both houses of the legislature. The remainder of the state was solidly Republican. Because of their overwhelming strength in the southeastern corner of the state, the Democrats have been able in the past to command a majority in most state-wide elections.

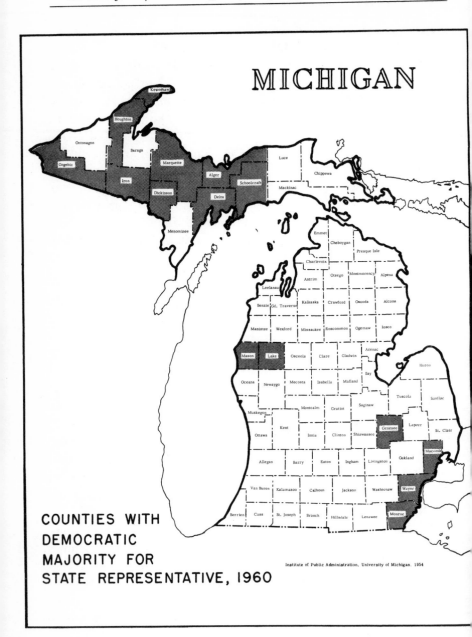

Figure 4

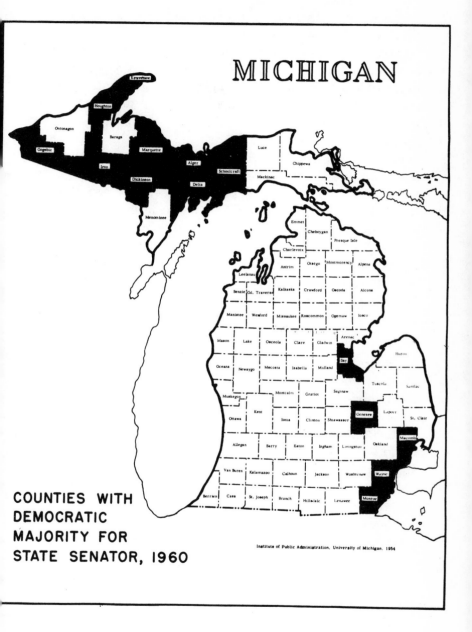

COUNTIES WITH
DEMOCRATIC
MAJORITY FOR
STATE SENATOR, 1960

Institute of Public Administration, University of Michigan, 1954

Figure 5

The marked discrepancy between sweeping Democratic success in the state-wide elections, and their consistent failure in legislative elections require some investigation in order to determine the extent to which distribution of their party's vote is responsible for the election results. It is also important to note the impact of the proposed apportionment system, again as opposed to the effects of the distribution of party strength. There are several ways in which this can be done. In Table 18, we have computed the comparison of actual seats to the full population entitlement of counties which voted Democratic in senatorial elections in 1960, and similar data for the apportionment which will take place under the new constitution. It will be noted that under the old constitution the Democratic party was seriously underrepresented, at least in those counties which have recently tended to vote Democratic in senatorial elections. While on a straight population basis, the 14 Democratic counties would be entitled to 16.80 seats, they have actually had only 12.21 seats, and thus have 4.59 seats less than a full population entitlement or, in other words, a representation index of 73.

Under the new constitution, however, the situation of these counties would improve markedly. In the 38-seat senate, the 14 counties would be entitled to 18.77 seats on a straight population basis, and will actually receive 17.20 under the illustrative apportionment we have been discussing. Any apportionment that could be made by the apportionment commission would not vary significantly from this figure. Thus, under the new constitution, the Democratic counties would have a representation of 92 percent of their full population entitlement. This is still a substantial disadvantage for the Democratic party, but it is far from their hopeless underrepresentation in the old senate.

Instead of losing the equivalent of 4.59 seats, the Democratic counties under the new system would be within 1.57 seats of their full entitlement on a population basis. An oddity of some interest is that under the new constitution 13 of the 14 Democratic counties would be overrepresented in the senate apportion-

Table 18

APPORTIONMENT OF SENATE SEATS TO DEMOCRATIC
COUNTIES COMPARED TO PURE POPULATION
APPORTIONMENT, 1908 AND 1962 CONSTITUTIONS*

Counties	Pct. of state pop., 1960	1908 Constitution (34 Seats)			1962 Constitution (38 Seats)		
		Actual apportion-ment-seats	Population entitle-ment-seats	Over- or underrep. seats	Actual apportion-ment-seats	Population entitle-ment-seats	Over- or underrep. seats
Alger	0.12	0.07	0.04	+0.03	0.08	0.05	+0.03
Bay	1.37	0.55	0.47	+0.08	0.58	0.52	+0.06
Delta	0.44	0.27	0.15	+0.12	0.36	0.17	+0.19
Dickinson	0.30	0.20	0.10	+0.10	0.21	0.11	+0.10
Genesee	4.78	1.00	1.62	−0.62	2.00	1.82	+0.18
Gogebic	0.31	0.20	0.11	+0.09	0.25	0.12	+0.13
Houghton	0.46	0.64	0.16	+0.48	0.37	0.17	+0.20
Iron	0.22	0.14	0.07	+0.07	0.18	0.08	+0.10
Keweenaw	0.03	0.04	0.01	+0.03	0.02	0.01	+0.01
Macomb	5.19	1.00	1.76	−0.76	2.00	1.97	+0.03
Marquette	0.72	0.46	0.24	+0.22	0.49	0.27	+0.22
Monroe	1.29	0.57	0.44	+0.13	0.57	0.49	+0.08
Schoolcraft	0.11	0.07	0.04	+0.03	0.09	0.04	+0.05
Wayne	34.08	7.00	11.59	−4.59	10.00	12.95	−2.95
Totals	49.42	12.21	16.80	−4.59	17.20	18.77	−1.57
Representation Index =		73		−4.59	92		−1.57

* Actual apportionment of seats to counties sharing a seat with one or more counties is calculated by dividing county population by district population. Population entitlement is calculated by multiplying county percentage of state population by the total number of senate seats (34 or 38). Democratic counties are those which cast a majority of votes for Democratic candidates for state senator in 1960.

ment, with Wayne County being the only underrepresented Democratic county. Of course, the underrepresentation of Wayne County is much greater than the combined overrepresentation of the other Democratic counties. Similar computations for the house of representatives are contained in Table 19. As we have observed before, the house of representatives was not far from a population base to begin with, and moved somewhat closer to straight population in the new constitution. The result is that the representation index of the Democratic counties in the house has increased from 97 to 98. Moreover, the Democratic counties under the new constitution would be less than half a seat short of their full population entitlement of 53.24 seats.

Despite the fact that the proposed apportionment system will not discriminate seriously against the Democratic counties, it is nevertheless true that given the present geographical distribution of Democratic party strength, it is most unlikely that the Democrats could capture the senate under the new constitution. In Table 20, we have applied the 1960 senatorial vote to the projected senatorial districts. No attempt has been made to draw district boundary lines within the counties entitled to more than one senate seat, and it cannot be predicted with certainty what the political complexion of such districts will be. Whether the Democrats will be able to retain their present monopoly of Wayne County senate seats is uncertain. If they do, this will give the Democrats a base from which to operate in building toward a senate majority. The neighboring county of Macomb is almost as heavily Democratic as Wayne County, and will gain an additional seat. Both the Macomb districts will very likely be Democratic. Genesee County is one of the most marginal counties in the state, but usually returns a small Democratic majority. In 1960, the Democratic candidate for the single senate seat from that county received 51.2 percent of the two-party vote. Under the new constitution, Genessee would be entitled to a second seat. Since the city of Flint is more heavily Democratic than the rest of the county, it is probable that one of the districts

Table 19

APPORTIONMENT OF HOUSE SEATS TO DEMOCRATIC COUNTIES
COMPARED TO PURE POPULATION APPORTIONMENT,
1908 AND 1962 CONSTITUTIONS*

County	Pct. of state pop. (seats)	Population entitlement (seats)	1952 apportionment (seats)	Over- or underrep. (seats)	1963 apportionment (seats)	Over- or underrep. (seats)
Alger	0.12	0.13	0.22	+0.09	0.14	+0.01
Delta	0.44	0.48	1.00	+0.52	0.58	+0.10
Dickinson	0.30	0.33	0.49	+0.16	0.37	+0.04
Genesee	4.78	5.26	4.00	−1.26	5.00	−0.26
Gogebic	0.31	0.34	0.70	+0.36	0.37	+0.03
Houghton	0.46	0.51	0.94	+0.43	0.64	+0.13
Iron	0.22	0.24	0.40	+0.16	0.26	+0.02
Keweenaw	0.03	0.03	0.06	+0.03	0.04	+0.01
Lake	0.07	0.08	0.13	+0.05	0.09	+0.01
Macomb	5.19	5.71	3.00	−2.71	6.00	+0.29
Marquette	0.72	0.79	1.00	+0.21	0.86	+0.07
Mason	0.28	0.31	0.54	+0.23	0.35	+0.04
Monroe	1.29	1.42	1.00	−0.42	1.00	−0.42
Schoolcraft	0.11	0.12	0.21	+0.09	0.15	+0.03
Wayne	34.08	37.49	38.00	+0.51	37.00	−0.49
Total	48.40	53.24	51.69	−1.55	52.85	−0.39
Index of Representation			97		98	

* See footnote to Table 18 for explanation of computations. Democratic counties are those casting a majority of their votes for Democratic house candidates in 1960.

Table 20

1960 SENATORIAL VOTE BY PROBABLE NEW SENATE DISTRICTS

Metropolitan districts	Democratic vote	Republican vote	Total	Democratic percentage
1-5, 17, 18, 20, 21, 38 (Wayne)	750,701	364,305	1,115,306	67.3
11, 35 (Macomb)	104,474	56,364	160,838	65.0
13, 36 (Genesee)	73,117	69,665	142,782	51.2
12, 15, 37 (Oakland)	132,361	156,295	288,656	45.6
16 (Kent)	61,784	90,995	152,779	40.4
Non-metropolitan districts				
6*	30,397	51,384	81,781	37.2
7*	29,043	44,308	77,351	37.5
8	24,771	50,052	74,823	33.1
9*	31,818	35,547	67,355	47.2
10*	26,123	41,786	67,909	38.5
14*	39,708	60,653	100,361	39.7
19*	29,861	36,990	66,851	44.7
22	40,751	53,244	93,998	43.4
23	41,586	60,878	102,464	40.6
24	32,322	41,729	74,051	43.6
25	16,954	33,784	50,738	33.4
26	18,088	32,196	50,284	36.0
27	16,880	34,294	51,174	33.0
28	21,313	38,347	59,660	35.7
29	14,253	20,627	34,880	40.9
30	17,988	18,067	36,055	49.9
31	25,190	21,418	46,608	54.0
32	24,509	21,205	45,714	53.6
33*	25,133	37,639	62,772	40.0
34	25,416	46,881	72,297	35.2

* Indicates districts existing under old constitution, and unchanged.

to be created (the one including Flint) will remain Democratic, but the other will probably be a normally Republican district. Oakland County, which, until the new constitution, has been the most underrepresented county in the state, has had a relatively small but reliable Republican majority. Its single seat has been held by Republicans ever since it was created in 1953.

The distribution of Democratic strength in Oakland County is a miniature version of the party's geographical distribution of strength in the state. That is, Democratic strength is heavily concentrated in a relatively small part of the county. The likely effect of this concentration of population is that when the county is divided into three senate districts, one of the districts will be Democratic and the other two Republican. Thus, given the pattern of party voting that has prevailed in recent years, the Democratic party could expect to pick up no more than 14 seats from the five largest counties, since the only remaining county in this group is Kent, which appears to be out of reach for the Democrats.

To add to these 14 seats from the Detroit-Flint area, the Democrats can expect to win the two western districts (i.e., the 31st and 32d) in the upper peninsula. In addition, the remaining upper peninsula district (the 30th), will be the most marginal of all the projected districts, and could well go Democratic. In the 1960 election, this projected district was Republican by 29 votes. Thus, the Democrats would end the election with approximately 17 of the 38 seats, provided they can retain control of all the Wayne County districts. As we have observed, the Democrats, in the 1960 election, received 52.1 percent of all the senatorial votes cast in the state. Under the projected apportionment they would receive 44.7 percent of the seats. Under the actual apportionment at the time of the 1960 election, with the identical distribution of votes, the Democrats received 12 of the 34 seats or 35.3 percent of the total. Thus, the apportionment provisions of the new constitution should substantially narrow the gap between the total party percentage and the percentage of seats won.

The remaining difference between these percentages, however, is primarily a product not of the apportionment system but of the geographical distribution of party strength. This was indicated by our previous analysis of the representation of Democratic counties in the senate and house, but further evidence may be obtained by comparing the outcome of an election using districts based entirely on population with the same distribution of party votes which were obtained in 1960. To facilitate this analysis, we have constructed an apportionment of a 38-seat senate, with district populations as nearly equal as possible, following county lines. This apportionment is plotted on the map in Figure 6, and population data and indices of representation are presented in Table 21. This apportionment shows the Michigan Senate approximately as it would be if the convention

Table 21

MODEL STRAIGHT POPULATION APPORTIONMENT
38-MEMBER SENATE*

Districts	Pop. per seat	Index
1-13	205,099	100
14-16	230,086	89
17, 18	202,902	101
19, 20	187,156	110
21, 22	181,594	113
23	178,909	115
24	210,673	98
25	201,639	102
26	211,296	97
27	188,542	109
28	212,044	97
29	235,192	88
30	188,186	109
31	207,354	99
32	234,057	88
33	215,447	96
34	214,469	96
35	211,701	97
36	199,983	103
37	211,726	97
38	202,116	102

* See Figure 6

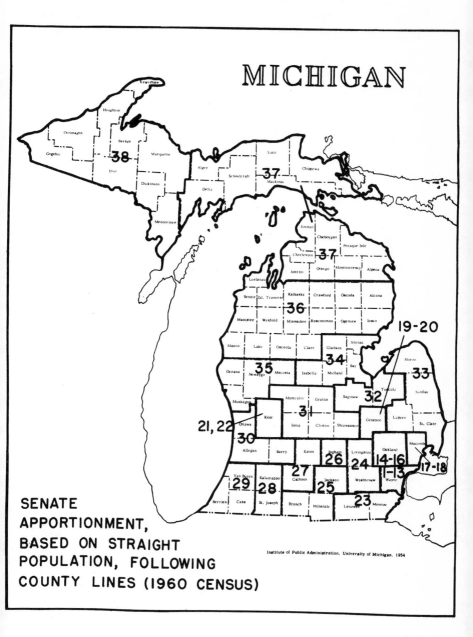

MICHIGAN

SENATE
APPORTIONMENT,
BASED ON STRAIGHT
POPULATION, FOLLOWING
COUNTY LINES (1960 CENSUS)

Institute of Public Administration, University of Michigan, 1954

Figure 6

had decided to place both houses on a population basis. The range between the largest and the smallest districts is quite narrow. The largest district would be the 32d, including Saginaw and Tuscola Counties, with a population of 234,057, while the smallest district would be the 23d, including Lenewee and Monroe Counties with a population of 178,909. Thus the largest district would be only 1.3 times the population of the smallest district.

Table 22

1960 SENATORIAL VOTE BY STRAIGHT POPULATION DISTRICTS*

Metropolitan districts	Democratic vote	Republican vote	Total	Democratic percentage
1-13 (Wayne)	750,701	364,305	1,115,306	67.3
14-16 (Oakland)	132,361	156,295	288,656	45.6
17, 18 (Macomb)	104,474	56,364	160,838	65.0
19, 20 (Genesee)	73,117	69,665	142,782	51.2
21, 22 (Kent)	61,784	90,995	152,779	40.6
Non-metropolitan districts				
23	29,861	36,990	66,851	44.7
24	30,638	47,530	78,168	39.2
25	31,285	49,656	80,941	38.7
26	34,203	50,762	84,965	40.3
27	33,487	41,113	74,600	44.9
28	30,397	51,384	81,781	37.2
29	35,975	62,329	98,304	36.6
30	23,013	54,988	78,001	29.5
31	25,048	47,169	72,217	34.7
32	37,752	51,495	89,247	42.3
33	30,497	56,480	86,977	35.1
34	36,440	46,358	82,798	44.0
35	37,578	46,113	83,691	44.9
36	30,012	56,245	86,256	34.8
37	38,539	47,023	85,562	45.0
38	47,389	41,137	88,526	53.5

* See Figure 6

Of course, in order to achieve these results, some sacrifices must be made in dealing with other considerations usually involved in apportionment. While all of the districts are reasonably compact, one district (the 37th) is not contiguous by land, since it spans the straits of Mackinac.

Due to the population size of the upper peninsula, a straight population apportionment cannot be achieved unless a district is created which includes area in both peninsulas. In addition, this straight population apportionment necessarily changes the composition of existing districts which were not excessively far from a straight population ratio, but which could be improved upon if population is the only or at least the dominant consideration in all calculations.

What would be the political effects of this ideal population apportionment, as compared to the 80-20 plan? The five metropolitan counties would have four more seats than under the new constitution. Of these, Wayne would receive three additional seats, for a total of 13, while Kent County would qualify for a second seat. Macomb, Genesee, and Oakland Counties would have the same number of seats as under the new constitution. If the Democratic party were able to win all three of the additional Wayne County seats, it would make a substantial net gain. However, it should be remembered that as the number of seats in Wayne County increases, the less likely it is that the Democrats will capture all of them. It will be difficult enough for the Democrats to win all ten of the Wayne seats under the 80-20 plan, but much more difficult to win all 13 seats under a straight population apportionment. The Republican party polls approximately one-third of the total senatorial vote in Wayne County. Certainly the Republicans should win at least one of the 13 seats.

Since no change would be made in Macomb, Genesee, and Oakland Counties, the only remaining difference between the proposed apportionment and the straight population in the metropolitan counties would be the addition of a second seat in

Kent. This additional seat would be reliably Republican. Thus, instead of the 14 seats to be expected from the new constitution, the Democrats could win 16, or a maximum of 17, seats in the metropolitan counties. This net gain of two or possibly three seats, however, must be balanced by the effect of the changes on the out-state districts. The principal effect of moving to straight population is to take seats away from the upper peninsula and the northern lower peninsula and give them to Wayne and Kent Counties. As we have seen, the only real area of Democratic strength in the state outside the Detroit-Flint metropolitan area is in the upper peninsula. We have noted that of the three upper peninsula districts which would be provided under the convention's apportionment plan, two would be reliably Democratic and the third would be extremely marginal. The straight population apportionment, however, removes two of the upper peninsula districts, leaving only one district wholly within the upper peninsula. This district, comprising roughly the western half of the upper peninsula would continue to be a Democratic district. However, the combination district made up of the eastern upper peninsula and the northern lower peninsula would have a clear Republican majority. Thus, instead of having a certainty of two and an excellent possibility of three out-state senate seats, the Democratic party under straight population would be reduced to one such seat. In summary, then, it appears that the net political effect of straight population apportionment in the senate would be a Democratic gain of one or a maximum of two seats. Depending on how the additional Wayne seats are allocated, the Democrats might even win fewer seats under straight population than under the new formula. Table 23 compares the probable party distribution of the senate seats under the existing constitution, the new constitution, and the hypothetical straight population apportionment we have been discussing.

Under all three apportionments, given the 1960 distribution of party strength, the Republican party would control the senate,

Table 23

PROBABLE PARTY DISTRIBUTION OF SENATE SEATS, ASSUMING 1960
DISTRIBUTION OF PARTY VOTE FOR SENATE CANDIDATES

	1908 constitution (34 seats)		1962 constitution (38 seats)		Straight population apportionment (38 seats)	
	Dem.	Rep.	Dem.	Rep.	Dem.	Rep.
Wayne	7	0	10	0	12–13	0–1
Oakland	0	1	1	2	1	2
Macomb	1	0	2	0	2	0
Genesee	1	0	1	1	1	1
Kent	0	2	0	1	0	2
Upper peninsula	3	0	2–3	0–1	1	1/2
Remainder of state	0	19	0	17	0	14–1/2
Totals	12	22	16–17	21–22	17–18	20–21

although the Democrats would be markedly better off under either the 80-20 plan or a straight population system.

This suggests a more important question. Does the very uneven distribution of party strength in Michigan make a "constitutionally Republican" senate inevitable, given a system of single-member districts following county lines? If so, how can a majority, even a very sizable majority, of the state's voters make a meaningful choice between the policies and personnel of the two parties? If Democratic control of both houses of the legislature requires an impossibly large percentage of the total vote, and if there is a reasonably durable state-wide Democratic majority, a partisan deadlock between the governor and the legislature is likely to be a persistent feature of the political landscape. Both parties are weakened. The Democrats sink into frustration, unable ever to carry out their programs. The Republicans find it difficult to compete effectively in state-wide elections because their party comes to be perceived by most voters as the last bastion of a hostile and obstructionist minority. Something very like this has happened in Michigan since 1948. Despite their brilliant string of successes in state-wide elections, the Democrats never had the slightest hope of controlling the state senate, nor the Republicans the remotest fear of losing that control.

There are only two ways out of the dilemma. One would be the introduction of an entirely new system of representation designed specifically to translate state-wide votes directly into legislative seats in both houses. As we have seen, the "tote-board" plan advocated by the Democrats at the Constitutional Convention was designed for this purpose. Given the heavy Republican majority in the convention, there was never any chance that the plan would be accepted. But some such plan, or possibly some form of proportional representation could be introduced directly by the people through the constitutional initiative provisions found in both the old and the new Michigan constitutions. A sufficiently determined Democratic state-wide majority could introduce any sort of apportionment plan it might desire.

Realistically, however, there seems very little chance that such a thoroughgoing change in the representative system could succeed. It would face the strongest opposition, not only from Republicans but from many Democrats who would resist the introduction of any such radical new system. After all, it was as recently as 1952 that a heavy majority of Michigan voters rejected a much less sweeping change which would have kept the traditional system of geographic districts, and simply required relative population equality.

The remaining possibility is that, either under the 80-20 plan or under a conventional equal-population apportionment, the Democrats will be able to gain enough strength in a sufficient number of senate districts so that they will have a reasonable hope of controlling the legislature when they have a clear state-wide popular mandate. What would be the components of a possible Democratic majority under the 80-20 plan? If the Democrats can win all of the ten Wayne County seats, two more in Macomb County, one each in Oakland and Genesee Counties, and three in the upper peninsula, they would have 17 seats, and would be three seats away from a majority. The second seat in

Genesee County would be an obvious target, since the party division there is already close. Another possibility is that the further spread of the Detroit metropolitan area into previously Republican parts of Oakland County bring another seat into the Democratic column. Finally, the Calhoun-Branch County senate district was 47.2 percent Democratic in 1960, and is certainly not out of reach. If the Democrats carried all three of these districts, plus the 17 previously discussed, they would have a senate majority. As Table 24 indicates, the population contained in these districts is 55.1 percent of the total state population.

Under the model population apportionment discussed earlier, the Democrats would have to win all 13 of the seats that would be allotted to Wayne County. They would carry only one seat in the upper peninsula (the only district wholly within that area), and would still need to gain control of additional seats in Genesee and Oakland Counties, just as under the 80-20 plan. The Calhoun-Branch district would no longer exist. This hypothetical Demo-

Table 24

MINIMUM DEMOCRATIC SENATE MAJORITY, 80-20 PLAN

Districts	Democratic percentage 1960	Population
10 Wayne districts	67.3	2,666,297
2 Macomb districts	65.0	405,804
2 Genesee districts	51.2	374,313
2 Oakland districts	45.6	460,173
30th district (upper peninsula)	49.9	94,586
31st district (upper peninsula)	54.0	114,006
32d district (upper peninsula)	53.6	97,360
9th district (Calhoun-Branch)	47.2	152,449
Total population		4,334,901
Percentage of state population		55.41

cratic majority would include 52.51 percent of the state population in the counties involved. Although this is a slightly smaller percentage than that required for the minimum Democratic majority under the 80-20 plan, it is not clear that it would be easier for the Democrats to control a population-only senate. Everything would hinge on whether they were able to control all of the 13 Wayne districts. As noted earlier, the larger the number of districts in Wayne County, the harder it will be for the Democrats to win all of them.

In any event, we can say that while it would not be easy for the Democratic party to control the new senate, it would not be impossible by any means. It would not require a major social upheaval or a resettlement of Democrats from the Detroit area to the rural counties, as would have been the case under the old constitution.

Both under a population-based apportionment and under the 80-20 plan, the Democrats will need more than a simple majority of the total state vote in order to control the senate. Unless and until Democrats are more evenly distributed geographically, that will continue to be the case, so long as representation is based on single-member districts following county lines.

Table 25

MINIMUM DEMOCRATIC SENATE MAJORITY
STRAIGHT POPULATION APPORTIONMENT*

13 Wayne districts	67.3	2,666,297
2 Macomb districts	65.0	405,804
2 Genesee districts	51.2	374,313
2 Oakland districts	45.6	460,173
38th district (upper peninsula)	53.5	202,116
Total population		4,108,702
Percentage of state population		52.51

*See Figure 6

CONCLUSIONS

APPORTIONMENT SYSTEMS are constantly evaluated on two levels which should be clearly defined and kept separate, but which unfortunately tend to be blurred or merged together in political and judicial controversies.

The first of these levels has to do with the objectives of the system, and the philosophy or theory of representation which the system apparently articulates. The major contemporary question here is whether a state apportionment system must be based on population in both houses, in one house, or in neither. At the root of this question is one of the classic "grand problems" of politics and government: What should be the basis of representation? Should a system seek to represent individuals directly, or should it represent the individual as a member of a community? Are legislators the spokesmen of well-defined political and social groupings which ought to be respected and accorded consideration in apportionment actions? Or, on the other hand, should a legislative district be viewed only as an administrative device for insuring that each legislator will have the task of representing approximately the same number of individual citizens?

These are, in the deepest sense, philosophic questions, and none of them can be answered with a flat "yes" or "no" without reliance on a set of higher values. These higher values may be derived from the personal value system of an individual. They may also be derived from the philosophy of law and constitutional government which at any given time is being articulated and put into practice by the courts.

It has not been the purpose of this study to argue for or against the philosophic and legal bases of the contending arguments in the current apportionment controversy. Our concern has been with a second level of analysis and evaluation.

That second level has to do with the more practical problem of whether or not an apportionment system under examination appears to be successful in carrying out its basic philosophic, constitutional, and administrative goals, however they may be defined. In other words, does the apportionment system really do what it claims to do? Many systems adopt one set of norms in theory and quite another in practice. For example, many American state constitutions include apportionment provisions which require periodic reapportionment according to population. For various reasons, and especially for lack of any means of enforcing the constitutional mandate, these provisions have been highly ineffective. In Michigan, the mandate of the 1908 constitution regarding the decenniel reapportionment of both houses was never effective. In 1952, the so-called "balanced legislature" amendment attempted to compromise the difference between those who wished the constitutional mandates to be carried out fully, and those who wished the constitutional provisions to remain a dead letter. The "compromise" involved a guarantee of reapportionment in one house (accomplished by setting a time limit on reapportionment, and turning the job over to the State Board of Canvassers in the event of legislative inaction), in return for a complete freezing of senatorial districts.

Since 1952, Michigan has not been in violation of its own constitution, but since *Baker* v. *Carr* and *Scholle* v. *Hare* the question has been raised as to whether the doctrines and theories of apportionment articulated in the 1952 amendment do violence to the equal protection clause of the fourteenth amendment to the United States Constitution. The 1952 amendment is based on the idea that if one house of the legislature is reasonably close to population, the other need have no close relationship to population, and that there need be no provision whatever for reflecting population change of any magnitude.

Rightly or wrongly, most political leaders in Michigan, and most constitutional convention delegates seem to have interpreted the court decisions in *Baker* v. *Carr* and subsequent cases as dooming the frozen district system.

The Constitutional Convention was forced to make an implicit prediction about future rulings of the United States Supreme Court, and to shape the new constitution in such a way that if the predictions turn out to be correct, the apportionment system will be upheld. These implicit predictions can be summarized as follows:

1. The Court is likely to insist that one of the two houses of a state legislature be based closely on population, but that this insistence will not be so literal as to preclude the use of county lines and single-member districts, even though these devices will inevitably produce significant inequalities in the size of district populations.

2. The Court is not likely to insist on such a strict population standard in the other house, and will even permit very large deviations from average population size, so long as these deviations are based on a rational standard, uniformly applied, and so long as metropolitan population majorities are not grossly under-represented.

3. In determining the degree of latitude a state will be given in the apportionment of the second or non-straight population house, the Court will be influenced by considerations of practicality and judicial self-restraint. It will also be influenced by respect for the constitutional status of the states in the federal system, and will not attempt a total reconstruction of the representative systems of all 50 states. It will therefore tend to compare a challenged apportionment system to the systems in effect in other states. Specifically, in scrutinizing deviations from average population size and in evaluating the representation accorded to metropolitan areas, the Court is likely to pay considerable attention to how similarly situated persons in other states are treated by their apportionment systems. If, on such an examination, the challenged state appears to have one of the most defensible systems, the Court is not likely to overturn it.

4. The Court is likely to be concerned about the degree to which apportionment practice follows constitutional prescription. It will therefore be concerned with the question of effective remedies against malapportionment (i.e., apportionment contrary to the terms of the state constitution), and will tend not to intervene when effective remedies are available within the state.

These assumptions or predictions concerning emergent constitutional law themselves add up to a reasonably complete theory of state legislative apportionment. That theory is probably not quite the same as the personal preference or private philosophies of the majority of the convention delegates. Had it not been for the Baker and Scholle cases, the Michigan apportionment provisions would probably not be the same as those finally approved. Comparison of the pre-Baker apportionment plans being advanced by leaders of the majority Republican delegates with the final product seems to bear this out. However that may be, the plan finally adopted is the one that must be judged. To what extent is the Michigan plan successful in establishing the kind of apportionment system implied by the legal, theoretical, and practical considerations involved in the predictions discussed above?

1. The house apportionment under the new constitution will be, by any objective standards, one of the most nearly perfect approximations of straight population apportionment ever put into practice in the United States. Granting the acceptability of following county lines and using single-member districts (and no serious legal objection has been raised to these practices), the only flaw in the system is the residuum of the moiety clause first introduced in Michigan in 1850. The clause is greatly attenuated under the new constitution, and has only minor vestigial effects on the allocation of seats. But it clearly prevents the Michigan house apportionment from being a model of the equal population, single-member district system, following county lines. Even so, no existing state house of representatives will approach the status of a model apportionment system as closely as will the Michigan house apportionment plan.

2. The senate apportionment system is unlike that of any other state. Paradoxically, its strongest point is achieved at the cost of creating its greatest weakness. Its strength (always assuming the validity of its objectives) is that it makes provision for controlled overrepresentation of sparsely populated areas through a system that is automatic and uniform in its application, and which insures that the representation of metropolitan areas will always be at a considerably better level than has been customary in most states in recent years. Given the objective of creating one house in which the claims of local community are given special consideration, the plan seems far preferable to the usual practice of allowing apportionment authorities more or less unbridled freedom to discriminate heavily, freely, and even

capriciously against one or a few urban counties. Under this plan, the urban counties can never receive less than approximately 80 percent of their full population entitlement of seats. No inaction, chicanery, or gerrymandering is permitted to reduce the metropolitan counties' representation below that prescribed by the apportionment formula. Metropolitan senate seats are always allotted first, and the total number of metropolitan seats is allocated to the respective metropolitan counties by the impersonal and mathematical device of equal proportions.

Unfortunately, this precision and certainty is achieved by introducing into the apportionment formula the concept of direct representation of land area. It is literally true, as critics of the plan have pointed out, that 19.05 acres of land are given precisely the same weight in calculating the apportionment factors as one person. As population increases and land area remains constant, the acres per people equation will find a smaller number of acres required to equal one inhabitant. Such an equation, whatever its practical consequences, is certain to arouse repugnance even among some of those who find the final product of the whole system fair and reasonable. Opponents of the plan charge that it flies in the face of the most fundamental value of Western democracy: that of the supreme worth of the individual human person. It is said that the plan makes people equivalent to dirt.

Of course, area as such has no interests and cannot be represented. Only people can be represented, and only people are represented by the Michigan senate plan. The basic question is not whether land and people can both be represented, but whether people can be classified according to the density or sparsity of population in the areas in which they happen to reside. As we have demonstrated in this study, the senate plan is in reality a weighted population plan, and it would have been possible to rewrite the constitutional language so that exactly the same results could have been produced without any mention of land area components. We have seen that it is possible to draw up a population table showing precisely what percentage of total state population is necessary for a given number of senate seats in the metropolitan and in the non-metropolitan counties. Future changes in senate apportionments will be made for one purpose only: to reflect changes in population.

It might also be noted that any system of apportionment other than a perfect population apportionment in which every district has precisely the same population as all other districts contains a non-population or area component. Our comparative analysis makes it clear that in most states area is weighted more heavily than it would be under the Michigan plan, and it would not be very difficult to construct an acres per people equation for either house of any other state legislature. In all but a few cases, the equation would show that people are more highly valued under the Michigan system (relative to acres) than in the other states.

This would especially be true of highly urbanized states which have much less area than Michigan, but which despite their compactness and lack of sparsely populated areas have still found it desirable, for whatever reason, to allow wide deviations in the population size of legislative districts.[1] But, critics of apportion-

---

[1] To give only one example of how the people per acres equation could be derived for another state, let us look at the State of New Jersey. This is the most highly urbanized state in the union. It has 21 counties, ranging in population from 923,545 in Essex County, to 49,255 in Sussex County. Under New Jersey's "federal" plan of apportionment, each of the 21 counties has one state senator. There is no senate reapportionment provision in the state constitution. We can say, therefore, that the 20 counties which have populations smaller than that of Essex are granted representation on a non-population basis. The area of Sussex County, New Jersey, is granted recognition in the apportionment of the New Jersey senate just as surely as the area of Keweenaw County, Michigan, is weighted by the 80-20 plan. If the 20 New Jersey counties smaller in population than Essex all had the same population as that county (923,545), all senate districts would, of course, be identical in population. The 20 counties would have a combined population of 18,470,900. In fact, however, their population is only 5,143,237, so they are 13,327,663 people short of the number necessary to equalize the populations of all senate districts. In effect, then, the New Jersey system creates 13,327,663 artificial people, who must be equated with the 4,730,880 acres of land in the 20 counties. Dividing the land area by the synthetic population figure, we find that in

ment systems in those states cannot point to any specific constitutional ratio between population and area weightings, and usually do not charge that the system equates people with dirt in a precise way.

That the Michigan plan leaves itself wide open to such attacks must be admitted, and must be marked down as a major weakness of the plan. But unless all state legislative bodies are apportioned purely on population, anyone can calculate an acres per people equation for any of them as soon as he knows the populations of the districts and the number of acres in each. The question, therefore, is whether the inclusion in the new Michigan constitution of a mathematical ratio between area and population weightings is objectionable or unconstitutional simply because of the words themselves and without regard to their effect—since the same effect is inevitable once it is conceded that any basis other than population alone is acceptable in an apportionment system.

3. The various rank orderings of the states included in this study demonstrate clearly that on almost any measurement of equitability of representation likely to be applied to state legislative bodies, the Michigan senate would appear near the top of any listing of similar bodies in the various states. One is forced to the conclusion that if the courts should overturn the Michigan system, they will be hard pressed to avoid a complete reconstruction of state legislative representation systems.

4. There can be little doubt that the constitution seeks to provide foolproof guarantees that its provisions regarding apportionment will be scrupulously and completely carried out at all times. The major devices used are: (a) The use of essentially mathematical and statistical techniques for making major apportion-

---

New Jersey one person equals only 0.35 acres. This is only one way in which a people per acres equation can be arrived at, but however it is calculated, New Jersey will appear to place less relative value on population than the Michigan plan, because Michigan has much more area and a much smaller deviation in the population size of senate districts.

ment decisions; (b) The provision of detailed guide lines for use in constructing districts, once initial and basic allocations have been made mathematically. Included here are requirements that political boundaries be respected, that existing districts which conform to the constitutional requirements not be changed unless necessary, that irregularly shaped districts be avoided, and that in creating districts within counties entitled to more than one seat, populations shall be as nearly equal as possible, and in no event less than 75 nor more than 125 percent of the average population per district within the county; (c) The establishment of a bipartisan commission to accomplish the apportionment, with the proviso that a commission majority must approve an apportionment plan (thus insuring that neither party can control the Apportionment Commission's action); (d) The establishment of a 180-day deadline for completion of the commission's work, the period to begin as soon as decennial population statistics become available; (e) A provision for breaking deadlocks on the commission by requiring the Supreme Court to select one of the contending plans in the event no commission majority can be obtained; (f) Provision for judicial review of any plan adopted by the commission upon application of any elector, and for mandamus action against the commission should it fail in any way to perform its constitutional duties.

In short, little is left to chance or caprice. Almost every possible loophole has been closed, and insofar as a constitution can guarantee that its own provisions will be carried out, the apportionment provisions have the firmest of guarantees.

In final summary then, our conclusion must be that the proposed apportionment system successfully articulates the theory of legislative representation behind it. That theory is that a bicameral state legislature should have one house based closely on population, following county lines, and that the other house should be apportioned through a logical and uniform system of weighting population so as to give a relatively moderate but definitely significant overrepresentation to residents of sparsely populated areas, with effective limits on the degree to which metropolitan areas can be underrepresented.

Whether the underlying principles are prudent or desirable was a major question before the people in the 1963 referendum on the ratification of the new constitution must be decided by the people of the state. The federal courts must ultimately determine whether such a decision was within the competence of the people of the state. If the Supreme Court of the United States should ultimately hold that the fourteenth amendment to the United States Constitution requires that both houses of every state legislature must be apportioned according to population alone, the Michigan plan will be rendered null and void, along with the apportionment systems of practically every other state in the Union.

APPENDIX A

ARTICLE IV
Legislative Branch

Sec. 1. The legislative power of the State of Michigan is vested in a senate and a house of representatives.

Sec. 2. The senate shall consist of 38 members to be elected from single member districts at the same election as the governor for four-year terms concurrent with the term of office of the governor.

In districting the state for the purpose of electing senators after the official publication of the total population count of each federal decennial census, each county shall be assigned apportionment factors equal to the sum of its percentage of the state's population as shown by the last regular federal decennial census computed to the nearest one-one hundredth of one percent multiplied by four and its percentage of the state's land area computed to the nearest one-one hundredth of one percent.

In arranging the state into senatorial districts, the apportionment commission shall be governed by the following rules:

(1) Counties with 13 or more apportionment factors shall be entitled as a class to senators in the proportion that the total apportionment factors of such counties bear to the total apportionment factors of the state computed to the nearest whole number. After each such county has been allocated one senator, the remaining senators to which this class of counties is entitled shall be distributed among such counties by the method of equal proportions applied to the apportionment factors.

(2) Counties having less than 13 apportionment factors shall be entitled as a class to senators in the proportion that the total apportionment factors of such counties bear to the total apportionment factors of the state computed to the nearest whole number. Such counties shall thereafter be arranged into senatorial districts that are compact, convenient, and contiguous by land, as rectangular in shape as possible, and having as nearly as possible 13 apportionment factors, but in no event less than 10 or more than 16. Insofar as possible, existing senatorial districts at the time of reapportionment shall not be altered unless there is a failure to comply with the above standards.

(3) Counties entitled to two or more senators shall be divided into single member districts. The population of such districts shall be as nearly equal as possible but shall not be less than 75 percent nor more than 125 percent of a number determined by dividing the population of the county by the number of

senators to which it is entitled. Each such district shall follow incorporated city or township boundary lines to the extent possible and shall be compact, contiguous, and as nearly uniform in shape as possible.

Sec. 3. The house of representatives shall consist of 110 members elected for two-year terms from single member districts apportioned on a basis of population as provided in this article. The districts shall consist of compact and convenient territory contiguous by land.

Each county which has a population of not less than seventenths of one percent of the population of the state shall constitute a separate representative area. Each county having less than seven-tenths of one percent of the population of the state shall be combined with another county or counties to form a representative area of not less than seven-tenths of one percent of the population of the state. Any county which is isolated under the initial allocation as provided in this section shall be joined with that contiguous representative area having the smallest percentage of the state's population. Each such representative area shall be entitled initially to one representative.

After the assignment of one representative to each of the representative areas, the remaining house seats shall be apportioned among the representative areas on the basis of population by the method of equal proportions.

Any county comprising a representative area entitled to two or more representatives shall be divided into single member representative districts as follows:

(1) The population of such districts shall be as nearly equal as possible but shall not be less than 75 percent nor more than 125 percent of a number determined by dividing the population of the representative area by the number of representatives to which it is entitled.

(2) Such single member districts shall follow city and township boundaries where applicable and shall be composed of

compact and contiguous territory as nearly square in shape as possible.

Any representative area consisting of more than one county, entitled to more than one representative, shall be divided into single member districts as equal as possible in population, adhering to county lines.

Sec. 4. In counties having more than one representative or senatorial district, the territory in the same county annexed to or merged with a city between apportionments shall become a part of a contiguous representative or senatorial district in the city with which it is combined, if provided by ordinance of the city. The district or districts with which the territory shall be combined shall be determined by such ordinance certified to the secretary of state. No such change in the boundaries of a representative or senatorial district shall have the effect of removing a legislator from office during his term.

Sec. 5. Island areas are considered to be contiguous by land to the county of which they are a part.

Sec. 6. A commission on legislative apportionment is hereby established consisting of eight electors, four of whom shall be selected by the state organizations of each of the two political parties whose candidates for governor received the highest vote at the last general election at which a governor was elected preceding each apportionment. If a candidate for governor of a third political party has received at such election more than 25 percent of such gubernatorial vote, the commission shall consist of 12 members, four of whom shall be selected by the state organization of the third political party. One resident of each of the following four regions shall be selected by each political party organization: (1) the upper peninsula; (2) the northern part of the lower peninsula, north of a line drawn along the northern boundaries of the counties of Bay, Midland, Isabella, Mecosta, Newaygo and Oceana; (3) southwestern Michigan, those counties south of region (2) and west of a line drawn along

the western boundaries of the counties of Bay, Saginaw, Shia-
wassee, Ingham, Jackson and Hillsdale; (4) southeastern Michigan, the remaining counties of the state.

No officers or employees of the federal, state or local governments, excepting notaries public and members of the armed
forces reserve, shall be eligible for membership on the commission. Members of the commission shall not be eligible for election
to the legislature until two years after the apportionment in
which they participated becomes effective.

The commission shall be appointed immediately after the
adoption of this constitution and whenever apportionment or
districting of the legislature is required by the provisions of this
constitution. Members of the commission shall hold office until
each apportionment or districting plan becomes effective. Vacancies shall be filled in the same manner as for original appointment.

The secretary of state shall be secretary of the commission
without vote, and in that capacity shall furnish, under the direction of the commission, all necessary technical services. The
commission shall elect its own chairman, shall make its own rules
of procedure, and shall receive compensation provided by law.
The legislature shall appropriate funds to enable the commission
to carry out its activities.

Within 30 days after the adoption of this constitution, and
after the official total population count of each federal decennial
census of the state and its political subdivisions is available, the
secretary of state shall issue a call convening the commission not
less than 30 nor more than 45 days thereafter. The commission
shall complete its work within 180 days after all necessary census
information is available. The commission shall proceed to district
and apportion the senate and house of representatives according
to the provisions of this constitution. All final decisions shall require the concurrence of a majority of the members of the commission. The commission shall hold public hearings as may be
provided by law.

Each final apportionment and districting plan shall be published as provided by law within 30 days from the date of its adoption and shall become law 60 days after publication. The secretary of state shall keep a public record of all the proceedings of the commission and shall be responsible for the publication and distribution of each plan.

If a majority of the commission cannot agree on a plan, each member of the commission, individually or jointly with other members, may submit a proposed plan to the supreme court. The supreme court shall determine which plan complies most accurately with the constitutional requirements and shall direct that it be adopted by the commission and published as provided in this section.

Upon the application of any elector filed not later than 60 days after final publication of the plan, the supreme court, in the exercise of original jurisdiction, shall direct the secretary of state or the commission to perform their duties, may review any final plan adopted by the commission, and shall remand such plan to the commission for further action if it fails to comply with the requirements of this constitution.

APPENDIX B

Table 26

INDICES OF REPRESENTATION UNDER MICHIGAN CONSTITUTION OF
1908 AND NEW CONSTITUTION
(100 = STRAIGHT POPULATION)
(1960 POPULATION)

County	Senate		House	
	Old	New	Old	New
Alcona	245	248	138	117
Alger	179	181	167	109
Allegan	167	110	123	123
Alpena	236	248	138	117
Antrim	254	172	174	115
Arenac	245	135	205	115

Appendix B—Continued

County	Senate		House	
	Old	New	Old	New
Baraga	412	211	167	127
Barry	167	110	119	87
Bay	119	112	66	133
Benzie	254	172	174	129
Berrien	123	110	95	95
Branch	132	118	102	102
Calhoun	132	118	102	102
Cass	123	110	90	90
Charlevoix	236	172	174	115
Cheyboygan	236	248	187	115
Chippewa	179	218	139	118
Clare	245	135	151	115
Clinton	163	134	119	88
Crawford	245	248	200	117
Delta	179	218	207	121
Dickinson	189	110	146	109
Eaton	163	172	119	87
Emmet	236	110	187	115
Genessee	61	135	76	95
Gladwin	245	135	205	114
Gogebic	189	211	203	107
Grand Traverse	254	172	188	129
Gratiot	168	134	192	98
Hillsdale	138	123	102	102
Houghton	412	211	187	127
Huron	210	112	209	92
Ingham	92	83	101	101
Ionia	168	134	165	88
Iosco	245	135	138	115
Iron	189	211	167	109
Isabella	119	135	151	98
Jackson	138	123	108	108
Kalamazoo	109	97	84	84
Kalkaska	254	172	188	129
Kent	127	57	98	98
Keweenaw	412	211	187	127
Lake	264	169	174	126
Lapeer	154	113	170	96
Leelanau	254	172	174	129
Lenawee	129	115	91	91
Livingston	92	83	78	78

Appendix B—Continued

County	House		Senate	
	Old	New	Old	New
Luce	179	218	139	118
Mackinac	179	218	139	118
Macomb	57	101	53	105
Manistee	264	169	190	126
Marquette	189	181	127	109
Mason	264	169	174	114
Mecosta	168	169	125	125
Menominee	179	181	146	121
Midland	119	135	138	114
Missaukee	254	172	205	115
Monroe	129	115	70	70
Montcalm	168	134	125	125
Montmorency	236	248	200	117
Muskegon	93	83	95	95
Newaygo	264	169	175	114
Oakland	33	89	62	93
Oceana	264	169	175	114
Ogemaw	245	135	200	115
Ontonagon	412	211	203	127
Osceola	245	169	174	126
Oscoda	245	248	200	117
Otsego	236	248	187	115
Ottawa	93	83	72	72
Presque Isle	236	248	200	117
Roscommon	245	135	205	115
Saginaw	121	84	75	112
St. Claire	154	113	102	133
St. Joseph	109	97	90	90
Sanilac	210	113	102	96
Schoolcraft	179	218	167	118
Shiawassee	163	84	78	78
Tuscola	210	112	164	92
Van Buren	167	110	147	147
Washtenaw	133	119	82	82
Wayne	60	77	101	99
Wexford	254	172	190	126

APPENDIX C

The senate apportionment existing at the time of the Constitutional Convention is illustrated in Figure 7. This is the "frozen" apportionment introduced into the constitution by the "balanced legislature" amendment approved by the voters in 1952. Senate districts were described in the constitution, and were permanently fixed. It is this apportionment which was challenged in *Scholle* v. *Hare*.

352

Figure 7

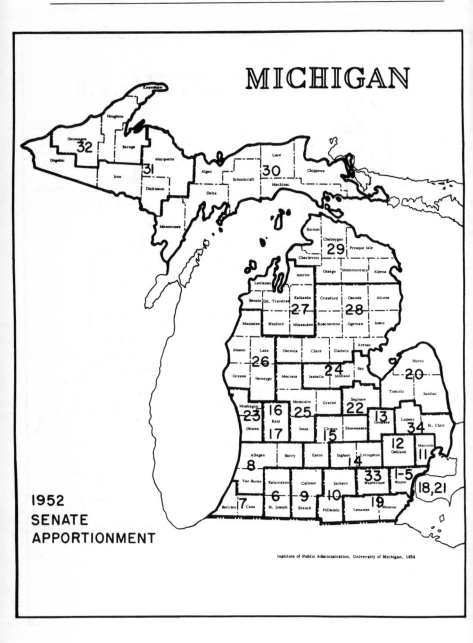

Figure 8

The house apportionment of 1953, illustrated in Figure 8, also resulted from the 1952 amendment. However, the house apportionment formula of 1908 (population, following county lines, and with a "moiety" clause granting a seat to counties or groups of counties with at least .5 percent of the state's population) was not significantly changed, except that the maximum house membership was increased from 100 to 110. The major innovation in house apportionment in 1952 was a guarantee of decennial reapportionment. If the legislature fails to act, the responsibility for reapportioning the house devolves upon the State Board of Canvassers, which is subject to mandamus action.

APPENDIX D

REPRESENTATION OF COUNTIES CONTAINING A MAJORITY OF THE STATE'S POPULATION

Table 8 presented statistics comparing the legislature representation of the five largest counties in each state. Apportionments under the new Michigan constitution would rank both houses sixth in the list of state legislative bodies which are, respectively, more and less favorable to the five largest counties in each state.

Since there is a considerable variation in the percentage of the state's population included in the five largest counties, computations were made of the representation of the smallest number of counties in each state which include a majority of the state's population. A rank ordering of the states on this basis is presented in Table 26. The proposed Michigan apportionment would rank both houses in seventh place, in relation to comparable legislative bodies in other states. Since the effective political power of the majority counties is determined by the combination of their representation in both houses of the legislature, their representation in both houses should be taken together in evaluating their position relative to similar counties in other states. In Figure 9, all states are plotted on the graph by using one axis for the legislative house more favorable to the majority counties and the other axis for the house less favorable to these counties. States where the majority counties have high representation indices in both houses are located in the upper right hand corner of the graph; those with very low indices in both houses in the lower left hand corner; and those with high majority county indices in one house and low indices in another will be found toward the upper left hand corner of the graph.

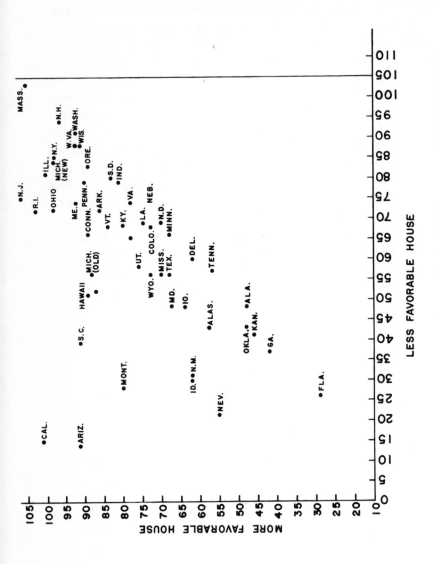

REPRESENTATION INDICES OF MAJORITY COUNTIES, IN AMERICAN STATE LEGISLATURES; 1960 AND NEW MICHIGAN CONSTITUTION

Figure 9

Table 27

RANK ORDER OF INDICES OF REPRESENTATION,
COUNTIES INCLUDING MAJORITY OF STATE POPULATION,
1960 CENSUS

I. House More Favorable to Majority Counties

		Number of Counties				
Rank	State	In state	Including majority of pop.	Pct. of state pop.	Repres. index	Upper or lower house
1	New Jersey	21	5	53.61	106	L
2	Massachusetts	14	3	50.76	105	L
3	Rhode Island	5	1	66.20	103	L
4	California	58	3	50.80	101	L
5	Illinois	102	1	50.88	100	L
6	Ohio	88	7	51.85	98	U
—New	Michigan Constitution	83	4	52.87	98	L
7	New York	62	5	52.80	97	U
8	New Hampshire	10	3	56.84	96	U
9	Washington	39	3	53.79	92	L
10	West Virginia	55	11	53.22	92	L
11	Maine	16	4	53.08	92	L
12	Wisconsin	71	8	51.21	91	U
13	South Carolina	46	9	50.39	91	L
14	Arizona	14	1	60.70	91	L
15	Pennsylvania	67	7	50.61	90	L
16	Hawaii	4	1	79.10	89	L
17	Oregon	36	4	51.99	89	L
18	Connecticut	8	2	53.20	89	U
19	Michigan (old const.)	83	4	52.87	88	L
20	Missouri	115	4	50.98	87	U
21	Arkansas	75	14	51.40	86	U
22	Vermont	14	4	52.96	84	U
23	South Dakota	67	13	51.52	83	L
24	Indiana	92	10	51.24	81	U
25	Montana	56	8	51.75	80	L
26	Kentucky	120	15	50.00	80	U
27	North Carolina	100	20	50.37	78	U
28	Virginia	98	17	50.70	78	U
29	Utah	29	2	55.44	76	L
30	Louisiana	64	7	50.61	75	U
31	Nebraska (Unicameral)	93	9	50.77	73	U
32	Wyoming	23	5	53.40	73	L
33	Colorado	63	4	50.50	73	L
34	North Dakota	53	10	50.63	70	L

Table 27—Continued

RANK ORDER OF INDICES OF REPRESENTATION,
COUNTIES INCLUDING MAJORITY OF STATE POPULATION,
1960 CENSUS

I. House More Favorable to Majority Counties—continued

		Number of Counties				
Rank	State	In state	Including majority of pop.	Pct. of state pop.	Repres. index	Upper or lower house
35	Mississippi	82	19	50.87	70	U
36	Minnesota	87	6	51.00	68	U
37	Texas	259	11	51.16	68	L
38	Maryland	24	3	57.69	67	L
39	Iowa	99	17	50.03	64	U
40	New Mexico	32	5	51.20	62	L
41	Delaware	3	1	68.90	62	L
42	Idaho	44	7	52.00	62	L
43	Alaska	24	2	55.80	58	L
44	Tennessee	95	8	50.87	57	U or L
45	Nevada	17	2	74.22	55	L
46	Oklahoma	77	9	50.52	49	L
47	Alabama	67	9	50.90	48	U or L
48	Kansas	105	10	50.77	46	U
49	Georgia	159	15	50.06	42	U
50	Florida	67	5	50.40	29	L

II. House Less Favorable to Majority Counties

		Number of Counties				
Rank	State	In state	Including majority of pop.	Pct. of state pop.	Repres. index	Upper or lower house
1	Massachusetts	14	3	53.61	103	U
2	New Hampshire	10	3	56.84	94	L
3	Washington	39	3	53.79	91	U
4	New York	62	5	52.80	89	L
5	West Virginia	55	11	53.22	88	U
6	Wisconsin	71	8	51.21	88	L
—New	Michigan Constitution	83	4	52.87	84	U
7	Oregon	36	4	51.99	83	U
8	Illinois	102	1	50.88	81	U
9	South Dakota	67	13	51.52	80	U
10	Indiana	92	10	51.24	79	L
11	Pennsylvania	67	7	50.61	79	U
12	Virginia	98	17	50.70	74	L
13	Maine	16	4	53.08	74	U

Table 27—Continued

RANK ORDER OF INDICES OF REPRESENTATION,
COUNTIES INCLUDING MAJORITY OF STATE POPULATION,
1960 CENSUS

II. House Less Favorable to Majority Counties—continued

Number of Counties

Rank	State	In state	Including majority of pop.	Pct. of state pop.	Repres. index	Upper or lower house
14	Nebraska (Unicameral)	93	9	50.77	73	U
15	Arkansas	75	14	51.40	72	L
16	Ohio	88	7	51.85	72	L
17	Rhode Island	5	1	66.20	72	U
18	Louisiana	64	7	50.61	69	L
19	North Dakota	53	10	50.63	69	U
20	Colorado	63	4	50.50	68	U
21	Kentucky	120	15	50.00	68	L
22	Vermont	14	4	52.96	68	U
23	Connecticut	8	2	53.20	66	L
24	Minnesota	87	6	51.00	66	L
25	North Carolina	100	20	50.37	65	L
26	Delaware	3	1	68.90	60	U
27	Utah	29	2	55.44	58	U
28	Tennessee	95	8	50.87	57	U or L
29	Mississippi	82	19	50.87	56	L
30	Michigan (old const.)	83	4	52.87	56	U
31	Texas	259	11	51.16	56	U
32	Wyoming	23	5	53.40	56	U
33	Missouri	115	4	50.98	52	L
34	Hawaii	4	1	79.10	51	U
35	Alabama	67	9	50.90	48	U or L
36	Iowa	99	17	50.03	48	L
37	Maryland	24	3	57.69	48	U
38	New Jersey	21	5	53.61	44	U
39	Alaska	24	2	55.80	43	U
40	Oklahoma	77	9	50.52	43	U
41	Kansas	105	10	50.77	41	L
42	South Carolina	46	9	50.39	39	U
43	Georgia	159	15	50.06	37	L
44	New Mexico	32	5	51.20	31	U
45	Idaho	44	7	52.00	30	U
46	Montana	56	8	51.75	28	U
47	Florida	67	5	50.40	26	U
48	Nevada	17	2	74.22	16	U
49	California	58	3	50.80	15	U
50	Arizona	14	1	60.70	14	U

SYSTEMS OF REPRESENTATION IN MICHIGAN: THE IMPACT OF A FEDERAL STANDARD

By Karl A. Lamb

THE TENNESSEE APPORTIONMENT decision, *Baker* v. *Carr*,[1] has won high praise for the United States Supreme Court. Litigation aimed at realizing the potential impact of the precedent has been initiated in several states. This case, according to some commentators, will rank second only to the school integration decision [2] as a milestone in the development of the American social and political structure. The Court has ruled that the apportionment of state legislative bodies, heretofore dismissed as a "politi-

---

[1] 369 U.S. 186 (1962).

[2] Brown v. Board of Education of Topeka, 347 U.S. 483 (1954).

cal question," is in fact a justiciable matter. It has also ruled that the guarantees of the fourteenth amendment do include a right to equitable representation—or at least a system of political representation in which "invidious discrimination" is not practiced.

The Baker decision unleashed a pent-up demand on the part of urban-centered political interest groups for some means of forcing the reapportionment of state legislatures in such a way as to reflect this century's movement of population to urban and suburban centers. In most states, it has been the legislature's duty to redesign the boundaries of legislative districts. Before the Supreme Court acted, the movement for increased urban representation had been met with massive inertia.

If the Supreme Court is indeed willing to define the nature of equitable representation in the manner their spokesmen predict, the urban interest groups should have cause for rejoicing as the real or fancied rural domination of legislatures is modified in state after state.[3] Many commentators on the development of a standard of representation as part of fourteenth amendment guarantees claim that the final outcome of the Court's deliberation must be to define the distribution of population as the primary, if not exclusive, basis for political representation. That is, they say, a legislative body which provides representation by districts must be apportioned so that the districts are substantially equal in population. The purpose of this paper is to examine the impact of such a federal or equal-populations standard on devices for political representation other than the state legislatures. The structure of political institutions in the State of Michigan is used to supply an example of the kinds of problems which would result in any of the 50 states when, or if, an equal-populations formula is imposed on such bodies as party conventions, city councils, and county boards of supervisors.

---

[3] Efforts to prove that underrepresented cities actually suffer at the hands of state legislatures have been far from conclusive. See Alfred de Grazia, *Essay on Apportionment and Representative Government* (Washington: American Enterprise Institute for Public Policy Research, 1963), pp. 96-128.

As is true in many other states, Michigan constitutions, since the acquisition of statehood, have stipulated an apportionment of the state legislature related in some manner to the distribution of population. Only in 1952 was the Michigan Constitution amended to freeze the existing senate districts into perpetual existence. But other representative institutions in Michigan have been related only slightly, if at all, to the population principle.[4]

One may qualify the prediction of chaos resulting from the redesign of such bodies with two limiting circumstances. It may be that the "unrepresentative" nature of such bodies has not operated in a manner that would deny the political desires of interests that could claim discrimination, in which case litigation is not likely to be initiated. Furthermore, if litigation is begun, there is no assurance that courts will be consistent in their decisions, and relief granted those complaining of malapportionment of a state legislature could be denied to those charging malapportionment of such a body as a county board of supervisors.[5]

Setting aside the possibility of judicial inconsistency, the question remains as to whether or not significant political frustrations are caused by the structure of representative systems in Michigan. Such frustrations could lead the injured parties to seek relief through a judicial application of a federal or equal-popula-

---

[4] Professor William Pierce points out on pp. 106 ff. in this volume that there is no legal principle which would prevent the application of a federal or equal-populations standard to local legislative bodies and similar institutions within a state.

[5] The apportionment of congressional districts has long been attacked for providing systematic discrimination against urban areas. Congressional districting in Michigan was chosen by the author of a recent popular article as a horrible example of the phenomenon. (J. Robert Moskin, "The Revolt Against Rural Rule," *Look*, January 15, 1963, p. 60.) But the matter of congressional districting poses a separate legal question. The guarantees of the Bill of Rights are perhaps not as directly applicable, so the problem will not be considered here. Article I, section 4, of the Constitution gives to Congress the authority to alter the method of electing members of the House of Representatives established by the states and gives to that House the power of judging the qualifications of its members. During its 1963 session, the Michigan legislature passed a congressional redistricting bill which was signed by Governor Romney.

tions standard of representation based upon the fourteenth amendment.

Four aspects of political representation in Michigan will be examined:

(1) The provision of the state constitution that only persons owning taxable real property may vote in local elections either on the question of approving bond issues or on that of raising the millage limit on local property taxes for a period of more than five years.

(2) The system of apportioning delegates to the county conventions of the political parties. One delegate represents each precinct, no matter how many voters reside therein.

(3) The apportionment of city councils, as presently constituted, and the problems posed by the possible creation of federated governmental authorities in metropolitan areas.

(4) The system of representation on county boards of supervisors. Michigan's Constitution provides that each township, regardless of population, shall have one member of this body, which serves as both executive and legislature for county government. Statute provides for the representation of cities according to a non-linear scale which favors small cities.

In each of these cases, substantial political advantages may accrue to groups within the electorate as a result of the system of representation. The imposition of an equal-population districts requirement could modify that advantage or even destroy that particular device for representation. The device used for effecting representation is the basic political problem of designing democratic governmental systems. Because of this, the definition of a federal or equal-populations standard of representation will involve the Supreme Court in intense political conflict at the state and local level.

THE PROPERTY QUALIFICATION

THE NOTION THAT the possession of substantial property in land should be the basic qualification for participation in the political process is usually traced to feudal times. With the industrial revolution, a rising merchant class demanded representation on the basis of movable property. Finally, those of "radical" bent in political philosophy began to claim that representation should be accorded to all men, regardless of their economic station. The establishment of a property qualification for voting in national elections was seriously considered by the Founding Fathers. During the first half of the 19th century, the states gradually abandoned property limitations on the right of democratic participation.[1] In some southern states, property limitations were reinstituted after 1880 to restrict Negro voting.

Michigan constitutions for half a century have provided that only owners of real property shall vote on local bond issues; the question of increasing the liabilities of local government is submitted only to those who will pay any increased taxes made necessary. Far from being a reversion to medieval theories of representation, this provision first came into being as a modest effort to expand the electorate.

Entering the Union in 1837 (paired with the slave state of Arkansas), Michigan adopted a constitution which provided comparatively liberal qualifications for voting. All white, male citizens over the age of 21 were made electors and no property qualification was included. These provisions were continued in the constitution of 1850; Negro males were admitted to the electorate by the fifteenth amendment. When Michigan next assembled a constitutional convention, in 1907, the demand for political participation by women had grown into a formidable force. A minor concession to suffragette sentiment was deemed necessary. The 1908 constitution provided that local bond issues would be voted on by property owners and their spouses.[2] Even in 1908, Michigan was essentially a rural state, and its system of land tenure in both town and country was based on a large number of small freeholders. No substantial tenant class had developed, and this provision did not operate to establish a discriminatory limitation on the right to vote. Neither did it reflect the economic status of voters. The ownership of land, then as now, is no indication of wealth.

A discrimination did come into being with the urbanization of the state. Michigan's industrial development was greatly accelerated by the automobile industry; the growth of the popu-

---

[1] The history and evolution of theories of representation and their influence in America are outlined in Alfred de Grazia, *Public and Republic* (New York: Knopf, 1951).

[2] Michigan Constitution, 1908, article III, section 4.

lous industrial areas after 1910 far exceeded the state's general population increase. City dwellers are more likely to be tenants than are rural residents. Furthermore, the most common purpose of local bond issues is to finance the construction of improvements in the school system. The result is that many parents are granted no voice in determining the support to be given to efforts aimed at improving the education of their own children. Yet the rentals paid by these parents probably compensate the landlord for the property taxes which he pays.

The record of bond issue elections in Michigan shows that public support for school construction and other public services can hardly be taken for granted. The 1963 school election in the city of Detroit provides an example of the operation of the property qualification. Two issues were before the voters: an increase in the mill levy, a question open to all voters for participation, and a bond issue, voted on only by property owners. As Table 1 shows, 90,000 fewer persons participated in the bond issue election, and 9 percent fewer "yes" votes were cast for the bond issue than for the increased millage. Complex factors influencing the election, including resentment of the newly adopted Detroit income tax, make it impossible to isolate property ownership as the single variable determining the 9 percent difference, and the election would have been just as catastrophic for the Detroit schools without the property qualification. But the potential influence of the property qualification in determining the outcome of school elections is clear.

The Michigan Education Association urged the Constitutional Convention of 1961-62 to eliminate the property qualification on the grounds that it hampers the development of effective city school systems. Indeed, there are only three other states (Arizona, New Mexico, and Utah) which limit voting on school taxes to property owners.[3] The resulting contraction of the electorate

[3] United States Department of Health, Education, and Welfare, Office of Education, *Monograph No. 5* (Washington, 1961) quoted in Michigan, State of, *Journal of the Constitutional Convention,* February 5, 1962, p. 512. (Cited hereafter as *Journal.*)

Table 1

VOTING ON SCHOOL REFERENDA IN DETROIT, APRIL 1, 1963

Proposition A

			Percent
(Increase in mill levy to finance operating expenses—all registered voters eligible)	NO	211,344	61.02
	YES	135,026	38.98
	TOTAL	346,370	100.00

Proposition B

			Percent
(Bond issue to finance school construction—only property owners eligible to vote)	NO	170,662	70.03
	YES	85,445	29.97
	TOTAL	256,107	100.00

Source: complete unofficial returns, *The Detroit Free Press*, April 2, 1963.

is not as numerically significant in Michigan as it would be in other states, for Michigan leads all other states in home ownership. According to the 1960 census, 74.4 percent of Michigan's housing units are owner-occupied.[4]

The property qualification was the province of the Committee on the Declaration of Rights, Suffrage and Elections of the Constitutional Convention. A majority of that committe favored retention of the 1908 provision as well as an additional provision that only property owners could vote on raising for more than five years the mill limitation on property taxes. The proposal brought forth a strongly worded minority report signed by six

[4] The owner-occupancy rates for other states with a property qualification for voting on school bonds are: Arizona, 63.9 percent; New Mexico, 65.3 percent; and Utah, 71.7 percent. U.S. Bureau of the Census, *Statistical Abstract of the United States: 1962* (Washington: U.S. Government Printing Office, 1962), p. 729.

of the 15-member committee.[5] But the majority viewpoint carried the full convention, and the property qualification was made part of the proposed constitution. The Michigan Education Association, apparently convinced that this rejection of one of its recommendations was not so important as the acceptance of certain others, later endorsed the new document.

Only by inference can these provisions of Michigan's constitutions be attacked under the precedent of *Baker* v. *Carr*. The United States Constitution clearly indicates that the qualifications for voting will be determined by each state.[6] This power reserved to the states has been modified only by the addition of the fifteenth and nineteenth amendments. They stipulate that the right of citizens to vote shall be neither abridged nor denied because of race or sex. The Supreme Court of the United States, since 1898, has refused to declare unconstitutional a property qualification for voting in the form of a poll tax.[7]

One of the strongest arguments in favor of the definition of a federal or equal-populations standard of representation holds that, just as the right to vote is not to be abridged on account of race or sex, neither should it be abridged because of the place of residence of the voter. The principle of prohibiting discrimination based on place of residence could be made part of the "equal protection of the laws" guarantee through *Baker* v. *Carr* and the decisions which follow it. If it is, interest groups may be emboldened to attack the property qualification on constitutional grounds, claiming that it frustrates the desires of city residents who are less likely to own the property in which they reside than are the residents of rural or suburban areas. It will be an easy matter for the defendants to claim that the equal protection clause, when citizens are given the right to vote, only requires that their votes have substantially equal weight with

---

[5] *Journal,* February 5, 1962, pp. 512-13.

[6] Article I, sections 2 and 4.

[7] Williams v. Mississippi, 170 U.S. 213 (1898). A constitutional amendment abolishing the poll tax is currently before state legislatures for ratification.

those of every other citizen. It does not affect the determination by the state of the original qualifications for voting.

Therefore, a different legal principle would be involved in such litigation than is involved in questions directly concerned with legislative apportionment. But any federal standard of fair representation would certainly be made part of the argument by analogy. The property qualification for voting on bond issues is not the most burning political controversy in present-day Michigan politics. It is, however, a method of representing the wishes of Michigan citizens which may be affected by the definition of a federal standard of fair representation.

THE CASE OF THE
PRECINCT DELEGATE

IN THE ORIGINAL CASE of *Scholle* v. *Hare*, Mr. August Scholle, president of the Michigan AFL-CIO, sought judicial relief for what he claimed was substantial discrimination resulting from the unequal population of the senate districts frozen into the constitution by an amendment passed in 1952. The population of his own senatorial district, comprising Oakland County, was 13 times as great as that of the least populous district. Michigan's attorney general defended the 1952 amendment on the grounds that the people of a state have the right to adopt a system of area representation, even though this choice may be misguided.

An entire section of the defendant's brief was devoted to the argument that to forbid area representation in the state legislature would require the elimination of similar representative methods throughout the democratic system. One example cited was Michigan's system of electing delegates to the county conventions of her political parties. County conventions elect delegates to the state convention of each party. State conventions choose delegates to the national convention, which nominates presidential candidates. This progression begins with the selection of a precinct delegate to the county or congressional district convention, and each precinct supplies one delegate, regardless of its population. In rural areas, when the population of a township is so small that it is not divided into precincts, the township sends one delegate to the county convention.

City officials determine the boundaries of precincts on the basis of administrative convenience, tradition, or any other motive. At the time the defendant's brief was written, the smallest precinct in the city of Detroit contained 122 voters, while the largest contained 1,168. No minimum number of voters per precinct is specified, and the maximum number depends on whether the precinct utilizes voting machines or the paper ballot. State law simply prescribes that paper-ballot precincts may contain up to 800 registered voters, while voting-machine precincts may contain up to 1,400 registered voters, with no more than 600 voters per machine. Thus does technological progress affect the democratic process; large city governments, not those of townships, have purchased voting machines and thus, after an initial capital outlay, reduced the cost of administering individual elections. In a given county, the effect is that the large city or cities will probably send fewer delegates to the county convention than their share of the county's population would warrant.[1] Even within cities, it would

---

[1] There is evidence that the use of voting machines affects the outcome of some elections. In particular, machines influence participation in referenda. Because of the mechanical complexity of registering a choice on such questions, voting on them falls off drastically in machine precincts.

be theoretically possible (although probably not worth the bother) for city officials to influence the decisions of the county convention through manipulation of the size of precincts sending delegates to the county convention.

The defendant's brief in *Scholle* v. *Hare* concluded that:

> Our election precincts, then, the very nuclei of our democratic system, are no more based on population than are the senatorial districts of which the petitioner complains.[2]

The United States Supreme Court, in the past, has differentiated between the "private" decisions of political parties and those carried on as part of the political process and therefore regulated by state action. The latter are to be judged by the fourteenth amendment.[3] Michigan's party conventions (and their apportionment) are prescribed by state law; a standard of representation based on the fourteenth amendment would probably apply to the party conventions as clearly as to the state legislature.

There is, however, little evidence in Michigan of a demand for changing the method of designing these basic building blocks of the political party system. There is no claim that the rights of individual citizens are being denied because of the unequal population of voting precincts. This may be due to the fact that the influence of an individual precinct delegate upon the actions of the county convention are not perceived as being of great importance.

The public pays little attention to the selection of the precinct

Because of the heavy use of machines in urban areas, rural areas enjoy a considerable advantage when referendum issues are concerned with a conflict between city and country attitudes. Such factors in large part explain the defeat of constitutional revision in Michigan in 1958. See John P. White, *Voting Machines and the 1958 Defeat of Constitutional Revision in Michigan* (Ann Arbor: Institute of Public Administration, University of Michigan, 1960).

[2] Michigan, State of, 360 *Supreme Court Records and Briefs,* p. 44.

[3] Nixon v. Herndon, 273 U.S. 536 (1927); United States v. Classic, 313 U.S. 299 (1941); Smith v. Allwright, 321 U.S. 649 (1944).

delegate; there is so little interest in the position, in fact, that the party organization is usually able to designate its choice for the position.

Two methods are provided for the election of precinct delegates. The most common procedure is by write-in vote at the fall primary election preceding the general election in November. It is not unusual for an interested person to win the delegate designation with a handful of votes—his own, his wife's, and perhaps a neighbor's. If the party organization leadership senses a revolt, however, it is a simple matter to print a few hundred stickers which can be passed out to the party faithful for pasting onto the ballots. This is, in fact, a common practice, even when the party leadership is unchallenged. Counties with a population in excess of 180,000 may, by vote, adopt a system requiring the circulation of nominating petitions for precinct delegate candidates. This provides a further chance for the organization, which, on an unofficial basis, can supply personnel for the petition campaigns of the candidates designated by the established leadership. In any case, a county or district convention is likely to be relatively docile with incipient conflict previously settled by agreement between the leaders of rival factions.[4] Precinct delegates usually do not insist upon the importance or nobility of their representative function.

When the county or district convention has selected its representatives to the state convention, the picture of representation changes considerably. The number of delegates sent to the state meeting by each county or district convention is based on the number of votes cast for the party's nominee for secretary of state in the preceeding election. In a sense, this is an apportionment of the state convention according to the distribution of

---

[4] An exception to this general statement is currently provided by the contest for control of the Republican party machinery in the fourteenth congressional district of Wayne County. The forces of Richard Durant, a former member of the John Birch Society, seem locked in perpetual conflict with another faction, which includes former Governor Wilbur Brucker. Durant is a political opponent of present Governor George Romney.

partisan population; it precludes delegates from areas contributing little to the party strength from being able to control the decisions made by the party. This fact puts a premium on winning the support of the large delegations from the urban districts.

Factional struggles within Michigan's parties have, in fact, taken place in the convenient arena of the state convention. State conventions held in even-numbered years nominate the running mates (such as the nominee for attorney general) who will stand with the gubernatorial candidate in the electoral contest.[5] The central party organization is also established at state conventions, held at present in odd-numbered years, through the election of the chairman and vice chairman of the State Central Committee. The members of the State Central Committee itself are chosen by congressional district caucuses at the state conventions.

Because of the system of apportioning delegates to the state convention, populous counties in which the party has proven its capacity to win votes are proportionately well represented. The result, when there is a clear contest between metropolitan and out-state interests, is that the metropolitan majorities can prevail. In practice, the leaders of party factions will fight against each other to win the votes of the populous county and congressional district caucuses.

One must conclude, therefore, that the method of electing one delegate per precinct to the county convention, regardless

[5] Under the provisions of the 1908 constitution, the candidates for governor and lieutenant governor are selected in primary elections, while the state convention selects the candidates for attorney general, secretary of state, auditor general, treasurer, highway commissioner, and superintendent of public instruction. Making several of these officials appointive, through one method or another, the 1963 constitution provides that the gubernatorial candidate shall be nominated in a primary election, while the party convention will select candidates for lieutenant governor, attorney general, and secretary of state. A single vote will be cast for the nominees for governor and lieutenant governor, so that at least these two officers will be of the same party.

of the number of voters in that precinct, has not caused visible discord in Michigan party organizations. Apparently, no particular sentiment favors the reapportionment of county conventions. This results from the crucial decisions of the state party being made at state conventions apportioned according to the distribution of party voting strength. The definition of a federal standard of representation based on population distribution would perhaps draw attention to the fact that basic representation in party councils is not based on population distribution, but it is unlikely to cause immediate political trauma.

LOCAL LEGISLATURES:
THE CITIES AND THEIR SATELLITES

MICHIGAN MUNICIPALITIES have enjoyed the benefits of home rule since adoption of the 1908 constitution and enactment of the necessary implementing legislation. The trend in Michigan local charters has been toward the increased adoption of two features of "model" city government: non-partisan nominations and election-at-large, rather than by wards. The argument for at-large election is straightforward. The councilman is more likely to concern himself with the needs of the entire city if he is accountable to all its citizens, rather than to the neighborhood minority and interest. Problems of representation may result, in that the voter does not have an individual councilman to supply attention to his needs. A convincing argument can be made for a ward system in large heterogeneous cities.[1]

Civic reformers, however, have preferred at-large election to the politics of patronage and influence that characterized the ward elections of an earlier era. Furthermore, professional social workers now perform some of the services which were a basic function of old-time ward organizations. A by-product of the at-large election system is the elimination of arguments concerning the apportionment of the city legislative body which could result from an unequal distribution of population in the city's wards.

In 1918, the city of Detroit established a nine member nonpartisan council elected at large. Nevertheless, this type of election to the city council is not a universal practice in Michigan. Michigan's Home Rule Act provides that cities of less than 2,000 population must elect councilmen at large, but the design of representative systems for larger cities is left to the charter commissions, provided that the charter designates at least one ward.

As Tables 2 and 3 demonstrate, 12 council-manager cities and four mayor-council cities elect councilmen by wards. A total of four cities attempt to combine both theories of representation by choosing some councilmen in wards and others at large. The incidence of at-large election of councilmen in Michigan is considerably higher than the national average, however, which indicates that the apportionment of city councils may be an issue of greater potential importance in other states.[2] Since ward

---

[1] Harold Zink, *Government of Cities in the United States* (New York: Macmillan, 1939), pp. 279-81.

[2] National figures for 1961 show that mayor-council cities of over 5,000 population elected councilmen 44 percent at large, 32 percent by wards, and 24 percent by a combination of the two methods. Council-manager cities in the same population category elected 77 percent at large, 12 percent by wards, and 11 percent through combining the two methods. *The Municipal Yearbook* (Chicago: International City Manager's Association, 1961). Quoted in Arthur W. Bromage, *Political Representation in Metropolitan Agencies* (Ann Arbor: Institute of Public Administration, University of Michigan, 1962), p. 13.

Table 2

METHOD OF NOMINATION AND ELECTION OF COUNCILMEN IN
COUNCIL-MANAGER CITIES AND VILLAGES IN MICHIGAN

	Municipalities according to population				
	Over 20,000	10,000– 19,999	5,000– 9,999	Under 5,000	Total
Nomination of councilmen:					
At large	7	18	12	23	60
By wards	6	2	3	1	12
Election of councilmen:					
At large	8	16	1	32	67
By wards	5	3	2	1	11
Combination	0	1	1	0	2
(Not considered a combination when mayor is only one elected at large)					

Source: Dale F. Bock and Harry R. Smith, *Michigan Council-Manager Charters* (Ann Arbor: Institute of Public Administration, University of Michigan, 1959), p. 5.

Table 3

METHOD OF ELECTING CITY COUNCILMEN IN MAYOR-COUNCIL
CITIES AND VILLAGES IN MICHIGAN

	Municipalities according to population				
	Under 2,000	2,000– 9,999	10,000– 40,000	Over 40,000	Total
Election of councilmen:					
At large	11	4	7	6	28
By wards		4			4
Combination		1		1	2

Source: Dodd A. Southern, *Michigan Mayor-Council Charters* (unpublished master's thesis, Institute of Public Administration, University of Michigan, 1961), p. 40.

boundaries are specified in city charters, the boundaries are unlikely to be changed to reflect population shifts. Such population redistributions may be quite dramatic, due to the clearing of land for freeway construction or urban renewal projects. Groups feeling disadvantaged by the resulting malapportionment may effect a change through the local procedures for charter revision. Judicial relief based on a federal or equal-populations standard of representation will probably be sought only if those desiring new districts fear that a charter amendment would be rejected by the city's voters. Such action would of course involve the courts in issues of local politics, because it seems unlikely that all groups within a given city will unite in seeking the equitable apportionment of city councils on the basis of abstract justice.

The most important impact of a federal definition of representation lies in the future. Some kind of multi-functional governmental unit must be developed to serve the needs of metropolitan areas which have a measure of geographic and economic unity but are governed by a maze of local municipalities, authorities, and commissions. In Michigan, the Detroit metropolitan area, even in 1957, contained three counties, 54 townships, 72 municipalities, 107 school districts, and 14 special districts.[3] The problem of such areas was recognized in Michigan's 1963 constitution by the addition of two new sections.[4] The first of these grants authority to the legislature to establish in metropolitan areas

> . . . additional forms of government or authorities with powers, duties, and jurisdictions as the legislature shall provide. Wherever possible, such additional forms of government or authorities shall be designed to perform multi-purpose functions rather than a single function.

---

[3] U.S. Bureau of the Census, *U.S. Census of Governments*, vol. I, no. 2 (Washington: Government Printing Office, 1957), p. 26. Quoted in Bromage, *op. cit.*, p. 42.

[4] Michigan Constitution, 1963, article VII, sections 27 and 28.

The following section grants to local units of government the power to enter into cooperative governmental and financial arrangements and permits the officers of established local governmental units to serve as officers of a newly established governmental body which would supervise the cooperative arrangement.

The new constitution, therefore, will provide alternative approaches to the metropolitan area problem. Either a federated form of metropolitan area supergovernment may be established or a confederate form may be initiated through the cooperation of existing local units. Perhaps wisely, the new constitution does not specify any particular form of representation for the legislative bodies of such new authorities. Yet, the constitution does anticipate that, in the confederate form, representation would be achieved indirectly through the service of elected officials of existing local units.

No particular form of political representation has in fact won recognition as the one best designed to answer the problems of metropolitan area government. Experiments to date have been limited by the two overriding considerations, "what will work?" and "what can we get adopted?" Professor Arthur W. Bromage has described the existence of eight different schemes of representation (ranging from direct election to state appointment) which are related to the nature of the device adopted for integrating the governmental concern of the area.[5] As Professor Bromage states, the "insertion of an actual government at the metropolitan level throws down a challenge to existing units."[6] If an upper tier council is proposed, with direct election of its members from districts (the scheme adopted in Dade County, Florida), feuding local communities are likely to appeal to any established federal standard of representation as a means of opposing the erection of the supergovernment. If districts of equal population must be established, in order to meet the requirements of such a standard, yet another confusing and

[5] Bromage, *op. cit.*, p. 6.
[6] *Ibid.*, p. 93.

arbitrary political boundary will be added to the existing maze of adjacent and overlapping political authorities. Thus the definition of a federal standard of representation may add another complexity to the tangle of problems which presently burden the governments of metropolitan areas. No metropolitan supergovernment is presently being constructed in Michigan, the problems which will be faced by the architects of such a system can be predicted. One of them will be the designing of a system of representation that will pacify the sentiments of localism but establish effective political control through an electoral system which will make sense to the individual voter. Local loyalties may preclude the establishment of an at-large election system; but new districts of equal population might prove just as unpalatable.

LOCAL LEGISLATURES: THE COUNTIES

IN MICHIGAN, as in other states established under the provisions of the Northwest Ordinance, the form of local government was influenced by legislation passed before statehood was achieved or the present federal constitution adopted. An ordinance of 1785 provided for the surveying of the "congressional township" of six square miles, while the Northwest Ordinance of 1787 gave to the territorial governor the power of organizing townships and counties and providing for the designation of their officials. Michigan Territory was settled by immigrants from New York and New England. Its early political development was presided over by Lewis Cass, governor of the Territory from 1813 to 1831. Cass was himself imbued with the values of New England town (township) government. By 1827, three principles of county government had been established in Michigan:

(1) The direct election of county and township officials;

(2) Recognition of the township as the basic political unit, the "pure and elementary republic" praised by Thomas Jefferson;

(3) Establishment of the township as the basic unit of representation on the county board of supervisors. Each township would have one supervisor by constitutional provision, with the representation of cities within the county to be determined by the legislature.

This framework for county government was imbedded in the Michigan constitutions of 1835, 1850, and 1908.[1] It is continued in the constitution of 1963, although its force may have been vitiated by the provision for permissive county home rule.

When the powers of Michigan's townships were originally established, Governor Cass probably did not realize that the genuine communities created by the New England towns were unlikely to be duplicated in the six-mile square township, which had its origin not in political history but in surveyor's convenience. It was assumed at that time that all of Michigan would provide fertile farmland; neither the growth of urban industry nor the vast and unproductive cut-over areas resulting from deforestation were envisaged. The original powers granted to

---

[1] The origins of Michigan county government are described in Arthur W. Bromage and Thomas H. Reed, *Organization and Cost of County and Township Government* (Detroit: Michigan Commission of Inquiry Into County, Township and School District Government, 1933), pp. 5-10. Thomas Jefferson's high opinion of township government is reported in Arthur W. Bromage, "County Government in Michigan," *Papers of the Michigan Academy of Science, Arts, and Letters*, vol. xvi (1931 meeting), pp. 439-40.

townships were considerable. The electors assembled in the
annual township meeting were expected to choose

> . . . one supervisor, one township clerk . . . five assessors, one
> collector, two overseers of the poor, and three commissioners of
> highways . . . and so many constables, fence-viewers, and pound
> masters as . . . shall seem necessary and convenient.[2]

Most of these functions have long since passed from the township. Social services are provided by the county or the state, and
townships no longer have any responsibilities for road building.
Because no particular interest has been shown for many years
in the annual township meeting, township officials are elected
at regular elections. But the township supervisor remains. He
is the tax assessor for the township (working under the super-
vision of a state board) and he is the representative of the township on the county board of supervisors. Each township, regardless of its population, elects one supervisor. Only three other
states (Wisconsin, Illinois, and New York) make the township
a unit of representation on the county board. Counties usually
contain 16 or more townships; when representation is given to
cities, the county board becomes a large and awkward body, but
it serves as both legislature and executive for county government.

The distribution of population was never intended to be a
determinant of the representation on county boards, but, in the
early stages of the development of local government, the assumption may have been made that townships within a county (or
even within the state) would in the natural course of events
contain roughly equal populations. Such an assumption was
unrealistic in the early 19th century; by the end of that century,
it was becoming an absurdity. If the ideal form of representative
government includes districts of equal population, then Michigan's practice of making the township a unit of representative
government has resulted in monstrous distortions of the democratic process.

---

[2] Act of the legislative council, March 30, 1827, 2 *Michigan Territorial
Laws*, p. 317, quoted in Bromage and Reed, *op. cit.*, p. 8.

According to the 1960 census, one of the smaller townships in Michigan is St. James Township in Charlevoix County.[3] St. James Township contains 34 persons, or two-tenths of 1 percent of the Charlevoix population; and the county has 25 members on its board of supervisors. As Table 4 shows, the value of a citizen's vote in electing a representative on the county board is 2,000 percent. The vote value enjoyed by residents of other townships in the county varies from 78 percent to 500 percent. If both the principle of township representation were retained and the establishment of equal-population districts required, St. James would establish the ratio of representation at 1:34. Charlevoix County (with a population of 13,421) would then require a county board of supervisors with 395 members.

At the opposite end of the scale, the most populous township in Michigan is Nankin Township, a suburb of Detroit, which, in 1960, contained 81,149 persons. The single Nankin supervisor was one of 108 members of the Wayne County Board. The value of a Nankin vote in electing a representative to the county board was three-tenths of 1 percent.

While these examples are at the extremes of the spectrum, the problem they illustrate is a general one. In the 1960 census, Michigan boasted 111 townships with a population of 300 citizens or less. Although such townships are not located in heavily populated counties, they are substantially overrepresented on their county boards. On the other hand, 46 townships contain populations in excess of 10,000; and such townships were found in 14 different counties of the state. High-rise structures permit the housing of many thousands of persons in six square miles, requiring the services of not a single fence viewer. Although concentrated in the Detroit metropolitan area, such urbanized townships are a common phenomenon, and their residents seem

---

[3] The smallest township in Michigan is not St. James. That dubious honor goes to Sheridan Township in Gladwin County, with a population of 27, or three-tenths of 1 percent of the county population of 10,769. The value of a vote cast in electing the Sheridan supervisor is 1,433 percent; the Gladwin County Board has 23 members.

Table 4

REPRESENTATION ON THE BOARD OF SUPERVISORS OF
CHARLEVOIX COUNTY, MICHIGAN

	Population	No. of supervisors	% of county population	% of representation	"Value of Vote" index[*]
Townships:					
Bay	348	1	2.6	4.0	154
Boyne Valley	688	1	5.1	4.0	78
Chandler	113	1	.8	4.0	500
Charlevoix	290	1	2.2	4.0	182
Evangeline	420	1	3.1	4.0	129
Eveline	602	1	4.5	4.0	89
Hayes	499	1	3.7	4.0	108
Hudson	162	1	1.2	4.0	333
Marion	516	1	3.8	4.0	105
Melrose	672	1	5.0	4.0	80
Norwood	243	1	1.8	4.0	222
Peaine	177	1	1.3	4.0	308
St. James	34	1	.2	4.0	2,000
South Arm	726	1	5.4	4.0	74
Wilson	464	1	3.5	4.0	114
Cities:					
Boyne City	2,797	4	20.8	16.0	77
Charlevoix	2,751	3	20.5	12.0	59
East Jordan	1,919	3	14.3	12.0	84
Totals:	13,421	25	100.0	100.0	100

[*] This is the familiar David-Eisenberg Index, developed in Paul T. David and Ralph Eisenberg, *The Devaluation of the Urban and Suburban Vote* (Charlottesville: Bureau of Public Administration, University of Virginia, 1961). It measures the degree of under- or overrepresentation. Perfect representation on the basis of population distribution is 100. A district with half the population which should be required to secure a single representative scores 200.

Source: 1960 census. Data concerning number of supervisors supplied by the Michigan Municipal League.

clearly to be excluded from adequate representation on their respective county boards of supervisors.[4] As a result, in some urban counties, the small cities (suburbs of the central city) enjoy substantial overrepresentation on the county board. As Table 5 shows, residents of suburban Belleville, in Wayne County, wielded a representative power on the county legislature valued at 1,286 percent. The swank suburb of Grosse Pointe enjoyed 450 percent of the representation to which it would have been entitled by population alone.

Table 5

REPRESENTATION ON THE BOARD OF SUPERVISORS OF WAYNE COUNTY, MICHIGAN

	Popu-lation	No. of super-visors	% of county popu-lation	% of repre-senta-tion	"Value of Vote" index*
Townships:					
Brownstown	17,191	1	.6	.9	150
Canton	5,313	1	.2	.9	450
Dearborn	79,809	1	3.0	.9	.3
Grosse Ile	6,318	1	.2	.9	450
Grosse Pointe	2,192	1	.08	.9	1,250
Huron	6,884	1	.3	.9	300
Nankin	81,149	1	3.0	.9	.3
Northville	7,673	1	.3	.9	300
Plymouth	8,364	1	.3	.9	300
Redford	71,276	1	2.7	.9	.333
Romulus	15,233	1	.6	.9	150
Sumpter	5,972	1	.2	.9	450
Taylor	49,658	1	1.9	.9	47
Van Buren	9,509	1	.4	.9	225
Totals:	360,866	14	13.5	13.0	96

[4] The problem of malapportioned county legislatures does not exist only in states which establish the township as a unit of government. When county legislators are elected from districts, the same effect results from a failure to re-draw the district boundaries to reflect population shifts. Recent legislation in California empowers county boards to appoint committees which will examine the apportionment of the boards and make recommendations for redistricting. Most district boundaries have not been changed in this century.

Table 5—Continued

Cities:	Population	No. of supervisors	% of county population	% of representation	"Value of Vote" index*
Allen Park	37,052	2	1.4	1.9	136
Belleville	1,921	1	.07	.9	1,286
Dearborn	112,007	5	4.2	4.6	110
Detroit	1,670,144	57	62.6	52.8	84
Ecorse	17,328	1	.6	.9	150
Garden City	38,017	2	1.4	1.9	136
Grosse Pointe	6,631	1	.2	.9	450
Grosse Pointe Farms	12,172	1	.5	.9	180
Grosse Pointe Park	15,457	1	.6	.9	150
Grosse Pointe Woods	18,580	1	.7	.9	129
Hamtramck	34,137	2	1.3	1.9	146
Harper Woods	19,995	1	.7	.9	129
Highland Park	38,063	2	1.4	1.9	136
Lincoln Park	53,933	3	2.0	2.8	140
Livonia	66,702	3	2.5	2.8	112
Melvindale	13,089	1	.5	.9	180
Northville	2,982	1	.1	.9	900
Plymouth	8,766	1	.3	.9	300
River Rouge	18,147	1	.7	.9	129
Riverview	7,237	1	.3	.9	300
Southgate	29,404	2	1.1	1.9	173
Trenton	18,439	1	.7	.9	129
Wayne	16,034	1	.6	.9	150
Wyandotte	43,519	3	1.6	2.8	175
Totals:	2,305,431	94	86.5	87.0	101
County Totals:	2,666,297	108	100.0	100.0	100

* This index is explained in the note to Table 4.

Source: 1960 census. Data concerning the number of supervisors supplied by the Michigan Municipal League.

The formula established by Michigan's legislature for providing city representation on county boards was judged in 1959 to entail discrimination in favor of cities with a population of less than 10,000, while establishing gross discrimination against cities with populations in excess of 500,000.[5] Townships and villages have taken advantage of this provision. A number of smaller villages have incorporated as fifth-class cities, thereby winning separate representation on the county board and removing themselves from the township tax base. Populous townships have incorporated as first-class cities. Livonia Township in Wayne County incorporated as a city and tripled its representation on the county board, so that its representation is now slightly greater than the distribution of population would warrant (Table 5). Such reactions have not been universal, however; Redford Township in Wayne County, with 71,000 persons, seems to take aggressive pride in its pastoral form of government.

The legislative provision for the representation of cities supplies a non-linear scale, based on population, but strongly biased towards representation for the smaller city. No invidious attempt to discriminate against large cities is necessarily involved. The simple fact of providing representation for individual political units, whether they be townships or incorporated cities, requires a non-linear scale if the number of members of the county board is to be kept down to a size that can somehow transact the business of the county. The result, however, is a monstrous perversion, if judged by the "one man, one vote" standard. According to the general provisions of the statute, a city of 750 is entitled to one representative, while a city of more than 100,000 receives only 12 representatives, with an additional representative added for every additional 10,000 citizens (Table 6). In Wayne County, a city must attain 25,001 persons before winning a second supervisor; but the smallest incorporated city, Belleville, has one supervisor with less than 2,000 constituents. The constitutional provision of one supervisor per township at the same time gives the single supervisor from Nankin Township over 80,000 constituents. This permits a variation in district population within a single urban county of 40 to 1.

---

[5] O. Charles Press, "The Supervisor System in Michigan's Metropolitan Counties," *Michigan Courthouse Review*, December 1959, p. 14.

Table 6

PROVISIONS FOR THE REPRESENTATION OF CITIES ON MICHIGAN COUNTY BOARDS OF SUPERVISORS

I. GENERAL PROVISIONS

Population of city	Number of Supervisors
750 or less	1
750 – 3,000	2
3,000 – 4,000	3
4,000 – 9,000	4
9,000 – 25,000	5
25,000 – 35,000	6
35,000 – 49,000	7
49,000 – 65,000	8
65,000 – 80,000	10
80,000 – 100,000	12
100,000 – 500,000	one additional supervisor for each additional 10,000 or fraction
500,000 or more	one additional supervisor for each additional 40,000 or fraction

II. COUNTIES OF MORE THAN 500,000 POPULATION BUT LESS THAN 1,000,000

7,500 or less	1
7,501 – 15,000	2
15,001 – 22,500	3
22,501 – 32,500	4
32,501 – 50,000	5
50,001 – 75,000	6
over 75,000	one additional supervisor for each additional 25,000 or fraction

III. COUNTIES OF MORE THAN 2,000,000 POPULATION (WAYNE COUNTY)

25,000 or less	1
25,000 – 40,000	2
40,000 – 70,000	3
over 70,000	one additional supervisor for each additional 30,000 or fraction

City with 53% or more of county population (Detroit) shall have at least 53% of representation on county board

Source: Michigan, *Compiled Laws* (1948) section 117.27, as last amended by Act No. 6, Public Acts of 1961.

The intent of representing political units as communities on the board of supervisors is indicated by the fact that most county supervisors are either ex officio members—the primary duties of the township supervisor are concerned with the township— or they are appointed by elected city officials. The legal powers of county boards indicate that they are intended to function as representative institutions, although their members may not be directly elected by the voters.

A federal standard of representation requiring equal-population districts, therefore, would require Michigan to abandon the practice of constructing county legislatures on the basis of representing the political units found within the borders of the county. The unit with the smallest population, be it township or city, would determine the ratio of representation. The resulting number of required legislative districts would be absurd. The price of maintaining a separate representative for the city of Belleville, with districts of equal population, would be the election of 2,073 members to the Wayne County Board of Supervisors.

It can be argued that, in modern America, tiny municipalities or townships ought not to win such an emotional attachment on the part of their citizens that those citizens will resist the absorption of their small and inefficient governmental units by larger and more sensible forms. But such emotional attachments do exist; and they are cultivated with some care by the elected officials of those very townships and cities. The federal system has nurtured a tradition of local autonomy in the design of governmental institutions; the municipal home rule movement has expanded that tradition within the states. One finds it hard to imagine that the Supreme Court of the United States is prepared to render a decision which would end the representation of individual political units on county boards of supervisors.

Michigan's system of providing representation on county boards has in fact occasioned considerable political strife in recent years. Such conflict has not been one of unincorporated rural areas refusing the demands of the cities. Rather, it has been a conflict between the central cities and their satellite, but independently incorporated, suburbs. Suburban residents are not the natural allies of the city dwellers. Indeed, many suburbanites fled the city to escape its life and have only contempt for the core city, its people, and its problems. In Michigan, this conflict was dramatized by Detroit's adoption of an income tax levied upon persons working in Detroit, regardless of their place of residence. Suburban mayors formed a "Vigilance Tax Committee" in order to institutionalize their sense of outrage at this action. This was only the most public conflict between Michigan central cities and their suburbs.

Michigan's formula, in fact, gives to the suburbs an amount of power on the county board that is much greater than the suburban population would warrant. As Table 5 shows, the representation of all cities in Wayne County is slightly greater than their total populations would warrant, with a "value of the vote" index of 101. But the city of Detroit is the only city with an index less than 100. With 62 percent of the county's population, it has only 53 percent of the representation on the county board. In 1955, a section was added to the governing statute which granted to any city containing 65 percent of the county population 52 percent of the board membership. This was replaced in 1961 by an amendment which provided that, in counties of over 2,000,000 population, a city with more than 53 percent of the county population but less than 51 percent of the members of the county board shall have its membership on the county board increased to 53 percent. Since Wayne is the only county with a population in excess of 2,000,000 and Detroit's population had fallen below the 65 percent level, the 1961 amendment was in fact special legislation to assure majority control of its county board to the city of Detroit. The core cities of other metropolitan counties were excluded, and the city of Grand Rapids was the first to seek a remedy.

When the suburb of Walker, in Kent County, was incorporated in 1962, the state formula awarded it four supervisors, increasing the Kent County Board to 74 members. The city of Grand Rapids then contained 55 percent of the Kent County population but provided only 24 supervisors, or 32 percent of the total. Grand Rapids' complaint was strengthened by the fact that state law requires a two-thirds vote of the board in order to make certain key decisions, such as the location of county facilities, including hospitals, and the authorization of new tax rolls.[6] Grand Rapids officials saw themselves unable to influence these crucial actions. Grand Rapids therefore sought to induce a friendly legislator from outside Kent County to propose legislation which would make the 53 percent rule applicable to all counties. The Grand Rapids city attorney wrote that

> . . . under the existing law, there is no foreseeable possibility of Grand Rapids obtaining a majority on the Board, no matter what proportion of the county's population it attains.[7]

As Table 7 demonstrates, the position of Grand Rapids is not unique. The cities of Lansing, Jackson, and Kalamazoo each contain a majority of the population in their respective counties but hold only one-third of the seats on their county boards. Battle Creek, with 32 percent of the population, holds only 19 percent of the seats on the Calhoun County Board. Because of recent and intense battles with its suburbs, Grand Rapids was the first city to complain of these inequities. But the potential for conflict exists in other urban counties of the state.

The legislation requested by Grand Rapids was introduced in the 1963 session of the Michigan legislature and referred to the Committee on City Corporations.[8] In testifying before the committee, the mayor of Grand Rapids suggested that the city would be forced to turn to the courts if the legislature did not provide the hoped-for relief. If forced to do this, the city would hope to appeal to a standard of fair representation based upon the Supreme Court's action in *Baker* v. *Carr*.

---

[6] *The Detroit Free Press*, December 6, 1962.

[7] Albert R. Dilley to Gilbert E. Bursley, December 19, 1962.

[8] Michigan, 72nd Legislature, 1963 Regular Session, House Bill No. 96.

Table 7

REPRESENTATION OF TWELVE MICHIGAN CITIES ON THEIR
RESPECTIVE COUNTY BOARDS OF SUPERVISORS

County	City	County population	City population	City % of population	% of supervisors	"Value of Vote" index*
Bay	Bay City	107,042	53,609	50.1	51.1	102
Calhoun	Battle Creek	138,858	44,169	31.8	18.9	59
Genesee	Flint	374,313	196,940	52.6	41.5	79
Ingham	Lansing	211,296	107,807	51.0	33.3	65
Jackson	Jackson	131,994	50,720	38.4	29.6	77
Kalamazoo	Kalamazoo	169,712	82,089	48.4	37.5	77
Kent	**Grand Rapids	363,187	201,113	55.3	32.4	59
Muskegon	Muskegon	149,943	46,485	31.0	26.8	86
Saginaw	Saginaw	190,752	98,265	51.5	45.3	88
St. Clair	Port Huron	107,201	36,084	33.7	31.5	93
Washtenaw	Ann Arbor	172,440	67,340	39.1	27.0	69
Wayne	Detroit	2,266,297	1,670,144	62.6	52.8	84

* This index is explained in the note to Table 4.

** Grand Rapids figures based on population of areas annexed and separately incorporated in 1962. Other figures are for 1960.

As noted above, Michigan's 1963 constitution permits the legislature to provide home rule for counties. The effectiveness of the constitutional provision will of course depend upon the nature of the home rule act which may be drafted. This in turn will depend on the various urban counties reaching agreement concerning what provisions will give them the greatest flexibility in meeting their problems. It seems unlikely that a large number of counties will be able to achieve home rule, particularly if small municipalities are permitted to veto its adoption. The pattern of representation on county boards by one member per township and a formula which must of necessity discriminate against the residents of large cities will continue in most counties. It seems safe to predict that any standard of representation based on the fourteenth amendment, defined because of the demand for the reapportionment of state legislatures, will be scrutinized carefully for its applicability to county boards of supervisors.

CONCLUSIONS

THE MOVEMENT for adding a definition of political representation to the rights guaranteed by the fourteenth amendment is led by interests seeking to accomplish the reapportionment of state legislatures in order to give city residents a full voice in those bodies. A constitutional argument, not surprisingly, is being used in hopes of achieving a change in political institutions and increasing the power of one group relative to another. There is considerable reason to question the assertion that the reapportionment of state legislatures will achieve the happy resolution of urban problems forecast by its proponents.[1] There are compelling reasons to predict that such a determination, when applied to local legislative bodies, will hamper the quest of core cities in metropolitan areas for the solutions of important political dilemmas.

The supporters of a federal standard requiring equal-population districts have given little, if any, consideration to the impact of such a standard upon other representative systems within the states. But no federal definition of equitable representation can logically exclude these other modes of representation. Certainly they must be judged by the same constitutional formula that is applied to the state legislature.

Although many states designed the system for apportioning their legislatures to reflect the distribution of population in one manner or another, the same has not necessarily been true of other devices of representation. The consistent application of a federal or equal-populations standard of representation is likely to involve the federal courts in substantial redesigning of the institutions of local government in various states. Michigan presents an example of the problems which would result.

Four systems of representation in Michigan have been discussed. Michigan's constitutional requirement that only property owners may vote on the bond issues of local government seems to discriminate against urban residents. Although a federal standard of representation could not be directly applied in an attack on the property qualification, it would certainly be appealed to by inference.

Michigan law provides for the conduct of the affairs of Michigan's political parties. The basic unit of party decision-making is the county or congressional district convention. Delegates to these conventions are chosen on the basis of one per precinct, regardless of the number of registered voters living in the pre-

---

[1] These matters are analyzed in de Grazia, *Essay on Apportionment and Representative Government, op. cit.*

cinct. There have been no demands to change this method of designating delegates, because no group so far has claimed discrimination due to the unequal population of precincts. Similarly, the apportionment of city councils has not provided a source of substantial political conflict in recent years.

The pattern of political representation in urban counties and in multi-county metropolitan areas is a source of substantial conflict. Michigan's form of county government was established by 1827, before Michigan became a state, and it is hardly equipped to perform 20th century services. The township remains a political unit, although its powers have, in the main, passed to the county and to the state, which are larger and more competent. Each township supplies one representative to the board of county supervisors, regardless of the township population. Townships with a handful of citizens are dramatically overrepresented on the boards of some counties; urbanized townships are just as obviously underrepresented on the boards of other counties. Any requirement of equal-population districts would tend to further the destruction of the township as a viable political unit. Such a destruction might benefit Michigan's citizens, once they had grown used to it, but it would arouse determined opposition on the part of incumbent township officials and other persons sentimentally attached to the Jeffersonian image of grass-roots democracy. Since township officials are unlikely to abandon their offices before every legal channel has been closed to them, the result would be to embroil the federal courts in redesigning Michigan's system of county government.

Present controversies over representation on county legislatures have not reflected a division between cities and townships, however. They have in fact reflected a contest between the core cities of a metropolitan area and the satellite communities. Michigan law establishes the representation of political units as the basis for apportioning county boards. In order to assure one representative to every organized political unit, a non-linear scale which favors small cities has been necessary in order to limit the size of county boards and make them even modestly functional. A definition of fair representation requiring districts of equal population would of necessity end the practice of representing political units on the county boards. Equal-population districts would furthermore require that representative districts be established within the counties without regard for the boundaries of existing political units, so that yet another arbitrary political boundary would be added to the existing maze of lines on the political map. The resulting confusion would supply a concrete example of Professor de Grazia's contention that "equal population apportionment brings about a defective organization of public opinion and policy activity." [2]

The most pressing need of American local government is the design of viable systems of government for metropolitan areas. These areas now sprawl across the boundaries of existing counties, municipalities, special-purpose districts, and even states. No one form of metropolitan authority is likely to be designed which will best serve the needs of all areas; the ingenuity of local officials in responding to local needs will be severely taxed. A federal or equal-populations standard of representation is likely to impede the search for a viable form of metropolitan area government. It could establish rigid mathematical standards which would needlessly complicate the task of designing such new forms of government; and it would certainly supply the defedants of the parochial interest with fuel to add to the flames of opposition.

The effect of a federal standard of fair representation upon the design of local legislatures and other representative devices within the several states has received little consideration by those who seek a judicial declaration of the necessity of equal-population districts. The impact of such a standard in Michigan is potentially very great.

The assertion of such authority by the United States Supreme

---

[2] *Ibid.*, p. 175.

Court would constitute a frontal assault upon the traditional balances of the federal system. It would embroil the federal courts in thousands of local political disputes, incurring the possibility of grave damage to both the dignity and the authority of the Court.

INDEX

13080